History of American Thought and Culture

Paul S. Boyer
General Editor

The Engineering of Consent

Democracy and Authority in Twentieth-Century America

WILLIAM GRAEBNER

THE UNIVERSITY OF WISCONSIN PRESS

Published 1987

The University of Wisconsin Press
114 North Murray Street
Madison, Wisconsin 53715

The University of Wisconsin Press, Ltd.
1 Gower Street
London WC1E 6HA, England

First printing

Printed in the United States of America

For LC CIP information see the colophon

ISBN 0-299-11170-9

For Ben and Riley

Contents

Preface

This book was born more than a decade ago. While working on a study of retirement I became interested in the history of the Golden Age Clubs, private social-work agencies for the aged founded in Cleveland in 1940. In tracing the intellectual roots of the clubs, I found a powerful social-engineering impulse at work, with its origins in interwar social psychology. Then, in 1978, my mother's chance and altogether loving recollection of my sister (b. 1938) as "the little dictator," a reference with obvious historical import, sent me into the child-rearing literature. What I found was that the child-rearing experts of the 1940s were advocating a mode of social engineering — a system of authority — not unlike that used by Cleveland's social gerontologists. In one sense, *The Engineering of Consent* is simply an effort to elaborate on, and to establish a context for, that perception.

The book is an attempt to shed light on the history of authority* in the twentieth-century United States. Even so, it does not deal equally with all forms of authority; readers will find little or nothing, for example, on television, CIA surveillance activities, the imperial presidency, the corporate state, or gender relations — all valid aspects of the history of authority in modern America. Instead, I have written a history of one form of authority that seems to me central to the past century of American history. I have labeled it "democratic social engineering." A definition and description of the term can be found in the Introduction.

As a profession, history is more aware than ever before of a variety of authority relationships. We have histories of education, elites, the military-industrial complex, asylums, prisons, child rearing, and gender rela-

---

*Two words — power and authority — are available to those writing in this field. Some scholars distinguish between them, using power to refer to the possibility of controlling or commanding others, and reserving authority to describe delegated, sanctioned, or deserved power. In this book, I have not made this distinction. With rare exceptions, the words are used interchangeably in the pages below, and both carry the meaning ascribed to power. This decision was not made arbitrarily. Indeed, it reflects a central argument in the book: that it is difficult, if not impossible, to distinguish between power and authority as they are traditionally defined.

tions. We have an extraordinary series of debates on authority wrapped up in the question of what it meant to be a slave. Yet until the publication in 1983 of John Kenneth Galbraith's *The Anatomy of Power*, there had been no systematic attempt to deal with the history of authority as a field of study. While *The Engineering of Consent* is not the systematic treatment of the history of authority that we need, it is a step toward such a treatment, a midlevel work between the subject-oriented studies that touch on authority and an eventual synthesis. I also have some hope that the book will generate interest in the history of authority as a way of organizing and understanding the past.

I am indebted to the Benjamin Rose Institute for allowing me access to their indispensable records of the history of the Golden Age Clubs. I wish to thank the Society for the Psychological Study of Social Issues for permission to reprint portions of my essay "The Small Group and Social Engineering" (*Journal of Social Issues*, no. 1 [1986]); the Organization of American Historians for permission to reprint portions of my "The Unstable World of Benjamin Spock: Social Engineering in a Democratic Culture, 1917–1950" (*Journal of American History*, 67 [Dec. 1980], 612–29); and the University of Chicago Press for permission to reprint portions of my "The Golden Age Clubs" (*Social Service Review*, 57 [Sept. 1983], 416–28).

Anonymous referees for the *Journal of American History*, the *Business History Review*, and the University of Wisconsin Press gave me invaluable criticism. I am grateful to John Diggins for a stimulating reading of a portion of the manuscript, and to Henry Shapiro for his incisive comments on a primitive summary of the general argument, delivered before the American Historical Association in 1979. Fred Konefsky and Ellen DuBois read the entire manuscript with the care and understanding that only friends can muster; their advice has changed the book in significant ways. Bill Warner shared with me his own interest in authority and introduced me to some books I might not otherwise have found; our conversations about democratic social engineering and many other subjects have been of enormous benefit. Throughout the difficult process of writing about a rather unusual subject, Hamilton Cravens has been a source of unflagging encouragement; I am deeply grateful. The State University of New York subsidized two summers of research, and the writing of the first draft was completed during several leaves of absence provided by the State University of New York at Fredonia. Mary Notaro and Gloria Aniebo typed various drafts of the manuscript with precision and intelligence.

Dianne Bennett, my wife, has heard so much about this project that she now sees democratic social engineering everywhere, as I do, and she is almost as sensitive to authority (nothing much in the way of controlling behavior escapes us). More important, she is strong and generous, brings home a good check, and is a nice person to live with. My son Ben must wonder how anyone as attuned to the nuances of authority as his father could order him about with such regularity. Riley knew nothing of any of this, except that Daddy worked upstairs and that, once a day, he was allowed to come in and "type." He has also taught me that the engineering of consent might most easily be accomplished with a smile.

Buffalo, New York
February 13, 1984
April 16, 1986

The Engineering
of Consent

Introduction

In the half century before the Great War, Americans threw off one set of frameworks for validating truth, understanding authority, and structuring and ordering society, and they took on another. This process took place at many levels of society, but it was especially obvious among scientists and social scientists, philosophers, the clergy, educators, and social settlement workers. Wherever it occurred, Americans jettisoned certain forms of religion, in part because the theology no longer made sense, in part because the autocratic way in which that theology had been handed down no longer seemed viable. They cast away a priori truth, first principles, and a system of ethics which focused on ends. Experimentation, the process of inquiry, the *search* for truth (i.e., scientific method) replaced the old emphasis on moral absolutes. Means replaced ends. Methods replaced goals.

Embedded within these changes was a new structure or system of authority, democratic in form if not always in substance, operating on groups rather than individuals and functioning through participatory rather than authoritarian, subject-object relationships. That new system of authority is the subject of this book. I have called it democratic social engineering.

Because the group, and processes within the group, were central to the creators of this new system of authority, the term "group process" captures reasonably well the activities and individuals I am writing about. "Group process" has the additional advantage of being value-neutral; it suggests nothing beyond a method. When I first came to the subject, this term seemed the natural one, and I have often used it in the pages below.

Nonetheless, I have elected to emphasize the term "democratic social engineering." This label is at once descriptive and interpretive; unlike "group process," it contains something of my analysis of the movement described. I make no apologies for this. Many terms — including "liberal state," "corporatism," "imperialism," and "imperial presidency" — carry much the same burden and yet function effectively.

3

Each of the three words that make up the term — "democratic," "social," and "engineering" — sheds some light on its meaning. The word "social" has essentially the same meaning as "group process"; it refers to *how* the engineers (I will get to them in a moment) hoped to accomplish their goals. Their method, derived from turn-of-the-century social psychology, pragmatic philosophy, and progressive educational theory, was based on society itself. The locus of democratic social engineering was the society in microcosm: the small group. Small groups that were actually used to engineer behavior included YMCA clubs, Boy Scout patrols, Bible study classes, foremen's clubs, classrooms of students, and families.

"Democratic" connotes ends and means. As an end, "democratic" reflected the desire of most social engineers for what they defined as a more democratic society. But "democratic" has greater import as a description of means. Democratic social engineers expected to modify beliefs and change behavior by utilizing, and entering into, a "democratic" process within the family, classroom, club, or other small group. I hasten to add, however, that not all those I have described as democratic social engineers would have recognized their activities as involving a method in some way based on, or shaped by, democracy. In that sense, the word "democratic" not only describes; it also represents my own reading of the past.

Among the constituent elements of this democratic process were the familiar mechanisms or features of traditional political democracy: choice (in political parlance, voting), participation, discussion, the provision of information, and responsible leadership. Just as in politics Americans believed that they should have a "choice" between candidates and policies, so did democratic social engineers use the offer of a "choice" between often predetermined alternatives to engineer behavior (the quotation marks suggest how illusory real choice could be). Similarly, democratic social engineering was explicitly participatory; those whose attitudes were to be changed, or whose behavior was to be modified, had to be part of the process, to participate or be made to *feel* that they had participated. The vehicles for this technique of participation included forums, debates, and, most commonly, group discussions. At the apex of the system, providing information, guidance, and discipline for the discussions and other group processes, were trained leaders — the shop-floor representatives, in a sense, of our democratic social engineers.

The word "engineering" is perhaps the most normative and hence most provocative of the three. "Engineering" implies consciousness. Democratic social engineering was, by and large, a conscious effort at control. Whether teachers, social workers, businessmen, or parents, democratic social engineers have, generally with forethought, attempted to modify the behavior of others. Yet the objects of this effort — students, senior citizens, foremen, children, and many others — have, by and large, been unaware of the totality of what was happening to them. The word "engineering," then, carries the connotation of manipulation, and thus ironizes the adjective "democratic." From the family to the school, institutions that we have generally understood to be not just private but in some measure genuinely democratic have in fact been neither. Processes of classroom inquiry that we have labeled democratic were, in fact, carefully orchestrated, and the orchestration was just as carefully performed; the foremen's clubs of the 1920s, structured as democratic institutions, were, in reality, the creatures of factory owners and managers, for whom the democratic process was a means to preconceived ends. All these terms are explained more fully, and placed in the historical context in which they developed, in the next chapter.

If this description of the operation of democratic social engineering suggests a certain ethical deficiency, it is well to remember that those responsible for it invariably saw themselves as the standard-bearers of a new kind of process-based authority that was much more humane than anything that had gone before it. The operation of democratic social engineering through process distinguishes the methodology from mechanisms of social control that were only marginally procedural — as, for example, the commands an overseer issued to a slave, or the sermon a minister delivered to his congregation. Historically, social engineering *as process* to some extent replaced exhortation, force, and other kinds of authority that did not entail, as democratic social engineering did, a series of continuous actions.

More important for the history of authority was the fusion, within democratic social engineering, of process and content, of means and ends. Process was not simply a medium for the teaching of any values the social engineer might possess; the process itself — a process that was designed to replicate responsible and orderly social conduct — was the subject of instruction.

The book is organized by chronology and subject. The reader is cautioned, however, not to make too much of the chronology. Democratic social engineering has not been transformed in any major way in the past century. Although the narrative emphasizes the special influence of democratic methods of social control during, and between, World Wars I and II, the existence of a "golden age" of democratic social engineering should not overshadow the essential unity of the period under investigation. This is hardly surprising, for the elements that came together in the late nineteenth century to produce a democratic mode of social control — the social sciences, a middle class fearful of social disorder and the "masses," the real or perceived decline of community, family, and church, the development of democracy into a potent ideology — remain with us in some form or another. Moreover, a method of social engineering that operates within "private," informal, and voluntary spheres is not likely to be easily dislodged.

Some would argue that democratic social engineering is less a mechanism of social control than a kind of socialization, and thus not really "engineering" at all. Others, acknowledging the manipulative nature of democratic social engineering, suggest that the wide availability of its central mechanism, the group, and of its basic skills, including discussion, has rendered the method harmless. One might also argue that democratic social engineering represents a mild, socially progressive form of authority, a triumph of modern liberalism over less humane and more coercive methods of control. As the reader may well have guessed, I have other opinions.

1

Origins

The nineteenth century was a world under siege. The forces of industrialization, urbanization, science, the market economy, and what a recent writer has called "interdependence" laid waste the village, the family, the church, the workplace, and other familiar settings and institutions.[1] The village found itself in competition with other villages and thus, by one definition, not a village at all; the family, heretofore a unified system of productive relations, was physically disjoined as men and women left the home to work in factories and shops owned by others; the workplace, once a comfortable and homogeneous setting, became increasingly anonymous.[2] Americans who came of age in the half century after 1850 experienced a more centralized politics, the rise of the metropolis and the giant corporation, and the apparent need for a new kind of collective existence.

At stake in these changes was the whole system of relations by which society was ordered. The authority of the church was threatened by new scientific explanations of the universe, the origin of man, and truth itself; Charles Darwin's *Origin of Species* (1859) undermined the theoretical basis for understanding man as the bearer of inherent moral qualities. The authority of the family was damaged by mobility and urbanization. Geographic mobility put barriers of distance between parents and offspring; economic mobility threw up barriers of class. As farming ceased to be what most people did, the family's role as a general training ground for future farmers and farmers' wives diminished correspondingly. Paternal authority — authority based on the ability of the father to transmit skill and learning to his children — was shaken by the new technology of industrial America.[3] And the contained authority of the village, based on personal knowledge and shared experience and values, yielded inevitably to the heterogeneous, distended confusion and disorder of the emerging city.

In response to this crisis of authority, Americans — or, should we say, those educated, middle- and upper-middle-class Americans who most

7

valued order and most savored control—fashioned a new system of authority, a new social glue. Because their own lives were lived half in the old world and half in the new, the system of authority they created looked both to the past and to the future. It sought the accommodation of certain fundamental antinomies—freedom and order; the collapse of moral principles and the need for ethics; individualism and collectivism; the need for action and efficiency and the requirements of "democracy"[4]—that separated the world of the nineteenth century from that of the twentieth.

Democratic social engineering seemed to reconcile the conflicting claims within each of these dualisms. It was inspired in part by a collective recollection of small-town community life, yet its code words—democracy and, especially, inquiry—belonged to the twentieth century. It denied the existence of absolutes and seemed, therefore, to participate in the growing skepticism of first principles, yet its practitioners invested the methodology itself with an ethical content and talked endlessly about "character" and "citizenship" as if there were, indeed, some moral principles to teach. Freedom found expression in the emphasis on democratic participation and in the voluntarist framework within which most group-process activity would take place, yet there was an order in the person of the group leader and in the elaborate guidelines established for group discussion. There was scope for individualism within the process of the group and within the frequent admonitions to character and personality development, yet the process was clearly collective and personality seen as a social phenomenon. Here, finally, was a system that claimed not to see any inherent conflict between efficiency and democracy in a century when world war and several varieties of fascism suggested to many that the two were mutually exclusive. Through the mediation of the mature leader, democratic social engineering ensured that the people would act wisely, and that they *would act.*

The greatest advantage of democratic social engineering lay in its subtlety. The new system neither trumpeted new social goals nor insisted on adherence to institutions of authority, old or new. It was founded on methods, not goals; on means, not ends; and on process, not preconceived ideals. Within this new structure, authority did not disappear; it was contained within the methodology, tucked away inside a process of inquiry that by the turn of the century was rapidly making inroads in classrooms, Bible schools, settlement houses, scouting organizations, families, and other agencies of socialization and social control.

This chapter has three sections. The first section sets the stage for democratic social engineering by describing the political, philosophic, and social preconditions that gave rise to this new system of authority, based on society and operating through the social sciences. The second section employs late-nineteenth and twentieth-century examples to describe and explain the five central ingredients of democratic social engineering: the group; process; inquiry; democratic participation; and leadership. The third section examines how democratic social engineering was pioneered in the Protestant churches.

The conditions for the emergence of the new system were ideal in the 1890s. Yet like all systems, democratic social engineering might be said to have roots, origins, a history – preconditions. As Mark Kann and John Diggins have recently emphasized in a collection of essays on authority, the doctrine of consent – of legitimizing dominance by claiming (rightly or wrongly) that the dominated have acceded to the arrangement – has a long history. Kann, in fact, traces the idea of consent back to the Puritan notion of "consenting" to a covenant with God, to the secular Lockean social contract, and to the sort of implied consent granted by active participation in a contractual marketplace.[5] Diggins, in reminding us of the power of Puritan community in establishing the terms for consent,[6] enables one to see the connection between seventeenth-century community and the twentieth-century small groups that were, in a limited sense, their descendants. Of course, social and religious authority remained intertwined in the Puritan community, and there was as yet little conscious recognition of the role social organizations – to say nothing of a science built around the notion of society – could play in regulating behavior.

Convinced that morality and religion could no longer serve as the foundation for a stable and productive social order, the founding fathers institutionalized democratic authority. The doctrine of consent was thus politicized – transferred to the arena of politics and stripped of religious meaning. As the nineteenth century wore on, more and more Americans would give their consent by voting for their representatives.[7]

Yet this democratization of authority was carried out with great caution. Fearful of majority rule, the founding fathers decentralized power, placing it in the states rather than the national government. A system of checks and balances ensured that the whims of the majority would have to run a gauntlet of Senate, president, and judiciary before having the force of law. To buttress this written Constitution, James Madison developed a theory of "factions" that advocated the dispersion of power over a wide geographical area in order to prevent conglomerations of influence inimical to order and stability.[8]

The problem, as Sheldon Wolin has put it, "was to secure a steady and continuous flow of legitimacy *from* the people without promoting steady and continuous interference *by* the people."[9] In the nineteenth-century democratic state, this was accomplished through John Locke's "thin theory of legitimacy." Under Locke's theory, the people granted their consent to government only in periodic elections while at the same time — in the same act — relinquishing control of administrative and decision-making functions. Superior, perhaps, to Thomas Hobbes's notion that consent could be given by "a single act of consent registered in one moment of time," Locke's idea of legitimacy nonetheless did not allow for extensive citizen participation in the workings of government.[10]

Yet there was something radical in the very idea of consent, for once its theoretical legitimacy had been granted it was difficult to circumscribe its applications. If consent by the vote was essential to political legitimacy, why might not other forms of consent — administrative consent, for example — also be justifiable? Similarly, if voting was so vital, then perhaps all persons — women, blacks, and the poor as well as white males with property — should have the suffrage.[11] In short, the logic of consent led to wholly new realms of consent and, therefore, to efforts to coopt or contain that consent.

The late-nineteenth-century emergence of democratic social engineering might, on the one hand, be understood as the working out of this "logic of consent" or, on the other hand, as an effort to locate authority outside the more threatening sphere of democratic politics. In any event, democratic social engineering involved, in part, a two-stage historical process through which the device of political consent was applied in new and nonpolitical spheres. In the first stage, the doctrine of consent was applied to the larger entity of "society"; that is, society itself was conceptualized as the critical mechanism of order and stability. In the second stage, the locus of consent was shifted from society to the family and other small groups, social microcosms that functioned, in a way, as surrogates for the whole society.

Although this transfer of authority to the social realm would take place with dramatic speed in the late nineteenth century, the idea of an essentially nonpolitical, social authority had been understood for some time. Within political philosophy, Locke, Jean-Jacques Rousseau, and Jeremy Bentham had all argued that society could be understood as distinct from political arrangements and yet be invested with an effective authority. Opinion, reputation, private groups — these forms of society, for Locke, were the stuff of authority; rather than risk disapproval, people would conform. Rousseau's contribution was in part to develop the Lockean notion of social authority into a principle of openness. In Rousseau's ideal society, every act would be viable and open to scrutiny. Transgressors would not be punished but prevented from wrongdoing by an overarching, social system of observation. Bentham added the idea of the

Panopticon, a technological surveillance device that mirrored nineteenth-century liberal hopes that a new system of social engineering could be fashioned from the atoms of society. "A whole kingdom," Bentham wrote, "the great globe itself, will become a gymnasium, in which every man exercises himself before the eyes of every other man. Every gesture, every turn of limb or feature, in those whose motions have a visible influence on the general happiness, will be noticed and marked down."[12]

Democratic social engineering would involve more than a generalized social authority; by definition, it was authority exercised within a group context. Here the work of James Madison and Alexis de Tocqueville is helpful, especially in appreciating what was *not* understood about groups in the late eighteenth and early nineteenth centuries. Madison's concept of the "faction," closely tied though it was to political authority, might be taken as an early recognition of the power of the small group. But unlike a latter-day engineer or therapist, Madison was not interested in how the processes *internal* to a faction might be restructured in order to change behavior and opinion. Instead, he took the faction as a given, and sought to understand how the power of factions to do damage to the body politic might be diffused or limited. His *external* understanding of the group, as an association operating in relationship to other associations and in the context of a larger society, has dominated modern-day political science.[13]

Writing in the 1830s, Tocqueville presented quite a different idea of the group. Tocqueville not only understood how enamored Americans were of assemblies, meetings, societies, and other groups; he also understood, almost as a modern psychologist might, how "society" could function as an authority by exerting "pressure" on individuals within it.[14] Had Tocqueville put the two ideas together and conceptualized the small group as a "society," he would have been a step closer to becoming a democratic social engineer. He did not. And there is no reason to believe that he ever considered therapeutic intervention in societies and small groups — the hallmark of the democratic social engineer. Nonetheless, he came much closer than Madison to articulating the world view of late-nineteenth-century social scientists.

By the middle decades of the nineteenth century, other, more concrete signs of the emergence of a new system of social control had begun to appear. These signs, however, were just that — signs; they were not democratic social engineering itself. Some were too general, indicative of the character or tone of democratic social engineering yet lacking is specificity. Others, very precise components of the system, lacked an adequate setting. A good example of the former is the nineteenth-century decline of what John Kenneth Galbraith has called "condign" power (i.e., the use of force in social relations). Slavery was abolished, ministers less often delivered the "hell-fire" sermon, corporal punishment of prison inmates abated, and schoolmasters now and then spared the rod.[15] And while Jacksonian Indian removal was clearly accomplished with legal coercion and military force, it was carried out under a rubric of democracy: the Indians could "choose" to remain on their lands and, with that choice, to destroy themselves.[16]

The best case study we have of the transition away from the use of condign power is a recent account of the mid-nineteenth-century naval reform campaign against flogging. According to historian Myra Glenn, this campaign had several sources. Some reformers, troubled by signs of social disorder, sought a new and more effective system of discipline than flogging could provide. Others were convinced that a "republican" social order characterized by laissez-faire individualism was incompatible with a system of social control based on external coercion. Still others objected to flogging because it signified the captain's "absolute power" and thus, by analogy, raised the issue of slavery.[17]

The naval reform campaign looks forward in several ways to the twentieth-century system of democratic social engineering. Like the discipline of social psychology that would underlie much of that system, naval reform was premised on a malleable persona. Both rejected the idea of innate depravity, and thus both were able to envision a system of social control that did more than merely punish. The naval reformers also resembled democratic social engineers in their insistence that genuine obedience was a matter of "self" — of "self-control," "self-discipline," and "internal moral reform."[18]

Lacking in the nineteenth-century view, however, was a clear sense of how this new vision of discipline might be implemented. How would "moral suasion" be made effective and "self-discipline" become something more than a shibboleth? Given such skepticism, there was some opposition to naval reform on the grounds that the new system would not work; one congressman, for example, questioned whether "moral suasion could govern anybody." Even some advocates of change, harboring similar doubts, wanted naval officers to retain the power to inflict corporal punishment if the need arose.[19]

No less unsure were many other Americans who also desired a new system of authority but who had no greater understanding than the naval reformers of where a suitable mechanism for its implementation might be found. As home, family, community, and religion failed as institutions of stability and control, the middle class sought to replace them with a new system of internal authority, rooted in "character."[20] But "character building," as it was called, was not democratic social engineering.

Although the nineteenth century witnessed the emergence of the institutions that would form the structural basis for democratic social engineering—the American YMCA was founded in 1851, the Boys' Clubs can trace their lineage to 1860, the first American settlement house dates to 1886, Sunday schools were well established in the United States by the 1820s[21]—it seems clear that nineteenth-century advocates of change in the structure of authority lacked any compelling interest in the group as a mechanism of such change. Like the naval reformers of the 1850s, they did not yet understand that there was a mechanism—the small group, society in microcosm—that could induce, reinforce, and even change what some labeled "self-discipline" and others called "character."[22]

SOCIAL AUTHORITY

To this point, the discussion has focused on some of the more amorphous antecedents of democratic social engineering, including the doctrine of consent, the rejection of some of the more obvious forms of coercion, and the emergence of a certain inchoate interest in group life. But democratic social engineering was more than the sum of these entities; it was a remarkably precise system of authority with identifiable ingredients, operating in a real world.

The new system of authority was given substance and shape in the forty years spanning the turn of the century. Those who shaped it could be classified as social scientists. Because democratic social engineering was designed to function through groups, those social sciences traditionally identified with the study of group processes—particularly sociology and psychology—were more central to the movement than others. Nonetheless, it would be misleading to suggest that these disciplines were causal to the entire movement. Because it was the product of social and cultural forces that cut across occupations and disciplines, democratic social engineering was assembled and practiced by sociologists, psychologists, political scientists, philosophers, scientists, religious leaders, educators, and social workers—by everyone who understood the social and procedural nature of modern authority. Put another way, the perceptions that produced an interest in groups, in scientific method, in leadership, and in other elements of what coalesced as group process knew no boundaries of discipline; Jane Addams understood about these things not because John Dewey was a visitor at Hull House, but because the two shared common perceptions about society and authority. Moreover, democratic social engineering was a complex system in which the group was only one entity, and disciplines other than psychology and sociology were often better suited to articulate certain of its qualities. For example, the central notion of engineering through process and inquiry was best articulated not by social psychologists studying small groups but by the pragmatic philosopher-psychologists, John Dewey and William James. Indeed, democratic social engineering was widespread decades before there was any significant body of scholarship on small groups.[23]

Of the historical forces that generated democratic social engineering in the late nineteenth century, arguably the most significant could be described as a culture-wide moral crisis. Many Americans experienced the decay of the old world and the rise of the new in just these terms. Moral principles which had once provided a satisfactory guide for conduct no longer seemed viable. Americans' belief in universal moral values was eroded by the mechanistic universe of evolutionary science. This process occurred on every level of American culture, including the philosophical. There, relativists like James and Dewey rejected a priori truths for "pragmatic" methods, in which truth was a mode of inquiry, a problem-solving method.[24] By 1910, the constellation of beliefs that Edward Purcell labels "scientific naturalism"—the denial of a priori truth, of metaphysics, and of universe-explaining rational principles—had left traditional religion, a national cultural cement since the seventeenth century, in a shambles.[25]

Although Progressive Era reformers by no means dropped the passionate rhetorical moralism of the 1890s, moral issues and moral approaches to social problems were increasingly subsumed into technical issues, claims of expertise, and a new emphasis on means.[26] As it was developed in the group-process movement, the "new morality" had one seminal characteristic: it was a morality of method, of means rather than ends. James insisted that pragmatism had no dogma, no doctrines, "save its method." For Dewey, there was no value in "eternal" categories; "movement and purpose," "fluent doubt and inquiry," were all that mattered. Educational theorist William H. Kilpatrick introduced his most influential statement on curriculum by emphasizing the need for "the factor of action, preferably wholehearted vigorous activity."[27]

There is no simple explanation for this overwhelming insistence on means rather than ends. Was the Progressive Era consensus on values and goals so complete that all attention came to be focused on means?[28] Or had the possibility of agreeing on ends become so unlikely, or so loathsome philosophically, that it was no longer considered viable? The Italian philosopher Papini implied as much when he likened James's pragmatism to "a corridor in a hotel, from which a hundred doors open into a hundred chambers. In one you may see a man on his knees praying to regain his faith; in another, a desk at which sits someone eager to destroy all metaphysics; in a third, a laboratory with an investigator looking for new footholds by which to advance toward wider horizons. *But the corridor belongs to all.*"[29]

Answers to these questions become possible only when we understand that the means/ends dichotomy was in one sense artificial. Group-process advocates realized that ends and means were identical. If agreement on ends had become impossible, consensus could be achieved and maintained through means alone. This was perhaps the most important insight of democratic social engineering: that one could teach a certain way of behaving not just (or not at all) by the force of argument, but rather by creating a particular behavior pattern in one's method. Concretely, group decision making (a method) produced democratic citizens (a goal).

The congruence of means and ends was a persistent theme in Kilpatrick's work. As methodologically oriented as he was, and as much a student of Dewey, his 1918 essay on the "project method" was laced with statements that suggest goals. He was concerned for "the ethical quality of conduct," interested in "democratic citizenship," and he disliked "selfish individualism." Though his writing emphasized method, it was always with clear goals in mind, and it was always with the recognition that means and ends were inseparable.[30]

No less significant than this crisis in morality was the growing sense that the society was coming apart at the seams. The signs of this disintegration — strikes, protests, third-party movements, the depression of 1893, urban poverty, the assassinations of James Garfield and William McKinley and the attempted murder of Henry Clay Frick, the growth of socialism, anarchism, and the trade union movement, the rise of giant corporations — the signs were everywhere. The cohesive, unified society of the past (a myth, to be sure), seemed to have given way to a chaos of self-serving individuals, organizations, and social abstractions.[31] Not the least threatening of these was the industrial working class, now locked into the world of the factory and separated, perhaps irrevocably, from the tools of production. Twentieth-century scholars of authority seem to agree that this new "mass," or perceptions of it, was of enormous concern to the middle class — European as well as American. Thomas Haskell, for example, notes the emergence in the nineteenth century of anxiety over a "mass public, one that threatened to withhold deference from all men, all traditions, and even the highest values."[32]

The study of society, and of the groups, large and small, that were now understood to be part of it, began in earnest. Many early studies, including Gustave LeBon's *The Crowd* (1898), emphasized the potentially irrational dynamics of the collective, group mind.[33] Others, most notably sociologist Charles H. Cooley's *Human Nature and the Social Order* (1902), examined human nature, the self, the personality, and morality as products of social experience and group interaction and standards.[34] Edward A. Ross coined the term "social control" in *Social Control: A Survey of the Foundations of Order* (1901), a remarkably optimistic book in which Ross argued for a natural social control marked by "sincerity, spontaneity, and elasticity . . . ." "The best control," wrote Ross, "is that which rises afresh whenever a handful of persons associate, which therefore, cannot be cornered and monopolized by a scheming class or profession. *Public opinion, suggestion, social religion,* and *art* are naturally diffuse. *Personal ideals, social valuations,* and *illusions* are less so. *Physical force, belief in the supernatural,* and *ceremony* are easily centralized and managed by the few."[35]

The concept of the primary group — the family, the church, the communal circle — came into its own with Cooley's discussion of intimate, cooperative, face-to-face associations in *Social Organization* (1909).[36] The first academic case study of the small group was published in the *American Journal of Psychology* in 1898. Among the significant early essays on small groups were J. A. Puffer's "Boys' Gangs" (1905) and Lewis M. Terman's "A Preliminary Study of the Psychology and Pedagogy of Leadership" (1904).[37]

Its links to the social sciences did not ensure that the new system of authority, fashioned from society and groups, would achieve general acceptance. Social scientists might have labored long and hard only to create a system lacking in widespread appeal. To be effective, the new system would have to mesh with basic American values. In the context of the nineteenth century, this above all meant reconciling the national heritage of individualism with the new thrust of collectivism. Some collective forms, such as national labor unions and giant corporations, threatened the public ideology of individualism that had been at the core of the American experience since the seventeenth century. Yet most Americans, and most intellectuals, had come to believe that the corrosive effects of industrialization, urbanization, and Darwinism could be attenuated only through the development of new forms of collective organization and consciousness. Charles Sanders Peirce, James Mark Baldwin, E. A. Ross, and others, came to advocate new forms of community that were collective and yet consistent with the tradition of individualism.[38]

Group process was an attempt to preserve individualism while outflanking collectivism. Although committed to forms of authority that were social, democratic social engineers were also deeply committed to the survival of individualism. They wrote of "internal authority" and of self-discipline and self-regulation because they believed, or wanted to believe, that genuine individualism could be reconciled with powerful collective mechanisms of decision making and social control.[39] This reconciliation would take place within nonauthoritarian, democratic small groups — within the system of democratic social engineering.

Critics of democratic social engineering might have argued that the new method was only power in another name; that the individual in a group was bound to submit to the demands of the aggregate, to bend to the will of the skillful leader, or to arrive at some conclusion predetermined by causes acting on all individuals. Dewey and James, whose peculiar brand of psychology and philosophy was at the center of group process, would have found such criticism wrongheaded, if only because each believed so deeply in free will. For Dewey, the dynamic process of group interaction itself served as a guarantee that individuals would make thoughtful and intelligent choices. For James, free will was a composite of genius, creative energy, and other manifestations of the power of the human mind to shape the life of the individual. Dewey's freedom of choice and James's free will were essential ideas for those who wished to forge a new collective structure while adhering to an older faith in the primacy of the individual.[40]

THE METHODOLOGY: COMPONENTS OF DEMOCRATIC SOCIAL ENGINEERING

On the eve of the Civil War, it would hardly have made sense to speak of a "system" of democratic social engineering. A search of the social landscape reveals pieces of it, of course: Madison's factions would become the next century's pluralism; Tocqueville had observed the American proclivity to groups; the doctrine of consent was operative in the political sphere; there was much discussion of "internal" authority; and one could see Americans of the 1850s turning away from physical force in the rearing of children, the disciplining of seamen, and the punishment of slaves. A perceptive observer might even have seen a harbinger of a democratic, open system of social control in the Republican party ideology of "free soil, free labor, and free men."[41]

To have projected these elements into a "system," however, would have required an act of faith. Much of the matrix of institutions in which democratic social engineering would operate did not exist in 1860. There were no settlement houses, few public schools, and the YMCA had only in the preceding decade developed an American presence. Sociology and social psychology would not emerge as cogent academic entities for another thirty-five years.

A half century later, one could speak with some clarity of a new "system" of democratic authority. Many of the requisite institutions, including schools, settlements, Bible study groups, the Christian associations, and the scouts, were either mature or very active. Social scientists had begun to publish detailed analyses of small groups. Although there remained an unconscious quality to democratic social engineering — there was as yet no organized profession of social group work, no school of human relations within the business community, no *theory* of "permissive" child rearing — one can, nonetheless, identify with some precision the essential components of democratic social engineering and observe something of its actual operation. In this section, I have set out the basic components of the methodology, drawing on examples largely, though not exclusively, from the core institutions of the late nineteenth and early twentieth centuries that played so central a role in its early development. In addition, the section explicates the strong links between group process, progressive educational theory, and pragmatic philosophy.

The Group

At the center of the methodology was the group. It was within this mechanism that the other elements — of inquiry, democratic participation, and leadership — were to be followed or carried out. The size of the group seems to have made little difference. Baby doctor Benjamin Spock conceptualized the mother/child relationship as a small group though it consisted of only two persons. Educator Kilpatrick, on the other hand, applied democratic social engineering to his own classes of more than six hundred students. The usual vehicle was a small, voluntary organization of five to fifty members. Nor did the circumstances under which groups were founded affect their usefulness for group-process concepts. Some groups, like the Golden Age Clubs of Cleveland (1940–), were organized explicitly for the practice of democratic social engineering. Others, like boys' gangs, were spontaneously created organizations that only later became vehicles for group work. The settlement houses, hardly creations of the "folk" and yet not specifically created for group process activities, lay somewhere in between.[42]

Process

What was new after 1890 or 1900 was not group life itself, but rather the conscious recognition that groups could be important agencies of social adjustment. The success of this therapeutic outlook depended on a further revelation: that the *content* of group experience might be less important in a social sense than the *process* of that experience. The success or failure, for example, of a club discussion on the League of Nations hinged not so much on the arguments made, or on the existence or content of a club consensus, as on the procedures and processes used to present arguments and reach conclusions.

This emphasis on process was the logical, inevitable result of the central assumption of pragmatic thought: absolute truth did not exist. This assumption was shared by the social settlement workers, teachers, and others who functioned as intermediaries between pragmatic philosophy and the objects of democratic social engineering. Thus group-process theorists and practitioners affirmed the need to avoid the teaching of absolutes and usually denied the very existence of absolutes. For example: in 1912 Herman Horne, professor of the history of education and the history of philosophy at New York University, wrote a Bible study manual for departments of Bible study in Young Men's Christian Associations located in colleges. Horne recommended the "conference" (i.e., discussion) method of study, and he cautioned study-group leaders to avoid issues of theology and metaphysics and to stick with the "practical." His message was widely disseminated, for Horne eventually taught some ten thousand students, sponsored over fifty doctoral candidates, published twenty-six books, and, in 1923, became the first professor to broadcast a classroom lecture over the new medium of radio.[43]

A second example comes from Pittsburgh, where social settlement worker Charles C. Cooper developed something of a reputation for the group discussions that took place at Kingsley House, of which Cooper was head resident, and for the intellectual forums known as the Hungry Club. Having originated as an intimate luncheon gathering, the Hungry Club was by the late 1920s attracting hundreds of Jewish, Catholic, and Protestant leaders to its forums. This growth, Cooper proudly emphasized, had taken place democratically, even anarchically, for the Hungry Club "has no organization, no officers, no rules, constitution, or by-laws. It lives simply by the precedents that have been established through its own experience." Cooper was especially pleased when participants in a 1928/29 lecture series on religion demonstrated indifference to matters of doctrine (i.e., to absolutes) once treated as primary and sacrosanct. Commenting on the "total lack of reference on the part of both speakers and audience to the creeds and dogmas of the church today," Cooper plumbed the possibility that this indifference might prefigure a new kind of bond: "Was there something of prophecy in this as to a new church of the future which, without the mechanical aid of creeds, would yet bind men to it as strongly as did the church of the past, through perhaps more profound and fundamental loyalties?" (Cooper was not entirely clear about what these "more profound and fundamental loyalties" were, though he went on to suggest that they were exemplified in the "deep loyalties to an ideal" which had nurtured the Hungry Club.)[44]

One finds a similar combination of spontaneity, self-government, and rejection of absolutes in John Lovejoy Elliott's work with the Ethical Culture Society and the Hudson Guild, a social settlement. In its relationship to the group-process movement, Elliott's career is a transitional one, since his work reveals shadows of group process while never coming to grips with it as a unified system of social engineering.

Elliott came under the influence of Felix Adler, the founder of the Ethical Culture movement, while a student at Cornell in the 1880s. The following decade, after receiving a Ph.D. at the University of Halle, he worked as Adler's assistant at the Ethical Culture School in New York City, where he met several persons, including Jane Addams and Mary Kingsbury Simkhovitch, who would later be identified with the group-process movement. By the late 1890s, Elliott's activities centered on the Chelsea neighborhood in New York City, where he helped organize local residents into clubs. When, in 1897, six or seven of these clubs came to think of themselves as one unit, the Hudson Guild was born.[45]

In structuring the Hudson Guild, and as a participant in the Ethical Culture movement, Elliott employed a nondirective approach to decision making and ethics. Because he believed in the capacity of ordinary people to govern themselves, his Progressive Era reorganization of the Hudson Guild resulted in a governance structure famed for its democratic characteristics. Under this new structure, each club or group sent delegates to a house council. Although Elliott could veto the decisions of the House Council, that body could override the veto with a two-thirds vote.[46]

The Ethical Culture movement, as Elliott described its fifty-year history in 1929, was an attempt to bring together agnostics, atheists, and theists under one ethical tent. Although Elliott did not deny that some objective standards existed (he talked about a "better way of life"), he emphasized that participants in the Ethical Culture movement were "not asked to adopt any creed, official philosophy, or metaphysics." Where the old religions appealed through drama and emotion, ethical culture "has today only its appeal to truth, which in modern times has been construed chiefly in terms of science."[47]

Elliott rejected as a bonding force for the Ethical Culture movement certain kinds of rigid, authoritative mechanisms — the creed, the "official" philosophy, even metaphysics (by definition, "the branch of philosophy that treats of first principles or the ultimate nature of existence, reality, and experience").[48] Instead, Ethical Culture was held together by "truth." But this truth was never defined as a fact or as a series of facts. Truth, indeed, was not something that *is.* It was, as Elliott said, "construed," and it was "construed" by "science." Truth, in short, was a *process* — the scientific process.

Inquiry

"Inquiry" was only one of several words and phrases used by democratic social engineers to describe this part of the methodology. Others were "group thinking," "conference," "discussion," and "science." In the final analysis, they had the same meaning, connoting process, a kind of objectivity, movement toward truth, and optimism. Authors in the group-process area usually assumed the close relationships between these terms. Occasionally, however, the similarities were consciously examined. For example, in a 1949 handbook on industrial conference methods, Henry M. Busch made the case for the similarity of the conference method and the scientific method. "In both," he wrote, "the basic attitude is honest inquiry, not partisan defense. Both require analysis of a problem, a search for a solution which squares with all the facts at hand, and practical testing of the solution."[49]

Having affirmed the objectivity of science, Busch went on to use that "fact" of objectivity to demonstrate that his own tool, the conference method, was also objective. This definition of science, however, denied to science and inquiry an important, even crucial quality given it by the leading theorists of the group-process movement: inquiry was the ultimate tool of social action. Dewey, the leading theorist of the movement, suggested as much in an 1891 letter to William James. "A tremendous movement is impending," he wrote, "when the intellectual forces which have been gathering since the Renascence and Reformation, shall demand complete free movement, and, by getting their physical leverage in the telegraph and printing press, shall, through free inquiry in a centralized way, demand the authority of all other so-called authorities."[50]

Here, in capsule form, are Dewey's rejection of philosophical idealism and his belief in inquiry as the methodology of the future.[51] Although this particular statement focused on centralized means of communication — the telegraph and the printing press — most of Dewey's work assumed that the inquiry method was available to, and appropriate to, the smallest and most intimate contexts of life: families, neighborhoods, play groups, the classroom, clubs, and so forth.[52]

Democratic Participation

Practitioners and theorists conceptualized group process as anti-elitist not only in the above sense of unrestricted availability of the methodology, but also in terms of the processes that were theoretically, or actually, carried out in the groups. John Lovejoy Elliott, as we have seen, reorganized his Hudson Guild settlement to reflect his sympathies for demo-

cratic participation in Guild decision-making processes. Equally important was the contribution of Harrison Sackett Elliott (no relation), who
pioneered democratic methods in the YMCA and at Union Theological
Seminary. Harrison Elliott took degrees at Ohio Wesleyan University,
Drew Theological Seminary, and Columbia University (where he was a
student of Dewey and Kilpatrick). After a career with the International
Committee of the YMCA, Elliott came to Union Theological Seminary
in 1922 as assistant professor of religious education. His contributions to
democratic social engineering will be treated at length in the following
chapter. For the moment, it is sufficient to note that his teaching methods —
typical of the group-process movement, and clearly influenced by his association with Kilpatrick — reflect the movement's interest in democratic participation. One of Elliott's students at Union wrote:

As I recall my own student days during Dr. Elliott's first years here, I feel that
students were intrigued and stimulated by his genuine faith in the values which
would come from group thinking and from individual student participation in the
work of his classes. We came to realize that he meant what he said when he urged
us to do our own thinking and to come to conclusions by a group process in which
issues were fairly faced and every person shared in the quest for the truth.

According to another Elliott student, those who took the professor's courses
"experienced the democratic method in group work. Skillful in the discussion method, which he employed almost exclusively in his classes, they
witnessed in him the actual practice of the techniques of non-directive
leadership."[53]

Democratic participation seems natural enough in the classroom, but
its scope was hardly limited to this area. The settlements were equally
important. Lillian Wald's Henry Street and Jane Addams' Hull House were
the scene of significant efforts in democratic social engineering. Hull House,
in fact, was described in 1923 as a prime example of "democratic religion"
in a study by liberal reformer and theologian William Adams Brown and
designed to analyze religious forms in the new language of social psychology.[54] In the 1920s, the YWCA Girl Reserve movement "democratized"
its program to allow for greater youth participation in program planning.
The theoretical perspective which culminated in the first Golden Age Clubs
in Cleveland in 1940 was shot through with the idea that the aged should
take an active role in every form of club activity. Industry was less
enamored of this particular aspect of group-process methodology, but even
so, many businessmen believed there were advantages to worker participation in certain kinds of corporate activities. The participatory ideal was,
for example, an aspect of the corporate-sponsored foremen's club movement which followed the First World War.[55] Wherever one finds demo-

cratic social engineering — in organized recreation, in religious education, in child rearing, or in geriatrics — one also finds this insistence on participation, often in association with the word "democratic," and sometimes contrasted with processes and modes of decision making characterized as autocratic, authoritarian, or by the 1940s totalitarian.

Leadership

The frequent, even obligatory use of these words does not prove that the group-process movement was democratic, or anti-elitist, or both. Participation in itself is not democracy. We have all "participated," even actively, in processes in which we had no real or ultimate power to affect policy or outcome. What can be said with some sureness is that the group-process movement may be defined in part by its tendency to trumpet its democratic ingredients.

Were immigrants running the Hudson Guild? Were Harrison Elliott's students functioning as teachers in his classes? Were the elderly in Cleveland's Golden Age Clubs and the workers in Dayton, Ohio's, foremen's clubs making policy? Were these and other objects of the group-process movement exerting significant influence in the organizations to which they belonged? Answers to these questions must take account of still another element in the group-process methodology: leadership. Just as democratic participation was obligatory in group-process parlance, so was leadership. At issue was not only the structure of group life — the shape and form of every sort of organization and institution — but also a vision, in microcosm, of American democracy. Behind most statements on group leadership was an implied framework of ideas about democratic government and the relationship between governors and governed, between experts and followers.

Group-process advocates considered themselves proponents of democracy. By this term, they generally rejected systems of social control which they believed allowed for too little guidance from above (sometimes labeled "laissez-faire") and systems which allowed for too much guidance (sometimes labeled "dictatorship," "totalitarianism," or "authoritarianism"). The area between laissez-faire and dictatorship they defined as "democracy." Even so, that area was so large that group-process advocates often differed on just how much leadership, and what kind, was appropriate to democratic social organization. After World War I, for example, two participants in The Inquiry, the organization which sought to diffuse racial, ethnic, and industrial conflict through group discussion, could differ significantly on the question of leadership. One, Bruno Lasker, emphasized a light-handed leadership which he called "the encouragement of democratic study." The other, Robert Park, the urban sociologist, insisted that group process could be effective only if shaped by the charismatic leader.[56]

Most group-process advocates avoided characterizations of democratic social engineering that required a "charismatic leader" to be effective, and most stood clear also of a nondirective group process in which leadership had no part. The usual problem lay in constructing a methodology that allowed, in theory at least, for the interplay of leadership and democratic participation. A case in point is the work of William Clayton Bower, who in 1929 published a leadership training curriculum for the International Council of Religious Education. Bower had absorbed the work of Dewey, Kilpatrick, Harold Rugg, and other progressive educators, and his curriculum fused education, psychology, and religion. He likened the teacher in a group-process situation to a coach, to a "human and educational engineer." Moreover, the teacher's leadership role apparently rested on some democratic sanction, for "his position in the group will not rest upon an authoritarian basis. . . ."[57]

Yet in at least one respect, the group leader's role was lacking in genuine democratic sanction: groups seldom chose their leaders. Children did not choose their parents, students did not choose their teachers, and the older persons who filled Cleveland's Golden Age Clubs in the 1940s did not choose their leaders. The American Boy Scouts were reluctant to give up the leadership control that a proper development of boy-led patrols would have implied; instead, they held tightly to the reins of power by focusing scouting activities around the adult-led troop.[58] Where the possibility of elected leadership did not exist — the case in most institutions of democratic social engineering — the literature is silent on the crucial question of where leaders come from. Indeed, they seem to appear out of nowhere.

Despite the failure to isolate a democratic source of leadership, social engineers invariably denied any desire to establish an authoritarian or autocratic system. Bower, for example, insisted that education could take place only through "responsible social participation in the life of the group," and he denounced authoritarian education for its neglect of the "complete sharing of experience," the sine qua non of "perfect comprehension." Yet Bower's characterization of the learning/teaching process as a relationship between "immature" and "mature" persons and his description of the guidance process (of the role of the group leader) make it difficult to establish the point of balance in this hypothetical democracy. In fact, Bower's leader is a powerful person with considerable latitude:

It is the function of the teacher as guide to help the learner locate and feel the crucial and problematical areas in his experience. He should assist the learner in analyzing his situation by seeing that he does not overlook or neglect essential factors which the learner because of his immaturity or inexperience might not see. He will assist the learner to search and criticize his own past experience so as to see at what points it is inadequate, erroneous, or merely a matter of assumption or prejudice. He will stimulate the learner to search for adequate facts and will suggest where he may find the sources of facts. He will help the learner to search diligently for all the possible outcomes to a situation and to evaluate them all in the light of the highest standards of the race. He will assist him in making wise choices and in planning economically and wisely for the carrying out of his purpose. He will stand by through the patient process and help the learner to sustain his purpose until he has carried through. He will help the learner to identify the qualities of character that are Christian and to integrate them into a consistent system of principles for the conduct of life. And throughout the process, he will assist the learner to discover the values involved in the process and to develop appreciations of the meaning and worth of life. Above all, he will help the learner to feel so deeply these appreciations that in their most intense and spiritual form they will ripen for him into a sense of the Divine companionship and of a vital co-operation with God in the achievement of the purposes of the Kingdom of God.[59]

Perhaps the most striking feature of this passage is the fusion of a particular methodology to very specific goals. Like the terminology "mature" and "immature" and the wide range of functions granted to the leader, this fusion of ends and means calls into question the distinction which Bower attempted to draw between participatory and authoritarian education. If the methodology is inseparable from clearly defined goals, as it seems to be here, then the scope for the learner's participation is considerably reduced.

One finds this advocacy of firm and aggressive leadership in almost every group-process manifesto. It is present in the writings of Grace Coyle and other theorists of social group work; in the work of recreational theorist Eduard C. Lindeman; and in Spock's classic, *The Common Sense Book of Baby and Child Care*.

Perhaps the earliest appearance of this notion of leadership in an identifiable literary genre occurred in the first decade of the twentieth century among writers, like Bower, who were bent on developing an improved system of religious education. Foremost among them was George Albert Coe, the first non-Presbyterian to teach at Union Theological Seminary and one of the first religious educators to find in the "New Psychology" procedures relevant to religious instruction. Like other group-process advocates, Coe was attracted to voluntary organizations as a vehicle of social engineering. The organizations were especially valuable because they provided the "opportunity for enlarged self-expression, especially under the influence and with the friendship of a mature leader."[60] Others saw similar possibilities in "self-governing Bible classes" in which a leader would encourage "freedom of thought" on the one hand and "lead his boys out of doubt and difficulty by the path of service" on the other. The Men and Religion Forward Movement, an interdenominational religious education movement formally launched in Buffalo, New York, in 1910, was explicitly organized to reflect the growing reliance on trained leadership. Traditional devices — large conventions and inspirational meetings — were no longer sufficient. "Where there is adequate leadership," read a tract published in 1912, "any one of the features of the message can be readily incorporated in the permanent program of the Church."[61]

Leadership — even the consciousness of leadership — is a universal in human history. The post-1900 interest in leadership, however, had two unique qualities. First, it took place within an academic environment. Those who used the language of leadership at this time were well aware that they were practitioners of a new social "science." Second, these ideas of leadership were being applied to primary and voluntary organizations, to small groups that heretofore had not seemed likely vehicles of social engineering. Early practitioners of group process were creating a system of social engineering ideally suited to a democratic culture.

FROM EXHORTATION TO ENGINEERING: THE CRISIS OF INSTITUTIONAL PROTESTANTISM

Of the major institutions of the 1800s, the church was perhaps the most troubled at the end of the century. Protestantism, especially, had not proved durable in its encounters with industrialization, cities, science, and the state. The urban masses had found the church unwilling to grapple with sweatshops, poverty, child labor, and other social products of the nineteenth-century political economy. Many were also distressed at the difficulty of reconciling Christian theology with Darwinian biology. The process of disestablishment, by which churches were separated from the state and denied its nurture, was completed in 1833; the result was a voluntary system under which the aggressive, evangelical denominations prospered, while those with traditional methods of gathering — the Congregationalists, Unitarians, and Presbyterians — entered into a long period of relative decline.[62]

The denominations responded to these challenges in many ways, most of them beyond the scope of this book. Some denominations, for example, developed retirement systems in an effort to attract a younger and more aggressive clergy. Methodists and Baptists recruited a lower-class immigrant population through an emotional evangelicalism. A segment of the nonevangelical Protestant clergy found relief in a sentimental alliance with women, another disestablished element of nineteenth-century American life.[63]

Nothing the church could do would preserve Christian religion as a way of interpreting every worldly event; but the church could, and did, project a new image that was at once less oriented toward individual soul saving and more attuned to the growing desires of many persons for social and communal experience.

Two aspects of this new sociological approach concern us here. One, the story of the social gospel, has been told often enough elsewhere. It will be retold here only to place it in the context of new social theories of personality. The second, the pioneering use of group-process techniques in turn-of-the-century Sunday schools, Bible study classes, Christian clubs, YMCAs, and other institutional offshoots of Protestantism, will receive more extended treatment. In essence, the church entered the nineteenth century a powerful institution, its fortunes linked to the state. It entered the twentieth century linked, instead, to a new and potent form of authority, in its own way just as political: the authority of the social sciences. Its story has been included here because the formidable challenge to the church's preeminence as an institution led it so quickly, and so dramatically, to group-process methods. Unique in its intensity, it was in other respects a typical nineteenth-century experience, and one that can be used to flesh out and set off the larger history of authority.

The Social Gospel

The main outlines of the social gospel are well known. In the last quarter of the nineteenth century, the nation's Protestant churches came to see the teachings of Jesus as a "social" gospel, a message of brotherly love and humanitarianism. Toe-to-toe with the problems of urban-industrial America, fearful of class divisions, and anxious to bring the masses into their churches, the Protestant clergy shed its Calvinist emphasis on salvation through individual regeneration for a new interest in meliorative social action. By 1912, according to historian Henry May, the social gospel was "the characteristic American religion of the articulate and up-to-date middle class."[64]

Interpreting the social gospel movement from the perspective of democratic social engineering adds an additional dimension to an explanation of why the clergy, and the American Protestant community, came to appreciate social reform. The substance of my argument is that by 1910, and perhaps earlier, the clergy's commitment to social action was, at least in part, generated by certain widely held and well-thought-out views on the structure of personality and of the role which personality could play in encouraging people to join the church. The gospel had become social in order to reach and convert the new "social" — i.e., socially defined — personality.

An earlier generation of clergy had seen personality and people as dual: secular and spiritual. This dualism was convenient. Because of it, the church could afford to ignore the secular side of human beings and depend on reaching people by appealing to their spiritual selves. Darwinian biology, however, brought the very idea of a spiritual nature into question. The comfortable dualism — which had allowed the Protestant church to avoid both social issues and evangelicalism's approach to redemption — collapsed.[65]

The problem, and even the potential for its solution in a social-scientific approach to personality, had been sensed long before the turn of the century. Late eighteenth- and nineteenth-century revivalism downplayed doctrine and emphasized Christianity as a social phenomenon. This was also the approach of Henry Ward Beecher, the embodiment of Northern, middle-class, liberal Protestantism. Never much concerned with fine distinctions between denominations, Beecher held consecutive posts in Presbyterian and Congregational churches. Similarly disdainful of theological subtleties, he designed his sermons as emotional experiences. By the early 1870s, Beecher had come to believe that the weaknesses of the church were traceable to the new social sciences. Where laymen had once consulted ministers to understand the nature of man, they now turned to professional students of human nature. The church could survive, Beecher argued, only if it adapted the modern tools of social analysis to its own uses. "You must know what men are in order to reach them," he said, "and that is part of the science of preaching."[66]

For the "New Psychology," influential in the work of Peirce, James, Dewey, and other intellectuals, personality was purely social, the product of social experience. This view of personality was absorbed quickly and completely in fields such as religious education, where it proved useful, and in institutions, such as the YMCA, that were part of the social gospel movement. It now became commonplace for religious educators to denigrate the idea of a dual personality, to assert that personality was social, and, because it was social, to insist that personality could be "realized" only in groups.[67]

One advocate of the social personality was Baptist clergyman and educator Clarence Barbour. During an eighteen-year Rochester, New York, pastorate that began in 1891, Barbour championed the causes of middle-class Progressivism, including improved public schools and "good" government. Resigning in 1909 to become associate secretary of the Religious

Works Department of the International Committee of the YMCA, Barbour became a leader in the evangelistic Men and Religion Forward Movement and developed a reputation as a superb public speaker. In *Making Religion Efficient,* a publication edited for the YMCA in 1912, Barbour summarized the issues of social personality as they applied to the recruitment of adolescent youth. "Too long," he wrote, "has the church . . . considered the boy as a dual personality and regarded life as both secular and spiritual. Today it is beginning to understand that all boyhood life is spiritual; that there are no secular activities in boyhood, but that every activity that a boy enters into has tremendous spiritual value, either for good or for bad."[68]

Another proponent of the social personality was Sherwood Eddy, international secretary of the YMCA and a theorist of that organization's endeavors. A genuine reformation, Eddy claimed in 1926, was dependent upon "human fellowship," for two reasons. First, associations had in the past been powerful agents of reformation. The Russian Revolution, the founding of the American republic, the Italian campaigns of Giuseppi Mazzini — all had been dependent on the cooperative unity of the group. Second, association was critical to personality. "It is in this active comradeship between personalities, in the battle for a common quest, that personality itself is transformed. Men are molded in association, whether with men or God. Isolated individuals are welded into an organism. Companionship leads in turn to coöperation, discovery, light, vision, courage, accomplishment." According to Eddy, the YMCA triangle symbolized a "fresh emphasis upon the unity of personality . . ." When the YWCA Girl Reserve program published a manual for advisers in 1921, this theory of personality was evident: "The girl is a whole girl, in any situation, with all of her personality involved; this means that she must be trained as a whole person."[69]

In his history of the YMCA, Eddy wrote that the major purpose of the organization — to help young men "grow as Christians" — had not changed since the organization's founding. The group's methods, however, had changed a great deal. From the religious meetings and personal contacts of the early days, the YMCA had gravitated toward the recreational, vocational, and citizenship education programs that made the organization an important participant in the social gospel movement. "What it meant to be a Christian," Eddy concluded, "was now understood in more comprehensive terms."[70]

The social gospel was a method for realizing older goals of individual salvation. Religious educator Bower, for example, claimed that Jesus had clearly suggested that "it was through the adequate perception and fulfilment of the human social relations that one would find the most open and illumined way to God. It may be said," Bower concluded, "that it is impossible for the isolated self to enter upon religious experience to the fullest extent."[71] Christianity came to be seen as a way of life (i.e., the gospel became social) because the church itself had come to see the *idea* of a "way of life" as a productive and useful one. The social gospel was one indication that Protestantism had been studying at the feet of the new social sciences.

The Protestant church had learned that it could grow and prosper only by abandoning outmoded techniques of soul saving for methods which activated the social personality. Armed with this knowledge, the church moved to create an organizational matrix appropriate to the new social techniques. Older institutions were remodeled to become vehicles for group process — for democratic social engineering. Organizations outside the church, such as boys' gangs, were examined for what they could contribute. New organizations, such as the Girl Reserves, were founded, and new organizational efforts, such as the Men and Religion Forward Movement, were mounted — largely to take advantage of this new social avenue into the hearts of men. Within these organizations, church authorities and religious educators applied a wide variety of techniques adapted from Dewey, James, Froebel, and others — the methodology described in the previous section of this chapter.

Some religious educators believed that Christian instruction should take place in the public schools. The most prominent and influential advocate of this view was Coe. Raised in a Methodist parsonage in the decade after the Civil War, Coe was troubled by his inability to have a conversion experience. While remaining committed to religion as a way of life and field of study, he made his peace with evolution and scientific method. Trained in theology and philosophy, Coe began his academic career at the University of Southern California, moving on to Northwestern University in 1893 as John Evans Professor of Philosophy of Religion. He helped found the Religious Education Association in 1903. Perhaps irresistibly drawn to New York City, the center of group-process thought and practice, Coe became professor of religious education and psychology of religion at Union Theological Seminary in 1909 and joined the faculty at Teachers College of Columbia University in 1922. The author of numerous books on religious education, he was an enormously influential figure within twentieth-century liberal Protestantism.[72]

Like Dewey, Coe had no desire to spearhead an attempt to reintroduce a "dogmatic religious instruction that has been properly excluded from the people's schools." He also rejected the "abrupt processes of the revival," preferring to pursue salvation of the young through education. Like Dewey, who was working on the idea that democracy and scientific method might be melded into a faith appropriate to the public school, Coe believed that religion, properly shaped, might find a place in the classroom. For this to happen, he argued, religious education had to become "modern," that is, modern in methodology. Religion could find a way into the public schools if it ceased to be dogmatic, if it shunned "authority" for the techniques of progressive education. In a sense, Coe sought to bypass the separation of church and state by making the gospel social in purpose and by teaching the gospel through group-process methods.[73]

Group-process advocates also believed that the family was a potential vehicle for social control through group methods. Although more difficult to shape than the public school and impossible to recreate, it had the advantage of being a preexisting, virtually universal institution. Very little needed to be done to perfect the family's social-control functions, since obedience, as Coe argued in his 1904 work, was a product of community life and the family was a natural community.[74]

Nonetheless, Coe and others apparently believed that some families were excessively authoritarian in structure and needed help in carrying out their community functions. The help they offered came in the form of progressive educational theory and group methods. Equating the commanding-parent/obeying-child concept with "the mediaeval conception of church authority and the Augustinian doctrine of divine decrees," Coe argued that authoritarian child rearing sacrificed the home's potential as an educational institution. Obedience and character emerged when the child exercised "the functions of a member of the family community."[75]

George Walter Fiske's 1910 study of boy life contained a similar conception of parental and familial authority. Fiske was a prolific author and frequent lecturer before ministers, teachers, and YMCA workers. His analysis may well have reflected his membership in the American Sociological Society. Like Coe's ideal family, Fiske's was a supervised partnership. Parents should offer "friendly encouragement, moral support, watchful interest, unobtrusive guidance, timely and definite suggestion, and a frank spirit of comradeship," while gradually withdrawing their control of the boy.[76]

Schools and families held great potential for social engineering through group process, but neither was entirely accessible to the church. The search for a more convenient vehicle brought many religious leaders to Sunday schools and Bible study clubs, traditional institutions that could be adapted easily to the new group methods.[77] Between 1900 and 1912, a substantial literature appeared that justified the Sunday schools and Bible clubs as suitable tools and set down both an elaborate educational theory and a specific methodology. A spirit of discovery permeates this literature, as if some remarkable new power had been placed at the service of religion.

Charles E. McKinley's perspective is typical in this regard. McKinley had worked with the Grinnell, Iowa, YMCA, attended Chicago Theological Seminary, and been ordained a Congregational minister in 1894. In *Educational Evangelism* (1905), McKinley claimed that "a moral magnetic field of particular character and well-nigh irresistible power" operated in "every community, neighborhood, or group." Because they were often naturally formed (and, therefore, somehow especially open to leadership), Sunday school groups offered unique opportunities for religious education. Writing in 1912, Barbour shared McKinley's faith in the power of the Bible class as a "means of direct and indirect evangelism."[78]

The theory and methodology of these and other authors were adapted from—and paralleled—the work of the pragmatic philosophers and progressive educators. Edwin F. See's YMCA-sponsored study, *The Teaching of Bible Classes*, demonstrated familiarity with the writings of Dewey, James, Charles De Garmo, and other progenitors of progressive education. See suggested that Bible classes utilize the "question method" of teaching in order to arouse student "self-activity"; his insistence that specific subject matter reflect the interests of the student amounted to an early, partial formulation of what Kilpatrick would later label the "project method." Behind Barbour's notion of a "conversational" approach lay a similar emphasis on nondirective teaching. The teacher, Barbour wrote, "is called to make men Bible students, not eager listeners to addresses." Several studies emphasized the importance of leadership. Written for departments of Bible study in college YMCAs, Herman Horne's *The Leadership of Bible Study Groups* offered the most explicit directions for group leaders. McKinley's vision was the pastor-as-teacher, entering into the "natural" groups formed by boys and girls, earning their confidence, becoming "one of their group, his influence . . . beyond estimation."[79]

Sunday schools and Bible clases were accessible to the clergy, but they possessed a major weakness: their membership was confined to those who had already been brought into some relationship to the church. How could one enlarge the pool of potential converts? Must one rely on groups with some clear religious content? Group-process enthusiasts found answers to these questions in the nascent theory of progressive education. Two elements of this theory are applicable here. First, learning was a function of "interest"; one learned when the subject matter was useful, and one did not learn when the subject matter failed to touch one's basic needs. Second, methodology was as important as subject matter. Certain things— especially ethics and morals—could be taught in any context, provided the instructional *method* was ethically and morally appropriate (or, in Barbour's framework, "there are no secular activities in boyhood . . .").[80]

Progressive education taught the traditional Protestant clergy that it could move beyond the Bible class and the Sunday school to groups as yet untouched by religion. In fact, "religion" might be more effectively presented in groups with no obvious religious function, but in which members had a vital "interest" in group activities.

The church found the proper vehicle in the clubs and gangs that were a feature of adolescent and preadolescent life at the turn of the century. In 1902, playground advocate Luther Gulick supervised a study of the social instincts of youth; a decade later, several studies of clubs and gangs had appeared, demonstrating that spontaneous associations were widespread among youth, especially those between the ages of seven and seventeen.[81] Fiske, having left the ministry to become professor of religious education and practical theology at Oberlin Graduate School of Theology, argued that boys' gangs and clubs, hostile though they might be to "the orderly forces of society," could be utilized in the quest for self-control and leadership. Instead of acting upon boys with adult-created organizations that were unlikely to appeal to youth, Fiske suggested that the gangs and clubs be examined and their methods and forms approximated in the work of the YMCA. McKinley and Barbour were also convinced that effective church work with boys must proceed through existing, spontaneously formed gangs and clubs. "The gang itself," wrote McKinley, "may be turned into an effective educational agency."[82]

The willingness to cast off theology and dogma for a more social approach to recruitment was also present in the Men and Religion Forward Movement, a short-lived but methodologically innovative experiment in interdenominational evangelism. Its major components — the denominations, the men's and boys' departments of the Sunday schools, and the YMCA — agreed that it was time to bring "efficiency" to religion and the church. In practice, this meant replacing a divisive and unproductive theology with a "universal appeal to all types of believers" (i.e., the social gospel), and rejecting large conventions and inspirational meetings for a program of education through smaller local groups under Movement-trained leaders.[83]

A final example of the larger process through which a religious world view was replaced by a secular, social, and ultimately "democratic" one brings us back to Coe. One of many students of religion who in the early years of the twentieth century came to apply "scientific psychology" to the conversion experience, Coe summarized the conclusions of these scholars in 1916, when he described conversion as "a step in the creation of society," an abrupt change occurring in the context of "self-realization within a social medium." That phrase — "self-realization within a social medium" — was nothing less than shorthand for the "project method," made famous by educational theorist Kilpatrick in 1918. According to Kilpatrick, the project method made knowledge instrumental to some other pursuit of the individual, group, or school class. Successful education required only that this pursuit, or "project," whether it be sewing a dress or flying a kite, be a "whole-hearted purposeful activity proceeding in a social environment."[84] Coe's adolescent was brought to the faith, and Kilpatrick's student was educated, *in society* — that is, in the presence of other persons who were interested in the particular goals.

CONCLUSION

On the eve of the Great War, democratic social engineering had come of age. What in the mid-nineteenth century had been a collage of ideas about factions, organizational life, democracy, and society had coalesced into a field of force, complete with a complex and well-defined methodology, an organizational and institutional support system, and philosophic underpinnings.

Behind the new system was the American middle class. Confused by industrialization, fearful of the immigrant and working-class masses, concerned with mobility in an age of big corporations and growing bureaucracies, this class looked to the social sciences to forge a system of authority that would explain and limit social change, control the masses, and guarantee its offspring respectability. The solution to these problems lay in creating a system of authority from the beast itself — from the threatening public, the feared crowd, the intimidating bureaucracy. Social scientists demonstrated how groups might themselves become mechanisms of social engineering, and how individuals might prosper in group environments. Pragmatic philosophers showed how the scientific idea of inquiry could be stood on its head to become a model of social stability and a mechanism of social control. Educational theorists transferred the whole system into the concrete plane of classrooms, clubs, Sunday schools, and gangs.

In an organizational sense, most of the pioneering was done in the churches, where an older system of authority, symbolized by the minister preaching to his congregation about the "wages of sin," had proved inadequate to the institution's needs, and where a new system promised revitalization and growth. A second area of influence, and one perhaps more vital in the long run to the rise of group-process methodology, was the schools. The schools had long been recognized as a major vehicle of socialization, a function underscored by the heavy influx of "new" immigrants in the half century after 1880. What we now refer to as progressive education or child-centered education, with its emphasis on classroom methodology over content, was conceptualized and practiced on a limited basis in the 1890s and refined theoretically in the Progressive Era.[85] When two of the problems central to the middle class — urbanization and immigration — came together in the 1880s, the settlement house became the third locus of democratic social engineering.

During the 1920s, each of these areas — education, religious education, and the settlements — were increasingly shaped by group constructs. At the same time, democratic methods moved into the mainstream of American life as the 1920s defined it. Elements of group process began to shape production, selling, public relations, and other aspects of the world of business. As the Progressive Era drew to a close, democratic social engineering was on the verge of a major expansion. That expansion would owe much to American participation in the First World War.

2

A New Religion: Democracy and the Great War

On the face of it, the attempt to create a system of authority based on the social sciences would seem to have been doomed to failure. To be sure, social authority had its strengths. Foremost among them was its subtlety. Social engineers might work their magic in a great variety of group situations, secure in the knowledge that the objects of their efforts would remain unaware that they were being engineered, controlled, or socialized. Moreover, the system promised to grow in strength rapidly, as the burgeoning disciplines of sociology, social psychology, and pragmatic philosophy each year shed new light on the nature of behavior, on groups, on group processes, and on other components of social authority.

But even to enumerate these strengths is to imply a critical weakness. In a word, social authority was top-heavy. As a system, it made superb sense to John Dewey, William James, William H. Kilpatrick, George Albert Coe, and dozens of other intellectuals and academics. It was comprehensible and even compelling for the hard-core social engineers — social workers, Boy Scout officials, Bible study-group and club leaders, parents, and teachers — who carried on the day-to-day labor of modifying behavior.

Still, authority functions best when both subject and object, engineers and engineered, have an emotional investment in it. The problem in creating an efficacious system of social authority lay, therefore, in getting the objects of control — the students, children, immigrants, workers, and others — to look enthusiastically on the set of processes called social authority, to feel as if they had some important stake in obedience.

The system contained a mechanism for generating such enthusiasm: participation. The theory had always been that control would be less likely to be resisted, and might even be welcomed, if its objects were involved, or felt involved, in what was happening to them. To this end, turn-of-the-century social engineers employed a variety of participatory devices, including discussions, forums, debates, and inquiry.

But these were essentially the technical paraphernalia of participation, not far removed from the textbooks of the social scientists. Social authority would work only if participation could be invested with some clearly emotional content — only, in short, if social authority could be elevated from a dry methodology of social science to a compelling ideology capable of eliciting feelings of affection and loyalty. Enter democracy.

The transformation of social authority into a democratic ideology did not happen overnight. Indeed, the ideology of democracy was always implicit in the participatory mechanism of group process. John Lovejoy Elliott's Hudson Guild was explicitly democratic. George Fiske's 1910 study of boy life was infused with ideas of self-government and democracy. In 1912, Clarence Barbour described the ideal Bible class as "self-governing," a word that partook of democracy without being quite as meaningful or stirring.[1] For the most part, however, the possibilities of converting mechanisms such as self-government into the ideological weapon of democracy remained unfulfilled until the era of the Great War. Only then, with the nation in desperate need of a powerful tool of social efficiency and control, did democracy take on the character of a full-blown American religion.

What had been a fragmented and obscure movement in 1900 or 1910 — a movement that could be easily visualized only historically, in retrospect — had by 1920 or 1925 become well developed and highly conceptualized and institutionalized. In 1910, the theoretical basis for democratic social engineering had been clearly explicated only in philosophy and education, and even in the latter field, the contributions of Dewey and Kilpatrick were six and eight years in the future, respectively. By 1920, Dewey had published *Democracy and Education*, Kilpatrick had described the "project method," and Mary Parker Follett had published *The New State*, practically a manual for democratic social engineering.[2] In 1900, only a few formal studies of groups had appeared in the new journals of the social sciences; by 1925, dozens were in print — a reflection of the growing belief that group life lay at the heart of social arrangements and, therefore, at the heart of social engineering.[3]

This growth and development were in no small way related to the war and its aftermath. Although democratic social engineering had always been peculiarly suited to the American social context, it was especially so in the decade after 1917, when Americans sought as never before to create and refine a system of authority that was at once opposed to German statism and yet efficient enough to bring victory in war; at once capable of utilizing the modern tools of education and leadership as the Creel Committee, the government's propaganda agency, had done, yet somehow distinct from "real" propaganda, manipulation, and elitism. At a time when youth rejected parents, clergy, and teachers who lectured them, nondirective authority, usually in the form of the group discussion, seemed ideal.[4] At a time when the ravages of war made all *goals* suspect, a system of authority based on *means* offered a solution. (Science was idealized in the 1920s not because it offered absolutes, but because it offered a *process* of inquiry that was experimental.)[5] In an era when conflict seemed the natural order of things, nothing seemed more useful than a structure of authority which utilized cooperative problem solving.[6] In a decade in which the "masses" seemed more dangerous than ever before, Americans — an important group of them at least — worked to create a structure of authority which obviated that threat by subsuming the dangerous element in a "democratic" structure.

MAKING THE WORLD SAFE

On an April day in 1917, Woodrow Wilson asked the Congress of the United States for a declaration of war against Germany. The enemy was autocracy: "the world must be made safe for democracy." This, one of the most famous lines ever delivered by an American president, has since been seen as a kind of overblown and unfortunate propaganda, the beginning of a misguided effort to market the war as a great democratic crusade. Thus, when the war failed to fulfill the promise that the president had claimed for it, the nation rejected Wilson and further involvement abroad for Warren Harding, normalcy, and isolation.

This familiar scenario may well be true. But it obscures a more important meaning in Wilson's famous remark: when Wilson reached for a word — indeed, for a methodology of social engineering — to move the Congress and the nation, he chose "democracy." He did not select that word because of its dictionary definitions of universal suffrage and popular government. He used it because it was charged with emotional meaning for millions of Americans in ways that went well beyond any rigorous definition of "democracy" as opposed to "autocracy." He used it because "democracy" had become an American religion.

Wilson's fusion of religion and democracy took place on two levels. One level featured Wilson the crusading evangelist, seeking, as historian David Kennedy has put it, "to sway the public mind with the power of his person and his rhetoric."[7] This was both old-fashioned (in that many churches, as we have seen, had already rejected the sermonizing approach) and forward-looking (in its implicit recognition of the power of propaganda). As evangelist, Wilson rhetorically linked democracy with religion.

As Harrison Sackett Elliott, one of the leading figures in the group-process movement in the 1920s, wrote of the speech: "Compare in their political, social, and religious idealism these two slogans: 'Make the World Safe for Democracy.' 'Repent, for the Kingdom of God is at Hand.'"[8]

The other level featured Wilson the democratic social engineer, seeking to convert his audience with democratic methods. Wilson ostensibly presented to the Congress the available "choices" of policy and, therefore, an implicit model of democracy as a field of options. But the president described only one policy "alternative," and he made every effort to convince his audience of the necessity of accepting that alternative. He was aware throughout of the power of the language of democracy.[9]

AN AMERICAN RELIGION

It is difficult to say precisely when democracy became a religion, but we can be reasonably sure it began to happen in the late nineteenth century. Surely the Puritans would not have justified their settlement at Massachusetts Bay for its contribution to "democracy," nor did the founding fathers see the Constitution in these terms, nor Abraham Lincoln the Civil War. The rallying cry of the Puritans was, of course, the purity of religion, the City on a Hill; for the founding fathers, it was social order and property; for Lincoln, it was liberty, free labor — what historian Eric Foner has described as the Republican ideology.[10] For Wilson, neither religion nor liberty would do. Liberty, like "freedom," evoked a spirit of individualism and atomism that was inappropriate to a land of giant corporations, big unions, interest-group lobbies and a nation girding for war. And religion, the victim of science, had, quite simply, ceased to be religious.

Group-process advocates were among the first to discover that as a way of motivating people, or as a set of symbols, traditional religion was moribund. This discovery took place in many ways, not the least of which was personal. Many of the leading theoreticians and practitioners of group methods had been born into traditionally religious families, only to reject that religion as youths or young adults. By the early 1890s, Dewey was looking to a new Reformation which clearly portended the decline of the old. He could see little purpose in traditional, dogmatic Christianity. Kilpatrick, the son of the pastor of the White Plains, Georgia, Baptist Church, had experienced a religious conversion at age fourteen, but only under extraordinary conditions of personal strife. In any event, Kilpatrick rejected immortality, the afterlife, and religious ritual after reading Charles Darwin's *The Origin of Species* as a college junior. Goodwin Watson, who would be associated with various aspects of the group-process movement for five decades after 1920, also grew up in a strong religious family, only to reject religious fundamentalism for "an extremely modernist position" while studying under Kilpatrick in the early 1920s.[11]

Something similar happened to Grace Longwell Coyle, a leading figure in the social group work movement of the 1930s. The child of a North Adams, Massachusetts, Congregationalist minister, Coyle, like Watson, came under the influence of Kilpatrick, Dewey, Herbert Croly, and others of similar persuasion while a student at Columbia, where she earned an M.A. in economics (1928) and a Ph.D. in sociology (1931). As early as 1933, Coyle was putting aside "emotion" for a religion steeped in "thinking," "science," and "philosophy." Although she believed in God, it was a God of design, a God that somehow confirmed for her that man was progressing, struggling toward what was better and higher. The struggle toward these higher values was God itself, and that struggle could take place only in the absence of older forms of religion. "Thought is the driver," wrote Coyle, "the engineer for religious emotion."[12]

The Great War did not create social engineering, or even democratic social engineering. But it did accelerate the process by which small groups and democracy itself came to be seen as reasonable alternatives to religion. The war's origins in a virulent nationalism had damaged the nation-state as an instrument of progressive authority and encouraged the belief that power might more appropriately reside in institutions that were smaller, more local, and more manageable than national government. For conservative politicos such as Warren Harding, this turn of events provided a convenient rationale for presiding over a do-nothing federal government. For our democratic social engineers, it intensified the feeling that there was something potentially spiritual in groups, group relations, and democracy.[13]

Evidence for this exists in the language and style that democratic social engineers brought to the new discipline. For *New Republic* editor Herbert Croly, groups and group discussion were the progenitors of a new moral awareness. "If the ordinary adult is to save himself," wrote Croly, "he must in association with a group of his fellows start gardens in which he can cultivate the vine and fig tree of a revived spiritual life." Croly hoped these associations would multiply rapidly and become spiritual universities, reuniting secular with religious education. "But whether they do or not," he concluded, "they will at least rescue many admirable people from premature moral senility by creating in them the practice of free experimental and disinterested activity carried on in intimate association with like-minded friends."[14]

Democratic social engineering also provided an outlet for charismatic people who in an earlier age might have become preachers. Ex-minister LeRoy Bowman made a career out of supervising group meetings. A friend wrote him in 1954: "There is just no one who can preside over these Religious Education meetings as well as you. . . . This is the ministry at its best and I think of you as one of the 'ministers' of the church." Oskar Schulze, the spirited co-founder of Cleveland's system of Golden Age Clubs, captivated his flock of senior citizens in much the same fashion.[15]

Just as those I have labeled democratic social engineers had come by the 1920s to perceive certain aspects of the social sciences as a new religion, so did they begin to understand that the group-process methodology taken from the social sciences bore some significant relationship to democracy. And as this relationship became clearer, so did democracy itself take on some of the religious aura that had heretofore enveloped the more technical notion of the science of society.

Bruno Lasker, whose organization, The Inquiry, was so influential in the group-process movement in the 1920s, understood the relationship between religion and democracy. He once described a professor who had stressed "democracy" as a viable approach to reform. "Few people in his neighborhood," Lasker commented, "take Protestant Christianity as seriously as they take Democracy."[16] This perception made democracy a vehicle for social reform and the modification of behavior. Where it had once been possible to bring people together and to precipitate behavioral change by demonstrating how far conduct diverged from the laws of God, it was now possible to accomplish the same ends by pointing out the gulf between professions of democracy and its practice. This was, in essence, what Lasker proposed to accomplish through The Inquiry: groups — democratic groups, society in democratic microcosm — would provide a new foundation for a system of moral choices that had once been rooted in religion and local experiences.

In a decade that was shaped by the Russian Revolution and, in America, by the upheavals of 1919, not everyone was as at ease with democracy as Lasker. Sociologist and political scientist Robert MacIver was among those who feared democracy and yet realized its potential as a mechanism of social engineering. Born in 1882, MacIver recalled struggling as a youth against the authoritarian pressures of religion. This experience made him critical of authority's "claims and pretensions" and drove him into the arms of democratic social theory. As a political arrangement, MacIver found democracy "aggravating," dependent upon an ignorant, inert electorate vulnerable to demagogic appeals. But in particular mechanisms of democracy — the group and "society" — MacIver found something genuinely spiritual. "Society," he wrote in his autobiography, "is belongingness, community, interdependence, intragroup and intergroup relations, schisms, combinations, dominances. Where there is a group, there is a purpose, and where there is a society, there is an invisible unity. The individual, the unit, is an individual only because society creates and shapes and informs his unit being."[17]

L. Cody Marsh, like Bowman an ex-minister, was one of several early practitioners of group psychotherapy who utilized certain democratic inspirational techniques adapted from religion in the group treatment of mental illness. In a 1931 paper, "Group Treatment of the Psychoses by the Psychological Equivalent of the Revival," Marsh described his "democratic" group-treatment methods. Like MacIver, Marsh was deeply disturbed by the specter of the masses, and, like MacIver, he constructed a therapy based on this very group. Working by the motto "By the crowd have they been broken / by the crowd shall they be healed," Marsh sought to heal through group singing, group calisthenics, and group field days. In sum, Marsh led a "psychological revival meeting," in which the mental patient was not so much cured as "converted."[18]

THE WAR

Woodrow Wilson, then, was neither the first nor the last to understand democracy as religion. In fact, the methods he employed in his war message were further developed and promoted in the work of the nation's wartime propaganda agency, the Committee on Public Information (CPI). Just as Wilson had understood the evocative power of the phrase "make the world safe for democracy," so did the CPI comprehend how potent, full, vivid, and potentially ideological that word "democracy" had become.

As it was used during the war, "democracy" had no single meaning. It certainly did not mean simply a set of identifiable institutions, such as the secret ballot, the referendum, or universal suffrage. CPI head George Creel once defined it as a "theory of spiritual progress. . . . the struggle everlasting." "Democracy," he said on another occasion, "is a religion with me, and throughout my whole adult life I have preached America as the hope of the world." Democracy was, then, often synonymous with the nation, with "Americanism," and with the perpetuation of what it meant to be American (whatever that was). It served, as historian Stephen Vaughn has written, as a "secular religion," an "ideological cement" which unified Americans for the struggle. Democracy, as the Creel Committee used the term, was — in the terms of the methodology developed in the preceding chapter of this book — a means, rather than an end.[19]

The Creel Committee defined democracy in the statements describing its own procedures and methods. Those procedures and methods were a near-perfect model of democratic social engineering. Here, too, the CPI followed Wilson. Just as the president had offered Congress "choices" in his war message, so did the Creel Committee attempt to set its work in an elaborate framework of freedom of choice. At the base of this framework was the crucial distinction between German "autocracy" and American "democracy," between German "authoritarianism" and American "antiauthoritarianism." These characterizations — or caricatures — of national ideals were reinforced by comparative analyses of how Germans and Americans learned (or were controlled, which seems to have been the same thing). The German ideal, wrote a CPI author, was *"external* control," while the American way was based on the *"inner* check upon the expansion of natural impulse."[20] Arthur Bullard, the former muckraking reporter and CPI pamphleteer, had in 1917 published a book, *Mobilising America*, of notable influence on both Wilson and his adviser, Colonel House. In it, Bullard argued that an American military buildup would require "an inward, spiritual mobilisation."[21]

Given their differences, each nation would — according to the framework, that is — fight the war in ways that reflected its system of authority. The Germans would do so with the tools of "Prussianism": coercion, state power, censorship, propaganda, and (by implication) lies.[22] Some Americans believed that a successful national effort would require similar tactics. "War," wrote Frederick Lewis Allen, "necessitates organization, system, routine, and discipline. . . . The only way to fight Prussianism is with Prussian tools." But the Creel Committee insisted — ironically, given the imprisonment of Eugene Debs, the IWW trials, and other wartime violations of civil liberties — that the war could be prosecuted with peculiarly American methods, methods which utilized the ideology of democracy in a system of democratic social engineering. At every point, these methods were set against the German model: not coercion but persuasion; not state power, but voluntarism and government by an informed public; not propaganda but publicity; not censorship but information, disclosure, and "entire openness"; not lies but "truth" and "facts."[23] And behind this methodology was the assumption — or rationale — that it all worked because the average citizen was a rational being. Therefore, said Creel, "no other argument was needed than the simple, straightforward presentation of facts." Democracy, added Bullard, was a "crazy ideal unless we can trust the people to sort the true from the false."[24]

Two historians, from whom the above account is derived, have recently examined the CPI. Vaughn insists that CPI members were "intelligent, sincere people," for whom the CPI effort was part of a commitment to "democracy" and to "democratic government." Vaughn applauds the efforts of the CPI to "avoid repression," efforts, he recognizes, that fell "short in . . . fulfillment." As he demonstrates, the CPI did engage in censorship, and in spite of "an intention to report only facts," it released biased news. In short, Vaughn accepts the essential distinction made by the CPI between its methods and those of the Germans; he regrets only that the CPI was unable to hew more closely to its announced intentions and stated methodology.[25]

David Kennedy also emphasizes the "sincerity" of the Creel Committee's "information-and-disclosure" approach to the war. He locates this approach in the context of a historic American "aversion to organize and lead — in short, to govern authoritatively." The First World War, Kennedy argues, provided "a great test of the historic American principles of voluntarism and laissez-faire in the face of modern crisis."[26]

What these views have in common is the assumption that Americans believed, for its own sake, in what Vaughn calls "democratic government" and what Kennedy refers to as a "reluctance to exercise power in a straightforward and necessarily forceful way." Vaughn implies, and Kennedy asserts, that the American way was somehow more restrained than the German — indeed, almost not a system of authority at all. For Kennedy, the Creel Committee's approach was a relic of nineteenth-century laissez-faire, an outmoded system unworthy of the modern world.[27]

These analyses ignore what Woodrow Wilson and the Creel Committee knew well: that the tools of the CPI, far from being relics of a bygone day, were the product of twentieth-century social science; that "democratic" social engineering, far from being an ineffective, lesser version of coercive state power, was a powerful device for shaping opinion and behavior; that "democracy," as Creel and Bullard understood it, was every bit as potent a system of authority as Prussian autocracy. Americans exercised power as they did in World War I because it was seen as a superior way of accomplishing essential goals. Far from having an "aversion" to organizing and leading, Americans were, in their own "democratic" way, experts at it.

The war did not create, or even significantly alter, the methodology of democratic social engineering. But the definition usually given that conflict — an ideological struggle between democracy and autocracy — encouraged scholars and planners in fields only tangentially related to the war effort to experiment with democratic techniques and to conceptualize more fully existing practices. The war produced an explosion of interest in democratic methods in the social settlements, the schools, and American industry.

The most elaborate conceptualization of existing technique took place in the field of education. Between 1914, when the war began in Europe, and 1918, when the war ended, two important expositions of progressive education appeared. The first was Dewey's *Democracy and Education*. Published in 1916, before American entry into the war, Dewey's study reflected an early emphasis on the group — the club, the gang, the school class—as the most significant element of the educational process. It also reflected Dewey's optimism that democratic, "progressive" education, by channeling interaction out of inappropriate, "antisocial" spheres (e.g., a gang) and into appropriate spheres (e.g., a club), could reduce isolation and selfishness and ultimately assist in the "breaking down of those barriers of class, race, and national territory which kept men from perceiving the full import of their activity."[28]

Two years later, the war had taken on the democracy/autocracy polarity.[29] Hence Kilpatrick's "project method," presented in 1918, inevitably conceptualized progressive education as appropriate to a democratic society. "The purposeful act," he wrote, "is . . . the typical unity of the worthy life in a democratic society." An act was "purposeful" only if the individual carrying it out had the opportunity "to purpose" (i.e., to determine in some way the course of action). Kilpatrick contrasted the purposeful act, in fact, with an act carried on under "dire compulsion." Thus the purposeful act was a participatory act, and in that sense, it was democratic. Kilpatrick also argued that the project method would discourage "selfish individualism" and encourage students "to determine one's conduct and attitudes with reference to the welfare of the group" (i.e., the social medium, "society," democracy by another definition). As Kilpatrick worked out the project method, it was at once a system of freedom (the purposeful act) and coercion (the welfare of the group as society), unified by the adjective "democratic."[30]

THE POSTWAR ERA

According to one reading of the historical record, the war, the peace, and the series of events associated with the Red Scare of 1919 (from the Russian Revolution through the Seattle general strike) brought an end to the fascination with democracy and to the use of democracy as a mechanism of social engineering. The evidence for this point of view is substantial. Events of the war years certainly undermined, or brought into serious question, the very idea of the reasonable and rational citizen upon which democracy was supposed to rest.[31] In response to such doubts, Walter Lippmann had suggested the creation of "intelligence bureaus," in which elites would guide the public toward appropriate and responsible solutions. Organizations such as the Brookings Institution offered "expert" opinion on a variety of matters in which open forums like commissions and committee hearings had proved undependable.[32] And H. L. Mencken used the *American Mercury* to rail at middle-class "homo boobiens."[33]

Interestingly, however, this antidemocratic reaction was accompanied by a new and profound *appreciation* for democratic modes of social control — i.e., for democratic social engineering. If the war years encouraged some to distrust the "masses," to see irrationality and conflict at every turn, it also served as an object lesson in the use of democratic methods for dealing with these problems. The message that emerged from the experience of the Creel Committee was that even the most complex tasks of social engineering — like the galvanizing of a nation for war — could be accomplished "democratically." This lesson was not lost on liberals, who continued to believe in the possibility, and the desirability, that conflict between classes, races, and nations could be attenuated.

The remainder of this chapter examines the impact of the war on a core group of persons interested in democratic group processes, explores the content of democratic social engineering in the 1920s, and describes how this method of social control found an institutional home in and around Columbia University in the city of New York.

Disillusionment and the Decline of Authority

Sherwood Eddy was one of several persons who played a major role in the growth of the YMCA. He was for many years its international secretary. In his autobiography, published in 1955, Eddy recalled how deeply the Great War had affected him. "Dwight Moody once said that the Civil War was his university," Eddy wrote. "The First World War was that for some of us." This "university," as Eddy called it, taught him a lesson that was significant precisely because it was so typical: conflict, not consensus, was the natural order of things. "Beneath the conflict," recalled Eddy, "I saw a world of perpetual strife between classes, races, and nations."[34]

The key word was perpetual. Those who lived through the Progressive Era, after all, could bear witness to the *Los Angeles Times* bombing, the Brownsville raid, and the German-English naval competition — that is, to undeniable evidence of "strife between classes, races, and nations." Yet that generation shared an optimism about the resolution of such conflict that was brought into question, if not shattered, by the First World War. Educator Kilpatrick summarized what many called "disillusionment" in a diary entry written in 1930. Since March 1918, Kilpatrick wrote, "every thing ideal has been in decline." George Coe, then teaching at Union Theological Seminary, understood the source of that "disillusionment." What the war had cast in doubt was the Progressive assumption that the "motives of men" (the title of Coe's 1928 book) were substantially similar, that "our" values were those of the "enemy."[35]

But there was more to this postwar disillusionment than a generalized sense of decline or conflict. Everywhere, the old institutions, the old mechanisms of authority and control, were subject to scrutiny, criticism, and even ridicule. Young people, some distrustful of a clergy that had supported the war, others resentful of anything resembling "propaganda," more and more distanced themselves from traditional denominational churches with their "creeds and dogmas."[36] No less vulnerable were parents, adults, and older persons, whose moral claims to the right to "demand loyalty and implicit trust," in the words of Goodwin Watson, seemed to have died in the trenches of Europe or been jeopardized by profiteering, propaganda, restrictions on free speech, and other signs of poor judgment.[37]

Institutions and disciplines that had seemed invaluable in 1910 appeared weak — in fact, as part of the problem — a decade later. Government, politics, political parties, collective bargaining, economics — all seemed less than satisfactory mechanisms for converting disorder into order and for resolving conflict.[38] For some democratic social engineers, the League of Nations was just another brittle and formal institution, an international version of the urban ward healers, in a sense; for many others, internationalism and the League held out the one hope for a cooperative solution to world conflict.[39]

The war not only led many Americans to question the efficacy of traditional institutions. It also accelerated and deepened an ongoing evaluation of the processes by which learning and control functioned in every kind of organizational setting. This evaluation took place partly because Americans had defined the war as a struggle against autocracy and for democracy — that is, as a contest between different systems of authority. Whether the perception was accurate or not, many believed that the German people had been rendered incapable of resisting the lure of war by systems of authority — "Prussianized" schools, "imperialistic religion" — that emphasized obedience and loyalty.[40]

A second reason for the increased interest in learning processes and control was the recognition given certain related concepts — the "masses," public opinion, propaganda, and manipulation — as a result of the war. Although none of these concepts was original with the war, all took on added importance during and after the conflict. Among the democratic social engineers, no one was more responsible for their dissemination than Mary Parker Follett. A Radcliffe graduate with a background in economics, government, and philosophy, Follett began her career at the Roxbury Neighborhood House in Boston, where she became involved in vocational guidance and what she called "school centers" — that is, using the public schools for discussion groups and recreation. In 1918, when she published *The New State*, Follett's interests were shifting from the immigrant to industry, and from the settlement to industrial relations.[41]

Widely recognized and well received by the scholarly community, *The New State* was a key document in the history of democratic social engineering. It described recent history in the language of manipulation. For

Follett, the "masses" or the "crowd" had been victimized by propa-
gandists—by Billy Sunday, political bosses, labor agitators, the Salvation Army, the purveyors of patriotism. Others agreed. Kilpatrick wrote
of how the war had revealed how easily "the passions of our people are
moved almost at will by hidden manipulators."[42]

Those individuals and organizations that were to be most influential
in the 1920s in the development of group-process techniques were well
aware of the pitfalls of irrationality. Alfred Dwight Sheffield, the Wellesley
College professor of English who created courses in group methods, shaped
his syllabi around assumptions of unreason. He accepted Lippmann's
notion that beliefs were fundamentally stereotypes, as well as psychologist Harry Overstreet's conclusion that many persons, governed by a "frustration complex," irrationally attributed their failures to villains.[43] At The
Inquiry, the New York City-based group-process organization treated later
in this chapter, national, racial, and class prejudices were always understood as a function of the pressure of "public opinion" and "propaganda."[44]

Thus the war significantly influenced the perspective of those who
were to take a prominent role in democratic social engineering. It made
them aware of deep-seated racial, class, and national conflict and skeptical
of resolving that conflict through traditional, formal methods, like politics,
or through traditional authorities, such as parents and clergy, at least as
these authorities were normally constituted. It increased consciousness of
how ordinary people could be, and were, manipulated and pressured into
patriotism, prejudice, or some other "irrational" and excessive stance. In
general, the war led to the downgrading of modes of learning and control
that were perceived as authoritarian; and it encouraged renewed interest
in processes that were perceived or defined as democratic.

Out of this wartime world view—and out of more than two decades
of experimentation described in the previous chapters—came a program
of democratic social engineering. This program (or philosophy, or series
of interrelated ideas) was designed to meet the needs of the postwar world
by relocating, restructuring, and idealizing authority. Relocating authority meant recreating authority in contexts that were local and/or private;
restructuring authority meant the systematic application of cooperative,
associative, and group processes; idealizing authority meant investing
social authority with the ideological power of democracy.[45]

The New York City Nexus

The geographical center of democratic social engineering was New York
City, and within it two institutions—Columbia University and Union

Theological Seminary. Between these institutions there was a considerable sharing of people, ideas, and programs. Columbia's prominence derived largely from the presence of Dewey in the Department of Philosophy and Kilpatrick (a Dewey student from 1907 through 1909) at Teachers College. Through his teaching and writing, Dewey's influence spread throughout the group-process movement. Dewey students who went on to make theoretical and/or practical contributions to democratic social engineering included Kilpatrick, Harrison Elliott (later affiliated with both Union Theological Seminary and the YMCA), and Goodwin Watson, who later worked with group process at Teachers College, at the Commission on Community Interrelations (after 1945), and with business corporations.[46] Group-process advocates for whom Dewey was an important influence included Benjamin Spock, the baby doctor; Eliza Butler, who as the first YWCA national student secretary for work in secondary schools (1910-) brought democratic techniques to high-school clubs; and recreational theorist Eduard C. Lindeman.[47]

Kilpatrick was a member of the Columbia faculty from 1909, when he was appointed instructor of the philosophy of education at Teachers College, until 1937, when he was forced to retire. He renounced the lecture method in favor of group discussions (he practiced what he preached) and acquired a reputation as a superb teacher. More than thirty-five thousand students took his courses, and the *New York Post*, having totaled the fees paid the university by Kilpatrick enrollees in one summer session, dubbed him the "Million Dollar Professor."[48] Kilpatrick's students included Harrison Elliott; Watson (for whom Kilpatrick was a more significant influence than Dewey); and Coyle, perhaps the single most important person in the history of social group work. Alfred Sheffield's training courses in group discussion were strongly influenced by Kilpatrick's theory of the learning process. In 1925-26, several national staffers of the YWCA Girl Reserve movement, including Coyle, studied at Teachers College.[49]

In 1910, Union Theological Seminary moved into new quarters near Columbia University, and in the next two decades, the seminary would play a role in the group-process movement second only to that of its larger neighbor. This influence was primarily due to the presence at Union of George Albert Coe, William Adams Brown, and Harrison Elliott. All labored in the gray area where Christian education met social activism and social control.

Coe's career at Union was clouded with controversy from his arrival in 1909. A Methodist, he was the school's first non-Presbyterian instructor. Nor was his distinction between "transmissive" and "creative" (i.e., lecture and participatory) methods in Christian education accepted with equanimity. A run-in with President Arthur Cushman McGiffert led to Coe's resignation in 1922 and a move to Teachers College. Coe's *Motives of Men* (1928) was an influential volume in the late 1920s.[50]

William Adams Brown, who joined the Union faculty in the 1890s, was a pioneer in the application of social psychology to Bible study classes. In late 1921, Brown joined with Sherwood Eddy of the YMCA, Kirby Page, a social gospel pamphleteer, and Harry Ward of the community center movement to create the Fellowship for a Christian Social Order, an organization dedicated to conflict resolution through group thinking.[51]

Ironically, Coe's replacement at Union in religious education became the quintessential democratic social engineer. Harrison Elliott had learned his group theory as secretary of the International Committee of the YMCA, for whom he wrote a manual on group discussion methods, and as a student of Dewey, Kilpatrick, and Coe.[52] During the war, while employed by the YMCA, Elliott carried out important if informal research designed to conceptualize the role of group methods in an army camp situation. Elliott was especially interested in the impact of a military/barracks life style on the morals and ideals of the Christian soldier. The problem, as he understood it, was the enormous power of the group — the barracks community — to influence the conduct of the soldier. And the solution, he believed, was to turn that very power to advantage. The focus of YMCA efforts, Elliott advised, should be an entire barracks, rather than the individual soldier. By first winning "key men" who could in turn "be organized to win their fellows," and then applying classic tactics of group discussion, YMCA workers could eventually "dominate the standards and ideals of an entire company, and indeed an entire army camp." In the group discussions in which this "winning" would take place, the group leader/"chairman" would act as guide, encouraging participation, ruling out irrelevant suggestions, and focusing attention on appropriate questions and "facts."[53]

Elliott's fame and influence spread rapidly in the 1920s as he found new contexts in which to implement a group-discussion methodology. Working alone or with Watson, his Union student, Elliott helped institutions convert their conference procedures to a discussion format. In 1923, for example, he organized the world conference of the YMCA on the basis of discussion groups. Similar efforts were made in the Country Life Association, the Christian Student Association Conference, the Girl Reserve movement of the YWCA, and several other organizations. For The Inquiry, Elliott helped draft materials for use in the organization's discussion groups and held training sessions for group leaders. Elliott's work was influential for Coe, Coyle, and, in the late 1940s, for Leland Bradford, one of the founders of the National Training Laboratory.[54]

If Columbia University and Union Theological Seminary provided the theoretical bedrock of the group-process movement, two other New York City-based organizations—The Inquiry and the YMCA/YWCA— were also important centers of activity in the 1920s. The Inquiry was founded in 1922 and remained viable until 1929. Active members were a cross section of the group-process movement. Day-to-day affairs of the organization were largely in the hands of former officials of the YWCA and YMCA. Rhoda McCulloch, an officer of the national YWCA and editor of a YWCA periodical, the *Women's Press*, was its secretary; Edward C. Carter, who had represented the YMCA in France, was its general sec- retary. Columbia University contributed its share of Inquiry members, notably Dewey, Kilpatrick, and Coyle. From Union Theological Seminary came Harrison Elliott and the founder of Union's Missionary Research Library, Charles Fahs. Editors at the *New Republic,* a batch of disillu- sioned Progressives that included Lindeman, Bruce Bliven, Francis Hackett, and Herbert Croly, became involved in the organization when its delibera- tions concerned the printed media. Social scientists who were members included sociologists George B. Haynes and Robert Park, psychologist Gordon Allport, and industrial-relations authority Ordway Tead. No one contributed more to the organization than Wellesley College English pro- fessor Sheffield, who drafted many of the organization's publications and regularly participated in the Inquiry effort to market the "conference experi- ence" to people "habituated to speech-making and propaganda."[55]

The founder of The Inquiry, and its moving spirit, was an intense and aggressive Jewish immigrant from Germany, Bruno Lasker. His life recapitulates much of the history of group process; by understanding Lasker, we can appreciate how he came to create an organization dedicated to democratic social engineering. Lasker was born in Hamburg in 1880. In size, Hamburg was a city. But for Lasker it was a small town, a com- munity. Like Dewey, Spock, and other youths who grew up to become democratic social engineers, Lasker felt comfortable and secure amidst the history of the city. "You got the feeling of the continuity of life," Lasker recalled, "of the antiquity of most of the things that were going on still." Lasker grew up appreciating Hamburg's strong local culture and his family's links to it.

A position with his father's coffee-exporting firm took him to Eng- land at the turn of the century. From his father's involvement with an anti- eviction society, Lasker learned the values of working in a local context — of helping a few people, rather than all of mankind—and he also became familiar with democratic methods while listening to the society's discus- sions of eviction cases. In Manchester, these lessons were reinforced in contacts with settlement houses and with visiting Americans, including Jane Addams (who had worked with Dewey in Chicago in the 1890s).[56]

Lasker was by self-definition a socialist, but his socialism closely resembled American Progressivism. The purpose of settlement work, according to Lasker, was to motivate people to "higher achievements" and to build a "stronger bridge [than charity] between different classes." (In the United States, where, Lasker claimed, there were no classes, the bridge was to be built between "groups.") This bit of insight had been distilled from Lasker's employment with British social investigator B. Seebohm Rowntree. Although Lasker and Rowntree carried out studies of unemployment, poverty, and diet, Lasker's recollection was that both of them were more impressed by the news from America that New York City Police Commissioner Theodore Roosevelt had managed to prevent juvenile delinquency with playgrounds. Rowntree went on to publish a pioneering work on the "human" approach to industrial relations; that is, he became a democratic social engineer within the field of labor relations.[57]

Therefore, when he arrived in the United States in about 1915, Lasker found institutions he could immediately appreciate, including Lovejoy Elliott's Hudson Guild settlement, the Ethical Culture Society's Madison House settlement, and Lillian Wald's Henry Street settlement, where Lasker was employed at the classic group-process task of forging gang members into a boys' club. Although at this juncture Lasker seems to have had no systematic approach to small-group social engineering, his settlement experience had stimulated his interest in local solutions, reinforced his Progressive inclination toward conflict resolution as a goal of social reform and, at Henry Street, brought him to what would soon be known as social group work.[58]

The war and its aftermath form the third basic ingredient in Lasker's makeup — the one, apparently, that turned him from a primitive practitioner of social group work at Henry Street to the ideological democratic social engineer who founded The Inquiry. In a sense, the war transformed Lasker's lack of insight into the causes of conflict into a full-blown methodology and ideology of conflict resolution. When the war broke out in Europe, the Lasker family was in Holland. Oddly, its reaction was one of amazement. "We knew that there was considerable political tension," recalled Lasker, "but it never occurred to me that it could mean war, and when there were rumors of war, I simply did not believe it, even when the newspapers failed to come and there was no mail." Perhaps the reason for Lasker's surprise had something to do with that protected feeling of community, acquired during the Hamburg years. In any event, Lasker felt little of the nationalism that was rampant in Europe. "My family," he recalled, "was not very political. They were not patriotic. They were Hanseatic in feeling, rather than patriotic . . ."[59] Whatever the reason, for Lasker the war (and later racism and labor-management problems) had no cause and no purpose. It was a misunderstanding, a conflict waiting to be resolved.

As an editor of *Survey* magazine, Lasker traveled to Europe in 1921. It was there, apparently, that his path crossed that of progressive education, giving Lasker a methodology to go with his theory of conflict. What he found was a virulent German youth movement and a variety of groups, including the military, the ultranationalists, and the Communists, seeking to turn that youth movement to their own purposes. He found a rising tide of anti-Semitism that must have been profoundly disturbing given his Jewish heritage. He also found educators who analyzed youth's inclination to excessive nationalism as a function of authoritarian education, and for whom some form of "progressive" or "democratic" education was the solution.[60] Lasker had, indeed, found a method — democracy — that he could harness for the purpose of conflict resolution. Returning to the United States, he had with him all he needed to create The Inquiry.

The Inquiry was held together in part by shared assumptions and beliefs about the extent and causes of conflict. At bottom, there was just too much of it, and it had become unmanageable.[61] Inquiry members believed that conflict might be rather easily eliminated, if only because of its origins. Conflict was the product of environmental, psychological, and informational influences. The cause of racial conflict and prejudice, for example, lay in "mental attitudes," in the lack of access to "information" (another word for facts), in "stereotyped attitudes" produced by schools, churches, newspapers, and comic strips, in "propaganda," in "social pressure." Racial prejudice was neither instinctive, nor was it, even in the South, the result of "a specific orthodox southern way of thinking on each question which must necessarily remain a distinct thing."[62] According to City College professor Julius Drachsler, who in early 1925 delivered a prominent series of lecture/discussions on the nature of prejudice to an Inquiry audience, the source of this new view of prejudice was the stimulus-response psychology pioneered by Russian physiologist Ivan Pavlov, psychologist John Watson, and social scientists at Teachers College. Watson's experiments, Drachsler argued, had revealed that fears and prejudices were not instinctive but acquired. Prejudice was socially conditioned.[63]

If prejudice was socially conditioned, it could be socially eliminated. The tools were those of democratic social engineering: groups, discussions, conferences, panels, inquiry, participation, leadership. "Our business," recalled Lasker, "was to bring all the overt conflicts, and also the more diffuse feeling of difference, out into the open in mixed group discussions, and to see to it that these discussions were conducted not only in the right spirit but by a tested method that was bound to bring results."[64]

This method was outlined for one social problem in an Inquiry pamphlet, "The Worker and His Job." In a situation characterized by conflict between workers and management, workers would participate in discussions guided by a leader. The leader would play an informational role, selecting words that conveyed "the idea but not the emotional weighting." Cynical workers would develop optimism; "militant" workers would "discover the necessity for a more discerning treatment." The method might also involve redesigning physical settings. At a national social work conference in Buffalo, for example, Lasker rearranged the chairs in a large ballroom to facilitate group discussion. He refused to use a platform or to face the audience as a single figure of authority.[65]

Those who served The Inquiry were aware that they were social engineers, that "the scientific study of human nature," as Sheffield put it, was "creating a body of knowledge by which organized relationships are made to generate social power."[66] They often differed, however, on the critical matter of what separated education from propaganda and on what distinguished democratic methods from coercive ones. Those who leaned toward the democratic side of things emphasized means over ends, "the encouragement of democratic study rather than . . . the results to be hoped for," and, especially, the role of group members in determining subject matter and arriving at conclusions.[67] Those who favored a more coercive approach emphasized more active guidance for the discussion process. Robert Park, for example, insisted that group process could be effective only if shaped by the charismatic leader. And William Adams Brown, according to Sheffield, favored "expert manipulation" in the cause of " 'putting over' an irreducible minimum of Christian essentials." Lasker would not go this far, but he did criticize Elliott's discussion techniques for their laissez-faire qualities. According to Lasker, Elliott "takes the original statements made by members of the group as basis for his process of weeding out and summarization. In no case, apparently, does he stimulate the group to correct its thought process, to go deeper than the statement that happens to spring to mind, to come to grips on an abstraction, to apply a process of logical analysis to a statement."[68]

The tension between these points of view — a tension, really, that was central to the American experience with democratic social engineering — was a constant theme of Inquiry deliberations. It was captured at a 1925 meeting of the organization's Committee on Race Attitudes in Children. The committee's report had pointed out the difficulties in inculcating proper attitudes in children when their parents believed differently. "If we were a propaganda committee," Lasker commented, "we would have to educate their parents. Since we are not, but a committee that believes in an open and flexible mind, we still have to educate the parents." "Why not," responded one committee member, "use the propaganda on the parents and educate the children?"[69]

The implementation of The Inquiry's methodology of small-group discussion took place through existing organizations. A large majority had some religious content, including the YMCA, the YWCA, the Missionary Education Movement, the Lutheran League, and the Baptist Young People's Union. Settlement houses, colleges, women's clubs, child-study and social work organizations were also important outlets. Among the sixty-eight students at Harrison Elliott's 1927 training conference for group leaders were representatives of the Amalgamated Clothing Workers, the American Country Life Association, the Brookwood Labor College, the Girl Scouts, and the League of Women Voters.[70]

These organizations were encouraged to form clubs and to sponsor conferences and study groups which would utilize The Inquiry's democratic methods, literature, and manuals to guide the process of group discussion. In Cleveland, the organization was in contact with settlement worker Alice Gannett and faculty from the Western Reserve School of Applied Social Sciences (SASS). SASS was a pioneer in group-work courses for social workers; years later, Gannett would figure prominently in the city's program of Golden Age Clubs, which were modeled on The Inquiry methodology. At the Federation for Child Study, work with children on race prejudice was carried out with group-discussion techniques. Some college teachers responded positively to Inquiry overtures. John Fitch adopted an Inquiry tool, the case method, for his industrial relations classes; historian Frank Tannenbaum wrote enthusiastically about converting courses from lecture to discussion format. Inquiry leaders also met with Croly, Bliven, Oswald Garrison Villard, Paul U. Kellogg, and other editors in an effort to bring the discussion method to the printed page. The *New Republic*'s Croly agreed "to make a definite experiment with the discussion method, even if costly in space."[71]

Yet there were problems. From the settlement houses came reports of the difficulties involved in establishing working clubs. One settlement head reported that of eighty groups in his house, only three were composed of boys "mature enough to take up such study and discussion." Another believed club work with Philadelphia blacks was worthwhile. But, he added, "the Negroes often feel they are being patronized. Such clubs often only last six months or less."[72] Others challenged Lasker's optimistic projection of what could be done about racial conflict in the South or pointed out the difficulties of establishing study and discussion groups in men's clubs, labor unions, and nonreligious organizations. The group could change its name from the National Conference on the Christian Way of Life to The Inquiry, but it could not entirely transcend its strong affiliations to religious organi-

zations or the industrial Northeast, or the powerful historical bonds between democratic social engineering and the churches.[73]

The YMCA and the YWCA were perhaps the outstanding consumers
of group-process methodology in the postwar years. By 1917, as we have
seen, the Christian associations had been using democratic techniques for
more than a decade as part of an effort to modernize (i.e., secularize) recruitment and instructional programs. After 1917, attention shifted from
a rather narrow approach centered on Bible study classes to a full-fledged
and rapidly growing program of clubs, most of them utilizing group
methods. The Girl Reserve program of the YWCA, for example, founded
in 1919 as "a democratic organization of youth with adult guidance," was
by 1925 providing club activity for almost two hundred thousand girls.
The YMCA responded with similar plans, recognizing the new primacy
of democratic methods by assisting in the publication of a manual for
leaders of boys' groups. Both youth associations worked closely with The
Inquiry, and various association affiliates, such as the Student Volunteer
Movement and the Student Department, provided a major market for
Inquiry study materials.[74]

The history of the Girl Reserve movement demonstrates how, after
the war, group process became less an adjunct to an organization with
limited, religious purposes, and more a general and flexible device applied
to a variety of social problems. The earlier phase is exemplified in the 1914
constitution of the high-school clubs operated by the YWCA. This constitution was adopted under the guidance of Eliza Butler, the YWCA's first
national student secretary for secondary schools and a teacher in the
Horace Mann School at Teachers College. Butler's method was democratic
— derived from Dewey — but her purpose was religious. The clubs were
to maintain a "strong, high moral sentiment; to bring students to a personal relation to Jesus Christ . . ." The ideal was old-fashioned evangelism.[75] After 1918, a more complex layer of reasoning replaced this evangelism. Especially prominent in this period was an emphasis on social responsibility. Perhaps because women had recently acquired the suffrage,
Girl Reserve documents emphasized the necessity of providing girls with
a "foundation which would help them 'make right decisions as to which
way they should go.'" A turbulent postwar world led some to advocate
democratic organization as a way of promoting "sane and tolerant" reasoning. And by the late 1920s and early 1930s, the rise of authoritarian
movements abroad contributed to a self-conscious emphasis on "choice"
in the Girl Reserve literature and to the determination to define the adult
club adviser as "a companion rather than dictator." ("The autocratic
method," added Abel Gregg in a manual intended for leaders of boys'
groups, "will produce a people who need dominant leaders.")[76]

CONCLUSION

As the decade of the 1920s wore on, there were some signs of a declining intensity of interest in democracy as a tool of social engineering. In the community centers, the religion of democracy was partially supplanted by the goal of efficiently delivering services into the neighborhoods. The Inquiry stopped functioning in 1929. Kilpatrick observed a mid-decade decline in graduate students interested in exploring nondirective education.[77]

Yet there were areas of growth. The YMCA and YWCA remained fully committed to democratic social engineering. Turn-of-the-century interest in clubs and associative activities had by the mid-1920s congealed into the discipline of recreation, where group methods would have great influence. Although The Inquiry had disappeared, the Columbia/Union Theological Seminary connection remained. An informal discussion group formed by Kilpatrick and including Dewey, Harrison Elliott, Goodwin Watson, and many others served as a "breeding ground" for the John Dewey Society and its journal, *Social Frontier*.[78] More important, group methods were just beginning to be utilized in social work and industrial relations.

These trends were not mutually exclusive. Democratic methods were more used in 1930 than in 1920, but they were also applied less obviously and less intensely. The war had not created group-process techniques. But it had made them seem especially useful, even indispensable, and it had heightened the awareness with which democratic methods were applied as well as the perception that it was democracy that lay at the core of the methodology. The Girl Reserves and The Inquiry were both highly self-conscious efforts, in which there was a good deal of talking and theorizing about democracy and its function. By the mid-1920s, the diminishing of the crisis caused by the war had brought an end to the religious aura that had surrounded democratic methods since 1917. As we shall see, this did not signify that democracy had fallen into disuse as a method of social engineering.

3

The Business of America . . .

In the years between the First World War and the
Second, American business came to appreciate some of the methods that
come under the broad term, democratic social engineering. Many corporations now utilized a post–Civil War mode of business governance called
"industrial democracy," a term including producers' cooperatives, profit
sharing, industrial councils, collective bargaining, human relations, and
arbitration and conciliation.[1] Some of these models of industrial democracy
involved major changes in the structure of capitalism; most, including
employee representation plans and the "human relations" approach to personnel,[2] were simply new methods of perpetuating capitalist hegemony.
Whatever their origin and purpose, these approaches to factory and industrial management were at least formulaically democratic.

Yet our knowledge of business methods exists within a remarkably
narrow range. Although business is concerned with both supply and
demand, production and consumption, what we know about the use of
democratic methods and group process is limited to the production side.
One section of this chapter remedies this deficiency by exploring some
of the uses of democratic methods in the consumption-side functions of
selling, advertising, and public relations. A second section probes the pro-
duction-side aspect of democratic methodology, concluding with an early
application of group process, the foremen's clubs. A final section employs
collective biography to suggest some possible relationships between the
First World War, the settlements, vocational guidance, and the human relations approach to labor-management problems.

CONSUMPTION

The American business system of 1930 was a very different creature from
its 1890 counterpart. The intervening years had brought enormous growth
in the production potential of the economy, and with that growth had

come the first fears that American consumers might prove inadequate to the task of purchasing all that the factories could make. One solution, almost unthinkable until the depression of the 1930s, was to give consumers more money to spend by distributing income from those who tended to save their marginal income (the rich) to those who tended to spend it (the poor). Another solution, also the outgrowth of the Great Depression, was to support personal consumption with an increased level of governmental expenditures.[3] But in the three relatively prosperous decades before the stock-market crash of 1929, those who thought about such things believed that consumers had sufficient money to support increased levels of production — if only they could be convinced to part with it. That burden fell to what in style, substance, and degree of sophistication were in 1900 or 1920 virtually new fields or professions: advertising, public relations, and selling (or what was then called salesmanship).

Advertising

On the face of it, advertising was ill suited to the democratic techniques described in this book. The printed page was an unlikely vehicle for group discussion; it might ask questions, but it could not respond to readers' answers. Unlike the student in a classroom situation, the reader had the last word. By the 1920s, advertisers were transcending these handicaps by focusing their efforts on small-group situations. Listerine sold mouthwash, and Prudential sold life insurance, by setting the product within a marital relationship, a family crisis, or some other social context.[4]

More important than how products were sold was the way in which advertising and consumption were together understood as part of a democratic process. For Edward Filene, department store magnate and industrial-democracy advocate, consuming was an act of democratic participation. People not only bought what they needed and wanted; they also, in the same process, carried out an electoral process. By purchasing the products of business, consumers elected the corporations that produced those products and democratically legitimized the place of business in American life. "The masses of America," wrote Filene, "have elected Henry Ford. They have elected General Motors. They have elected the General Electric Company, and Woolworth's and all the other great industrial and business leaders of the day."[5]

Public Relations

Edward L. Bernays, public-relations counsel for the American Tobacco Company in the 1920s, took the argument one step further, shaping it into a theory of advertising competition that resembled later theories of political pluralism. Although Bernays acknowledged that mass advertising was less education than propaganda, he believed that the competition between competing propagandas (i.e., between two advertisers) was equivalent to a kind of democracy. "The competition of ideas in the American market place," he wrote, "is an essential democratic process, for then the public can make its own choice. Even when ideas conflict and confuse, public debate clarifies the issues and makes for a sounder choice, in the long run."6 Neither Filene nor Bernays had a fully developed understanding of the potential uses of democratic techniques in advertising, and certainly Bernays appreciated just how much of an object the consumer was. Yet both also realized that their culture required that buying be established in a democratic context, and both did so in the same way, by emphasizing the concept of choice. To select this emphasis at the very moment when meaningful consumer choice was being rapidly circumscribed by oligopoly and its concomitants, advertising and public relations, suggests that democracy here had a mythic function, and further, that genuine choice existed in inverse relationship to affirmations of its continued viability.

Public relations did not exist as a self-conscious profession until after the turn of the century, when business came under the guns of Progressive muckrakers and began to realize that the tools existed to create and maintain a favorable public image — goodwill, in the terminology of the balance sheet. Because the railroads were at the center of Progressive regulatory efforts, and because frequent and dramatic railroad accidents were unavoidably public events, this industry was one of the first to hire public relations "counsel." Although more responsibly managed than some lines, the Pennsylvania faced the same pressures as other roads, and shortly after 1900 the company hired Ivey Ledbetter Lee to handle its public relations. Lee was born in 1877 in a small town in Georgia, the son of a Methodist minister. He had most of a college education at Emory University and Princeton before taking a job as a reporter on a daily newspaper in 1899. Lee left the newspaper several years later to open a primitive public-relations office with colleagues of similar mind, and it was not long thereafter that he took on the Pennsylvania as a customer. Over the years, Lee's clients would include Bethlehem Steel, the Chrysler Corporation, and, during World War I, the American Red Cross.

Lee's contribution to democratic social engineering is summarized in a story told about his activities in behalf of the Pennsylvania. When an accident occurred on the line, it was the usual procedure to restrict the press from the scene. On one occasion, however, Lee took a different tack. He escorted a carload of reporters to the scene of the accident. What those reporters saw, and how they reported the event, are unknown; but Lee had established a central tenet of public relations: openness, or the illusion of openness. While it is doubtful that Lee ever practiced complete openness, that he "advocated absolute frankness," in the words of one historian, seems entirely believable.[7]

It was perhaps inevitable that Lee, armed with the tactic of openness, would one day ply his trade for Standard Oil. By 1900 the company was infamous for its predatory relationship to competitors, having managed to swallow up ninety percent of the nation's oil-refining capacity. Before one official investigating body after another, company officials proved unable to recall critical moments in Standard's history. Henry Demarest Lloyd, Ida Tarbell, and other muckrakers had a field day with these corporate "barbarians," as Lloyd called them.[8]

Early in the century, Standard turned to public relations, and to the democratic ideology of openness, to refurbish its corporate image. Under the guidance of a former journalist, Joseph Clarke, the company jettisoned its long-standing policy of withholding information. When attacked, the company now countered with its own "facts." The reticent John D. Rockefeller, Sr., took to the pages of women's magazines to discuss his philosophy of giving. When in 1913 John D. Rockefeller, Jr., asked Lee to superintend the company's public relations efforts, he couched his request in the rhetoric of openness, as if the honest presentation of heretofore unreleased information would bridge the gulf between corporation and public. "I feel that my father and I are much misunderstood by the press and the people of this country," he said. "I should like to know what your advice would be on how to make our position clear."[9]

Lee's response to this query came in the context of events in Ludlow, Colorado, where forty strikers, eleven children, and two women had died in a pitched battle with state militia in the wake of a strike at the Rockefellers' Colorado Fuel and Iron Company. The Ludlow Massacre threatened to destroy what little Clarke had been able to recover of the Rockefeller reputation. Lee responded to this crisis, of course, with openness. Through a series of bulletins, the press learned what had "really" happened at Ludlow. And Lee's coaching gave Rockefeller junior the skills to answer, rather than evade, the questions posed at congressional inquiries into the incident.[10]

Through Lee's ministrations, the company was able to drop the confrontational style that had characterized its relationship with the Ludlow strikers and the general public. The new approach was dramatized in 1915, when Rockefeller junior appeared in Colorado to address employees and officers on the proposed Industrial Representation Plan. As an act of bravado, the speech is justly famous. But no one has captured more clearly what Rockefeller was trying to do than success theorist Dale Carnegie. At the time of Ludlow, Carnegie was teaching a course on effective speaking at the 23d Street YMCA in Manhattan, and — so history would prove —

gathering materials for his 1936 epic, *How to Win Friends and Influence People*. He thought the speech a "masterpiece." Although Carnegie was wrong to attribute almost magical powers to the address ("It calmed the tempestuous waves of hate that threatened to engulf Rockefeller. It won him a host of admirers"), he understood that Rockefeller had rejected a confrontational style of authority for a form of leadership. "Scolding parents and domineering bosses and husbands and nagging wives," Carnegie concluded, "ought to realize that people don't want to change their minds. They can't be forced or driven to agree with you or me. But they may possibly be led to, if we are gentle and friendly, ever so gentle and ever so friendly."[11]

Carnegie did not use the word "democratic" to describe Rockefeller's appeal to the strikers; for him "gentle" and "friendly" were analytically sufficient. But in this case, Rockefeller was being gentle, friendly, *and* democratic. Rockefeller's visit to the coal camps, and even the speech itself, were part of a larger effort to *involve* the miners in the process of reconciliation, to bring about their *participation* in the resolution of the conflict. In the address, Rockefeller attributed his very presence to a decision of the miners ("it is only by your courtesy that I am here"); he described his new relationship with the miners in terms which implied that the miners had taken an active role in forming that relationship ("that spirit of mutual friendship"); and he referred to the speech itself as a group process ("I am glad to have this opportunity to *discuss* with you our common interests"). The miners had decided, they had been active, they were participating in a group process — they were, in short, part of a democratic world. This was the message of Rockefeller and his teacher, Ivey Lee. "Crowds are led by symbols and phrases," Lee had once said. For the Colorado speech, he had armed his pupil with a democratic vocabulary of both.[12]

In 1915, Lee and Clarke were isolated practitioners of something a good deal less rigorous than a discipline. Five years later, they were part of a profession. The difference was the First World War, a conflict so unpopular with so many that enormous effort had to be expended in building a simple consensus in favor of American intervention and goals. This effort both absorbed the few already engaged in public relations (Lee, for example, served the Red Cross) and motivated others to fashion careers in the new field.

Among the latter was Edward Bernays. Born in Vienna in 1891, Bernays was the son of Anna Freud, Sigmund's sister. He came to the United States as a small child, earned a B.A. at Cornell University in 1912, and for five years practiced journalism and worked as a publicist in New York City's theater industry. When the war came to America in 1917, Bernays signed on with the Committee on Public Information, which he described as "the first organized use of propaganda by our Government." Its work, he wrote, "was the forerunner of modern psychological warfare." After the war, Bernays served for a short time on the American public relations staff at the Paris Peace Conference, supervising two war-related public relations campaigns: one to win American support for recognition of an independent Lithuania; another for the reemployment of ex-servicemen. These wartime and war-related activities, he later wrote, made him realize that "words and pictures" had been "powerful factors in helping win the war," and that "press-agentry had broader applications than theater, music or the ballet."[13] A generation of future public relations counselors had learned how easy it was to motivate and move entire populations. If a consensus could be reached on war, it could be reached on anything.

Bernays clarified the assumptions and described the tools of the new profession in *Crystallizing Public Opinion* (1923). The book appeared the year after Walter Lippmann's *Public Opinion,* and it shared with its more famous and more influential predecessor a whole range of ideas about why people believed what they did and how opinion — public opinion — could be shaped.[14]

Lippmann's world was full of ordinary people who were unprepared to understand the twentieth century. The world war had proved especially difficult to assimilate intelligently. Rural Americans — Lippmann uses the example of Miss Sherwin of Gopher Prairie, a character out of Sinclair Lewis' *Main Street* — saw the war not as a conflict involving millions of persons and hundreds of military divisions, but as a "personal duel" with the Kaiser. Others, including Attorney General A. Mitchell Palmer, fashioned their own "counterfeit of reality" from the war. But it was not just the war. The conflict had only worsened the tendency to analyze events and make decisions on the basis of superstitions, prejudices, myths, and stereotypes.[15]

For Lippmann, this irrationality was of great import for the history of democracy. If the masses did not respond with reason, then "representative government," whether in politics or industry or any other arena, was impossible. Democracy, however, could be salvaged in another form. Lippmann's reconstructed democracy had one specific ingredient: intelligence bureaus, staffed by "experts," and designed to provide decision makers and decision-making agencies with "facts."[16]

But the intelligence bureau was for Lippmann only a technical adjunct to a new system of democracy grounded in the arts of persuasion and implying group process. If the masses could not arrive spontaneously at right and reasonable decisions, they could be brought to reason by responsible leaders. This "creation of consent" would be achieved through "propaganda," a word that for Lippmann had benign as well as sinister meanings. In practice it meant a persuasive process, carried on under trained leadership. For example, the decision-making body could be made to understand and appreciate the expert's viewpoint — even in a typical confrontational, partisan proceeding — through the interposition of objective persons "who control enough facts and have the dialectical skill to sort out what is real perception from what is stereotype, pattern and elaboration. It is the Socratic dialogue, with all of Socrates' energy for breaking through words to meanings, and something more than that, because the dialectic in modern life must be done by men who have explored the environment as well as the human mind."[17]

Public Opinion has usually been interpreted as an antidemocratic book, and Lippmann's intelligence bureaus have become a famous example of antidemocratic elitism. This view is not so much incorrect as incomplete. Surely Lippmann had no great faith in the wisdom of the common people. Yet the system he designed to transcend the deficiencies of the masses was, so he believed, only a new brand of democracy based on the social sciences. The intelligence bureaus were elitist, but again, Lippmann recognized the necessity of linking the ordinary citizen with this new dispenser of the "facts" through a process democratic in form if not in substance. To define *Public Opinion* as an antidemocratic book is to fail to understand how committed Lippmann was to a system of social engineering based on the forms and processes of democracy.

Bernays' book was an attempt to locate the emerging profession of public relations within a general social theory. He began by defining public relations as the task of mediating between the client and the public. An immediate problem arose, for the "public" — what Lippmann called public opinion — could not be trusted. The opinions of the average individual were "dogmatic expressions," emotionally arrived at. Moreover, modern America was incredibly fragmented, composed of disparate populations unbound by common ideals and customs, and this characteristic made the task of reaching one "public" even more difficult.[18]

At the center of Bernays' analysis of the problem and basic to his solution of it, was man's primitive instinct for gregariousness. People acted irrationally not because they were ignorant, but because they were social, sensitive to the "voice of the herd." It was this very orientation to the crowd, this passion for participation, which opened doors for the public relations counsel, who could build a larger public opinion by working with the abundance of existing groups, focusing on areas of overlapping interest, creating unity of interest where once the appearance of irreconcilable difference had seemed overpowering.[19]

The herd instinct also allowed public relations counsel to operate within existing groups in a narrower sense. Since the people loved to *follow*, they could easily be *led*. It was the task of public relations to locate group leaders in existing organizations and associations and to use these group leaders to move the entire organization in the desired direction.[20]

The Bernays and Lippmann texts reveal some differences in approach. While Bernays was not uninterested in Lippmann's bias toward the technocratic presentation of information and "facts," neither was he as swept up in it as Lippmann was.[21] Nor did Bernays follow Lippmann in describing the specific procedures to be followed by group leaders in operating their organizations; the book contains no mention of the Socratic method and only an oblique reference to the technique of discussion. For his part, Lippmann's interest in Socratic dialogue at times appears perfunctory, an afterthought to his proposal for intelligence bureaus, and his book contains no systematic discussion of the group, as Bernays' does.

What unites these books, however, is more important than what separates them. Each is grounded in an extensive critique of democracy. Each seeks to establish a new and rational social consensus using one or another of the group-process techniques generated by the social sciences. Each emphasizes the role of leadership. And each employs a terminology that clouds the relationship between persuasion and force. Bernays made this last point most forthrightly when he wrote, "The advocacy of what we believe in is education. The advocacy of what we don't believe in is propaganda."[22]

Politics as Public Relations

Bernays' definition of public relations — mediation between client and public — is general enough to suggest that its techniques were applicable to fields other than business. Public relations methods proved especially useful in politics, where it fell to Herbert Hoover to play the first fullfledged role of client-president. According to Craig Lloyd's recent study of Hoover and public relations, the Iowa-born engineer inherited from Theodore Roosevelt and Woodrow Wilson a Progressive appreciation for the uses of publicity as one part of a process of "educational leadership." As food administrator during World War I, Hoover sold his programs through an education division that functioned much like the Committee on Public Information, and he became convinced of the important part that hard-sell public relations could play in politics. "Only by propaganda," he said in 1920, was "there any promise of educating the American public . . . in the ideals of democracy." This commitment led directly to the policies that characterized the Hoover administration's response to the stockmarket crash of 1929. Through his speeches and press releases, Hoover sought to restore "psychological confidence." He hired Bernays to handle public relations for the President's Emergency Committee for Employment. And he held a series of "no-business" meetings, as John Kenneth Galbraith has labeled them, because he believed that even meetings in which no business was transacted could have great value as propaganda.[23]

The side of Hoover that was engineer wanted to do more than propagandize. Hoover believed in the expertise of science, economics, and business, and in the necessity of utilizing that expertise to solve the problems of an increasingly complex society. But he was also aware of the difficulties of reconciling expertism with participatory democracy. That reconciliation would come, Hoover believed, through the mediation of public relations. Leadership, instruction, persuasion, propaganda—these were for Hoover tools for convincing ordinary Americans of appropriate courses of action while upholding their freedom of choice.[24] Here Hoover hewed close to *Public Opinion.* Although Hoover rejected Lippmann's emphasis on the irrational common man, he was no less committed to the leadership of technocrats and to finding ways of blending technocracy and the "expert" with democratic values. Hoover, like Lippmann, was a democratic social engineer.

Salesmanship

Selling seems somehow more timeless than public relations, and yet it, too, became a "profession" early in the twentieth century, complete with organizations, journals, and instructions for doing what until then had come naturally. That these instructions were permeated with psychology after 1915 should come as no surprise; no aspect of American culture escaped the brush of Freud or the behavioralists. Less recognized is that after 1920, the literature of salesmanship took on a democratic flavor traceable in part to an infusion of social psychology. Clarence Darrow summarized and poked fun at the new psychological salesmanship in an essay appearing in August 1925 in the *American Mercury.* The essay contains evidence of two ingredients of democratic social engineering: participation and leadership. According to Darrow, one book on selling suggested that a "Selling Talk" must take the prospect "to the point of *deciding* that he needs your goods more than he needs the money they cost." Another popular manual emphasized the importance of the buyer's voluntary commitment: "You get an order from a prospect because of what he *thinks.* Signing an order or handing over money must be a *voluntary* operation. The prospect must be *willing;* he must think certain thoughts. *You* must lead him *to think those thoughts.*"[25] In both these examples, selling meant involving the buyer in the process of deciding to purchase and consume; both suggested the necessity of leading the buyer to that decision.

These ideas of democratic participatory salesmanship were taken up in one of the century's most influential books, Dale Carnegie's *How to Win Friends and Influence People*, published in the midst of the Great Depression. The book may be interpreted as a guide to bureaucratic behavior or as a series of lessons in positive thinking in a decade of economic trauma.[26] But it may also be examined as a classic study in democratic salesmanship.

Carnegie's approach to selling was based on the standard assumptions of democratic social engineering. Like Lippmann and Bernays, Carnegie's salesmen operated in an environment of the irrational. "When dealing with people," Carnegie wrote, "let us remember we are not dealing with creatures of logic. We are dealing with creatures of emotion, creatures bristling with prejudices and motivated by pride and vanity." Like industrial psychologist Elton Mayo, for whom there were no real or irreconcilable differences between workers and bosses, Carnegie thought there were no fundamental conflicts between buyer and seller. An irritated customer, for example, frequently needed only a sympathetic ear. The salesman could diffuse whatever superficial conflict existed by emphasizing — in the quintessential way of democratic social engineering — that differences between buyer and seller were those of "method," not "purpose."[27]

Carnegie's instructions for salesmen contained two elements characteristic of democratic methodology. The first had to do with the presentation of authority. Just as Benjamin Spock would a decade later advise mothers to avoid arguments and direct disagreements with their children, so did Carnegie enjoin his salesmen from confronting buyers. "Real salesmanship," he wrote, "isn't argument. It isn't anything even remotely like argument. The human mind isn't changed that way." "*Always*," he emphasized, "*avoid the acute angle.*" In a short poem in which the salesman becomes a kind of teacher, Carnegie commented on the subtleties of the art of persuasion: "*Men must be taught as if you taught them not / And things unknown proposed as things forgot.*"[28]

The second instructional element characteristic of democratic methodology was Carnegie's suggestion that the decision-making process be in some sense democratized. There were several examples in *How to Win Friends and Influence People*. One featured an automobile sales manager who achieved substantial sales increases after instituting consultative procedures with his salesmen. Another involved Theodore Roosevelt, who as governor of New York had sought the advice of the state's political bosses on an appointment. When the bosses finally presented an acceptable candidate, Roosevelt took their advice and appointed him, noting (as if to suggest that his function was one of ratification), *"I would let them take the credit for the appointment."*[29]

For his most complete example, Carnegie tapped the field of child rearing, specifically the parental task of training an older child out of the habit of bed-wetting. Rather than scold the boy, his mother uses her son's desire for a bed of his own to create a proper motivational climate. She escorts the boy to a department store. With a surreptitious wink to the salesgirl, she introduces him and says, "Here is a little gentleman who would like to do some shopping." The remainder of the story contains the crucial elements of the "participatory" experience:

> The sales girl made him feel important by saying: "Young man, what can I show you?"
>
> He stood a couple of inches taller and said: "I want to buy a bed for myself."
>
> When he was shown the one his mother wanted him to buy, she winked at the sales girl and the boy was persuaded to buy it.

Carnegie concludes that the boy would not wet his bed because "That was *his* bed. *He* and *he* alone had bought it."[30]

The scene presented here is a familiar one. Many parents have played out such little farces with their children. But Carnegie is not really talking about children; he is talking about business, about selling. Transferred to the business world, the department store drama, with all its winks and persuasion, takes on the character of a real con game: two against one, with all the knowledge and all the cards on one side. Carnegie wanted certain results (he was a social engineer), and to obtain these results he had chosen certain "democratic" (participatory) techniques (he was a democratic social engineer). Whereas Lippmann and Hoover continued to see the process as a legitimately democratic one, for Carnegie the process was more obviously manipulative. But it was the same process.

PRODUCTION

Industrial Democracy

Inside the nation's factories and offices, employers were discovering how useful democratic processes could be. In the decades that bridged the two world wars, hundreds of corporations — and dozens of major ones — experimented with a variety of forms of what had become known as industrial democracy. During the Progressive Era, these experiments had usually been mere forays into collective bargaining, a process that Mary Parker Follett, a leading theorist of democratic social engineering, looked on as an example of an old-fashioned, confrontational process, one outside the framework of genuine democratic social engineering. As labor unions grew in strength, and as industrial conflict intensified, more far-reaching forms of democratic control seemed reasonable and necessary. Writing in 1914, Walter Lippmann called on American industry to "prepare itself for democratic control." Unions, he wrote, "are the first feeble effort to conquer the industrial jungle for democratic life."[31] The troubled year 1919 brought two Woodrow Wilson-sponsored conferences on industrial cooperation. The report of the second conference, issued in March 1920, analyzed the source of labor-management conflict and recommended resolution through the extension of democratic forms of industrial governance:

It can not be denied that unrest to-day is characterized more than ever before by purposes and desires which go beyond the mere demand for higher wages and shorter hours. Aspirations inherent in this form of restlessness are to a greater extent psychological and intangible. They are not for that reason any less significant. They reveal a desire on the part of workers to exert a larger and more organic influence upon the processes of industrial life. This impulse is not to be discouraged but made helpful and cooperative. With comprehending and sympathetic appreciation, it can be converted into a force working for a better spirit and understanding between capital and labor, and for more effective cooperation.[32]

Employers responded with the now-familiar tools of industrial democracy, including employee-representation plans (there were well over a million workers in over eight hundred plans in 1924) and new programs of personnel relations. Too much has been written on employee representation to warrant a full treatment of the subject here. The plans were controversial, even as they were put in place. Contemporaries disagreed on whether they were intended to create genuinely democratic environments, or only the facade of democracy; on whether they were designed to undercut union development or simply transcend it. Follett argued in 1926 that employee representation had begun as a conservative reaction and gradually taken on more positive characteristics.[33]

As vital as the alternatives posed above are for the history of industrial relations, they are largely irrelevant for our purposes. No matter what their aims or content, employee-representation plans were based on a democratic, as opposed to an autocratic, model of authority. Clarence Hicks's account of his tenure as industrial relations adviser to International Harvester, Standard Oil of New Jersey, and the Colorado Fuel and Iron Company demonstrates that a plan could be at once conservative in purpose and yet firmly grounded in democratic theory. In 1915 Hicks helped create a representation plan for Colorado Fuel and Iron, "under which representatives of employees and management could discuss and settle on a friendly basis all matters of mutual interest." The intent of the plan, Hicks acknowledged, was to prevent "class warfare."[34] It was the adherence to democracy, regardless of intent, that defined the era.

Personnel Relations

The second area of management to be made over in the democratic mold was personnel relations, a field concerned with the hundreds of ways in which management and labor contacted each other every working day. The story as generally outlined is true enough: in the four decades after 1900, personnel relations changed from the authoritarian methodology of Frederick W. Taylor and other early apostles of "scientific management" to the "human relations" approach based on the philosophy of Follett and Tead and the research of Elton Mayo.[35] Most scholars accept the designation of Taylor as an authoritarian, a case perhaps overstated, as Taylor's Socratic approach to his guinea pig/worker Schmidt attests.[36] Nonetheless, whatever Taylor's notions of democracy, they were raised to the level of consciousness only when scientific management found itself under attack.[37] It is also no secret that "human relations" was neither less profit based than scientific management nor more humane or "human." It was simply another way of getting things done, this time using groups, discussion, and other devices of democracy.

The transition from an authoritarian to a democratic style of personnel relations was made in the decade after 1920. Practically, of course, it took place in the nation's factories and shops. But it also required a theoretical underpinning, and that underpinning in turn depended on new ways of thinking about how and why workers behaved as they did. Among the prominent theoreticians of the democratic school of personnel relations was educator, editor, and lecturer Tead. Tead arrived at democracy as the proper mode of industrial relations by way of a psychological system that was an amalgam of social psychology, Freudian psychology, and a psychology of intuition. From personal observation of his environment and from the existence of the "herd instinct," Tead concluded that the world functioned through groups — among them neighborhoods, labor unions, employers' associations, churches, and nations. "The conduct of men," he asserted, was "[largely] determined by their group associations."[38]

Besides the herd instinct, Tead identified nine other instincts, from the sex instinct to the instinct of workmanship. When groups suppressed a "compelling instinct," they took on "pathological characteristics." Something like that, Tead believed, had happened to labor unions; created in response to intolerable working conditions, they had become — through a process of repression — "zealous," "uncritical," and "aggressive." Tead reserved a special place in his system for the "instinctive will to think," a concept he claimed to share with Lippmann and John Dewey. According to this instinct, man was a "rationalizing" (if not rational) animal. When this instinct — to think, to discuss, to reason, to be curious — was suppressed, the suppression undermined the other instincts. Tead was "particularly interested," therefore, "to discover how, if at all, the functioning of this instinct can modify the operation of all the rest as they manifest themselves in industrial behavior," and to recreate the conditions under which the thinking instinct might flourish. This involved doing away with institutions or situations that fostered submission and conformity. More important, it meant creating a "method of thinking," generating formal stimuli to "intellection," and developing environments in which the "habit of thought" could take root. The free play of this and other instincts, Tead concluded, naturally required democratic institutional arrangements, i.e., "democracy in industry."[39]

Tead had elevated the group to prominence as a therapeutic environment. He had defined some groups — especially labor unions — as pathological and, therefore, in need of therapy. He had fashioned a device — the thinking instinct — which he believed would allow therapists (i.e., social engineers) to reach inside the group and control its behavior. And he had summed it up, curiously, as "democracy in industry." What Tead had done was to appropriate the whole realm of discourse and social exchange as a tool of social control. (Tead was not alone in his boldness. Educator William H. Kilpatrick had done much the same thing in his "project method" of education.[40] But few accomplished the task as forthrightly as Tead.)

Judging from the frequency with which her name appears in the literature, Mary Parker Follett was one of the most influential theorists of democratic social engineering. She achieved this position because, like Dewey, she understood in the broadest terms the movement of which she was a part and because, unlike Dewey, she wrote clearly and concretely and moved easily between fields as different as education, social work, and business. A brief examination of her work reveals more representativeness than uniqueness. Follett's ideas were not that different from Tead's, Lippmann's, or Bernays', and her journey to industrial relations and personnel management — by way of settlement work and vocational guidance — was nothing less than a biographical replication of the history of social engineering in the second and third decades of the century.

Like many others whose thought we have examined in this chapter, Follett both feared groups and realized their potential as mechanisms of social engineering. She, too, believed in something like the "herd instinct." Yet if groups were dangerous, they were also the source of regeneration, control, and unity. Proper groups — democratic groups, groups that used discussion shaped through noncoercive leadership — fostered creativity, individual fulfillment, and social responsibility. "There is only one way to get democratic control," Follett wrote, "by people learning how to evolve collective ideas."[41]

Follett is perhaps most remembered as an advocate of rejuvenated neighborhoods and community centers, and there was a period in her life — roughly the decade after 1915 — when she was devoted to these causes.[42] They were, after all, natural causes for one whose first work experience was in Boston's active social-settlement community.[43] But Follett was not so committed to these issues, nor were they so primary in her thinking, that she was unable to shift fields as the times changed, or to seek out the most appropriate vehicles for her ideas.

Something of the kind happened after 1920. Social engineering in the Progressive Era had been in no small measure dominated by the problem of assimilating the immigrant, and for this purpose the settlement houses, the schools, and the community centers were reasonable solutions. As the flow of immigrants was restricted in the 1920s, attention shifted to an older clientele and to a new environment that was increasingly defined as the critical site of conflict — the factory. With many others, Follett made this transition from social work to business management. She had to do so, she explained to an English audience in 1926, because she believed in "unifying" and in "control" (of the business cycle or people, for example) and because the most advanced and sophisticated work in these areas was taking place in business. For almost a decade — from 1924 through 1932, the year before she died, Follett probed the world of business.[44]

If there was an assumption that held Follett's work in business management together, it was that conflict — in the sense of irreconcilable differences — was not an essential ingredient of social processes. Conflict existed, but it could be *"integrated"*; that is, solutions could be found in which "neither side has . . . to sacrifice anything."[45] Armed with this assumption, Follett went on to construct an ideal system of authority that verged on the anarchic. Orders, commands, coercion, the power that some had over others — all were unnecessary because every situation — no matter how obvious the conflict within it seemed — had an "order" that was "integral" to it. Conflict was integrated by figuring out what this "order" was in any particular situation.[46]

Once this is understood, all conflicts are resolvable, and no one orders anyone else about. Foremen are not in conflict with rank-and-file workers, nor do they issue orders to them. The head of the sales department is not in conflict with the head of production, nor does he relate to the production head as a superior. Instead, these pairs "take their orders from the situation." Gone is the need even for the tactics that most group-process advocates believed necessary, including certain kinds of leadership and persuasion. Follett's schema does not do away with the leader, but her leader is a mere facilitator, someone who could "organize the experience of the group," i.e., help the group discover the "order" in a given situation. "The best type of leader," Follett concluded, "does not seek *his* ends, but the ends disclosed by an evolving process in which each has his special part."[47]

Follett had taken the idea of democracy in personnel relations to its logical conclusion, until manipulation, propaganda, persuasion, and other descriptions of leadership that satisfied others had been banished from her vocabulary and vision. What she had arrived at, however, was based on the same kind of thinking as the scientific management which she criticized as coercive. Although she would never have countenanced a manager's verbally abusing an employee, as Taylor had abused the iron carrier Schmidt in an attempt to get him to move more iron, her system shared with Taylor's the pretense of science. Taylor had argued that there was one best way of doing every task, and that it was the task of the scientific manager to discover it and present it to the worker; Follett claimed, analogously, that every situation had its order and that it was the task of the leader/manager to help everyone involved in that situation to see the order inherent in it. Each sought to do away with conflict by assuming the existence of some natural order of things waiting to be discovered.

It was one thing to suggest a general approach to groups and behavior modification, as Tead had done; or to lecture on the theory of human relations as it applied to contacts between foremen and workers or managers and foremen, as Follett had. It remained for Mayo to demonstrate convincingly the utility of a human relations approach to conditions at the actual point of production. Born in 1880 in Australia, Mayo studied psychology at Adelaide University. During World War I he helped organize a psychiatric treatment program for soldiers suffering from shell shock. In 1923, equipped with Rockefeller and Carnegie Foundation grants, he became an associate in research at the University of Pennsylvania. Four years later, having made the move to Harvard University, Mayo began a famous series of experiments at Western Electric's Hawthorne plant in Chicago.[48]

These experiments have been described and analyzed in great detail by others. In essence, Mayo brought to the problem of production several critical elements in the human-relations approach. First, his experiments suggested that groups — even an informal network of interpersonal associations existing in a workroom — could and did influence levels of production. A second observation involved what became known as the "Hawthorne effect": that workers produced more because of enhanced status resulting from participation in the experiments. The third contribution of the experiments speaks most directly to the question of democratic organization. Mayo and his staff at some point recognized that productivity had increased because the workers had been drawn into the process of making decisions about their own working conditions.[49]

Of the three leading theorists of group process in industry, Mayo was perhaps the most broadly analytical and certainly the most historical. In several books published between 1919 and 1947, Mayo sought to explain the origins of his theories and to establish a historical focus for the Hawthorne experiments. Not surprisingly, his ideas closely paralleled those of Tead and Follett. Although Mayo did not call it the "herd instinct," he did believe that large-scale social organisms — such as corporations and labor unions — led indirectly to irresponsible social behavior. Deprived of community and of group experiences which might foster some sense of the corporate (group) nature of experience and, therefore, some notion of social responsibility, individuals developed habits of interaction and personality characteristics dangerous to a democratic society. Mayo labeled the result the "obsessive" personality, from the work of psychologist Pierre Janet, whose impact on his thinking was profound. Defined by his complete social inadequacy, the obsessive was unable to perform even the simplest and most routine of social acts — like seating oneself at a dining table in the presence of others — without feeling fear and anxiety. Obsessives were believed to have been deprived of the kind of ordinary, extrafamilial relationships that over time allowed the development of interpersonal association and collaboration. Unadapted to this crucial social aspect of reality, the unhappy, outcast obsessive was easily victimized and often drawn compulsively to extremist causes.[50]

In this schema — as for Tead and Follett — conflict between workers and management was unrelated to any fundamental or objective difference, class or otherwise, between the two. "Hates" existed, but they were "irrational," the product of a decline in "spontaneous collaboration" in the wake of the artificial collaborative forms (i.e., unions) established during, and as a result of, the Industrial Revolution.[51] According to T. North Whitehead, Mayo's fellow researcher at Hawthorne, labor unions were not to be considered evidence of substantive differences between capital and labor; they were, instead, essentially social clubs, designed to meet psychological and social needs.[52]

Fortunately, this decline in spontaneous collaboration, though rooted deep in history, could be stemmed, hatred eliminated, and business efficiency increased. The mechanism for this turnaround was, of course, the group, and through it, the reestablishment of spontaneous, unconscious collaboration. In one sense, Mayo's methods seemed to be far removed from Tead's. Where Tead had called for the restoration of thoughtful reason to the industrial process, Mayo defined his spontaneous collaboration as so natural and unconscious as to exclude thoughtful deliberation and discussion. In another sense, however, both Tead and Mayo were searching for the same thing: an organic way out of rigid existing frameworks, such as collective bargaining, for the settlement of industrial problems. For Tead this required an "anal" small group, practicing an intellectual process; for Mayo it required an "oral" small group, operating with ostensible freedom except for some natural preindustrial rules that were hardly definable. Neither Mayo nor Tead, however, could tolerate leaving this small group to its own devices. Each sought to enter it. Spontaneous it might be and natural as the medieval world, but Mayo's collaboration was a collaboration through leadership, persuasion, and "intelligent administration."[53]

Business and Democratic Methods

What we know of the practices of American business in the two decades after 1930 indicates that businessmen did not fear to adapt Mayo's emphases on groups or participation to their own purposes. Historian Loren Baritz has described the development in 1937 of H. H. Carey's "consultative supervision," a procedure, as Carey put it, "whereby supervisors and executives consult with employees or their representatives as equals on all matters affecting the employees' welfare or interest prior to formulating policies or taking action." During World War II, corporations turned increasingly to small, problem-solving groups under the guidance of trained leaders.[54] Henry M. Busch's manual on this "conference method" acknowledged debts to Kilpatrick, Dewey, Harrison Elliott, Tead, and other leading theorists of democratic social engineering, and it carefully distinguished the conference method from "pseudo-democratic procedures." Busch had trained executives of the Standard Oil Company of Ohio in conference methods.[55]

Another form of evidence for business's attachment to democratic techniques exists in the creation and operation of the National Training Laboratory on Group Development in Bethel, Maine. The laboratory grew out of the thought of Kurt Lewin. The German-born psychologist had in 1920 published a paper on the Taylor system that revealed an interest in the use of psychology to resolve labor-management disputes. Lewin hoped to find a way to make work more satisfying while maintaining productivity. Soon after his arrival in the United States in 1932, Lewin developed a strong friendship with social psychologist Gardner Murphy and ties with leading group-process intellectuals, including Kilpatrick and Dewey. In the mid-1930s, he supervised a series of experiments at the Iowa Child Welfare Research Station, in which he sought to test the effectiveness of democratic, autocratic, and laissez-faire structures of authority. Although most of this research dealt with children, after 1939 Lewin worked with the Harwood Manufacturing Corporation on labor productivity, emphasizing the use of small groups in helping workers build confidence that self-established production goals could be attained.[56]

The key element in the group process, Lewin argued, was democratic decision making: "Motivation alone does not suffice to lead to change. This link is provided by decisions. A process like decision making, which takes only a few minutes, is able to affect conduct for many months to come. The decision seems to have a 'freezing' effect which is partly due to the individual's tendency to 'stick to his decision' and partly to the 'commitment to a group.'"[57] By 1940 Lewin had a well-developed democratic theory and more than passing interest in its application to business environments.

As group-process ideas found a wider audience, Lewin moved to establish facilities that would train leaders from diverse fields in group procedures. One effort, aimed specifically at business leaders, proved short-lived.[58] More enduring was the National Training Laboratory (NTL), founded in 1947, the year Lewin died. The original planning for the laboratory was carried out by a team of consultants, including Lewin; his colleague at Iowa in the 1930s, Ronald Lippitt; Leland Bradford from the National Education Association (NEA); and Kenneth Benne from Teachers College, Columbia. The first laboratory, held in the summer of 1947, was sponsored by the NEA and the Research Center for Group Dynamics at the Massachusetts Institute of Technology. From 1950 through 1953 the NTL was supported by a grant from the Carnegie Corporation of New York.[59]

Although the Bethel laboratory served more educators than any other single group, it was also intended to train business leaders in group-process methods. The "central theme" of the 1947 laboratory was "productivity," measured individually and in a group context. An NTL prospectus suggested that the laboratory might be used to train management and workers to "collaborate in meeting the disruptive problems of technological change." Grace Coyle, a leading figure in social group work, described the NTL as "tied up with big business in certain ways and . . . doing counseling with personnel people in some of the large industries." In the early 1950s, more than ten percent of the NTL's substantial consulting business involved business organizations.[60]

Some persons trained in social group work were ambivalent and even sharply critical of the group ideas being taught at Bethel. Coyle, especially, tried to distinguish between her own field of group work, based on the educational theories of Kilpatrick and Dewey and on the discussion method developed in the early 1920s by agencies such as The Inquiry, and "group dynamics," built on Lewin's work and Gestalt psychology.[61] Not everyone accepted the distinction. Writing in 1967, psychologist Gordon Allport noted "a striking kinship between the work of Kurt Lewin and the work of John Dewey. Both agreed," wrote Allport, "that democracy must be learned anew in each generation, and that it is a far more difficult form of social structure to attain and to maintain than is autocracy. Both see the intimate dependence of democracy upon social science. Without knowledge of, and obedience to, the laws of human nature in group settings, democracy cannot succeed." Allport believed that Lewin, more than any other person, had demonstrated in "concrete, operational terms what it means to be a democratic leader, and to create a democratic group structure."[62]

Coyle's participation at the 1947 summer laboratory had convinced her that group dynamics, because it eschewed psychiatry and, therefore, the whole notion of individual behavior, tended to treat people as if they were "counters on a board, not full-bodied human beings."[63] Although neither Lippitt nor Lewin would have appreciated Coyle's way of putting the issue, they might have admitted to elevating the group vis-à-vis the individual in the training/learning process. Evaluating Lewin's contribution to psychology in 1967, Lippitt described his views in terms that reflected the new emphasis on group dynamics: "To Kurt Lewin the American culture ideal of the 'self-made-man,' of everyone 'standing on his own feet' seemed as tragic a picture as the initiative-destroying dependence on a benevolent despot. He felt and perceived clearly that we all need continuous help from each other and that this type of interdependence is the greatest challenge to maturity of individual and group functioning."[64]

At the heart of Coyle's discomfort with group dynamics was her belief that the group-dynamics approach, in contrast to that of social group work, assumed that behavior was "externally controlled" rather than "internally motivated . . . by complex emotions."[65] This distinction between external and internal modes of instruction, learning, and control runs deep in the history of group process, through the work of the movement's philosophers, religious educators, and educational theorists. Even the most practical documents of the group-process movement insisted on the importance of internalizing authority. A 1920 handbook for scoutmasters, for example, instructed its readers in the virtues of *self control and direction* as opposed to *outside control and direction.* The "highest and most effective control," stated the manual, is that "which is based on *consent,* on agreement with and the active *desire* to do what is asked . . ." "The chasm between the internal and the external," the manual insisted, "is real and steep and deep. Scouting has much to offer for bridging it as scouting pushes from *within* not from *without*."[66]

Valid or not, this distinction was central to the new system of democratic authority. When Coyle questioned group dynamics' commitment to internal authority, she was challenging the right of the Lewin/Lippitt school to consider its approach "democratic." Certainly the NTL's methods were far removed from those of the 1920 scoutmasters. When the laboratory described the content of its programs, it used some of the familiar language of democracy. For example, a report describing what was supposed to take place at the 1947 laboratory — where Coyle formed her negative impressions — mentioned discussion, group decision making, and conference planning as well as techniques like role playing more strongly identified with Lewin's group dynamics. The report paid lip service, at least, to the idea of democracy: "It is vital for survival that democratically effective leaders be developed to work with groups in all areas of face-to-face living. There is a great need for group life and leadership within which the individual can find security and insight, and can realize his capacity for positive change." In addition, an NTL internal memorandum on its training operations said that "every effort must be made to resolve differences by a process of collaborative participation," and it emphasized the need for an "attitude of 'permissiveness' toward the free expression of a variety of viewpoints." ("Permissiveness" was a word then being applied to the child-rearing ideas of Benjamin Spock; it was jargon for democracy.)[67]

But the same memorandum also described the "cultural island" theory on which the NTL functioned. According to this theory, training effectiveness depended on the "cohesiveness" of the laboratory, on its "psychological power" over the trainees. To create this cohesiveness, laboratory supervisors tried to isolate the trainee from the "back-home" situation.[68] Perhaps this was the atmosphere that Coyle found at Bethel in the summer of 1947.

A Case Study: Foremen's Clubs

One of the first occupations to experience the group, group process, and the club as a consciously applied methodology of social engineering was that of foreman. In the strained climate of labor relations created by the First World War and its aftermath, employers in Dayton, Ohio, brought the city's foremen into the first of many clubs. The club movement nearly collapsed in the wake of the stock market crash of 1929, only to be revived in the late 1930s and during the Second World War. Although they were not created with a single purpose or by a single interest group, on the whole the clubs — and the democratic methodology they entailed — were designed to improve efficiency and to reduce conflict between labor and capital by educating foremen — and, indirectly, ordinary workers — to the needs of American business.

The initial effort to bring foremen together in an informal, nonunion context took the form of a class for foremen, sponsored by the local Dayton YMCA and offered in 1917 or 1918. This effort was an outgrowth of the YMCA's program in industrial work. Launched in 1882 and enlarged after 1902, the program rejected paternalism for an emphasis on employee participation in welfare work. In this sense, its approach was "democratic."[69]

The YMCA's efforts found fertile soil in Dayton, and there and elsewhere foremen's clubs became a factor in industrial relations. The clubs were either shop clubs (with membership confined to a single plant) or city clubs (with club or individual membership drawn from several plants). In Dayton, some companies such as the Frigidaire Corporation had their own clubs, and the city's foremen were organized in 1918 in the Dayton Foremen's Club. The state's city and shop clubs were brought together in 1923 in the Ohio Federation of Foremen's Clubs. Three years later, Ohio had twenty major clubs with over 5,000 paid members. The Dayton club alone had 1,400 members. Although there is no clear record of club activity in neighboring Indiana, that state's services for foremanship training were extensive and utilized foremen's clubs. Between 1923 and 1936, Purdue University trained 10,000 foremen from 616 companies in 87 cities.[70]

Growth was much slower in the East, where by mid-decade there were perhaps a dozen active foremen's clubs.[71] Nonetheless, activity outside Ohio was sufficient to justify the organization of the National Association of Foremen (NAF) in 1925. The NAF's first convention in 1926 drew more than 1,500 delegates to what one observer described as a "crusade," reminiscent of bygone meetings of the YMCA Older Boy Conferences and the Men and Religion Forward Movement. Like other organizations, from trade unions to trade associations, this one proved difficult to maintain against the impact of the Great Depression. Membership declined from 30,000 in 1930 to about 4,000 in 1933. By 1936, when Franklin Roosevelt was elected to a second term, the organization of foremen — though not entirely in clubs or in the NAF — had entered the first phase of a recovery that would continue through the Second World War.[72]

The clubs were created for many reasons, several of them related to the climate of reaction against organized labor that hung over the decade after 1917. The clubs were in part an employer response to long-term changes in the status and organization of foremen. In 1875, foremen in many industries were essentially bosses, with real control over hiring, firing, and other crucial aspects of the lives of workers.[73] By 1935, mass production and scientific management had stripped most foremen of their managerial functions and their independence. As supervisory personnel began to think of themselves as workers rather than managers, they formed unions — on the railroads, in government, in the printing trades, in the maritime industry.[74] Business used groups and group process and the particular institution of the foremen's club not just to counter or prevent the organization of foremen, but to modify *attitudes:* to convince foremen that the economic changes of the past fifty years had not fundamentally changed the nature of foremanship and that allegiance ought naturally to be granted to capital rather than labor.

The foremen's clubs were designed and structured to accomplish these objectives. Many clubs were actually run by superintendents rather than foremen, and officers of the national association were generally above the rank of foreman. At the Carter's Ink Company, initiative for a foremen's club came from management, and the result was the Foremen and Supervisor's Club, attended by foremen, supervisors, and the company president, general manager, and plant superintendent. Carter's created a simple foremen's club only when foremen objected to the original format. Even then, Carter's management expected to penetrate the organization with its own objectives. "The Foreman's Club," said the company's works manager, "should be a place in which the company can inspire its lieutenants with a vision of the company's projects, its aims, its hopes and its good faith. It should be a place in which the foremen can unify their faith in the company, can come to a sympathetic understanding of the company's difficulties and its hopes, and can go out into the various parts of the factory to represent the company at its best, not by propaganda, but by work."[75]

At Cluett, Peabody, and Co., where a foremen's club was organized in 1919, management faced a similar problem. When foremen, apparently intimidated by the presence at club meetings of superintendents and other managers, refused to express themselves (an omission of no small consequence in the modern, communication-oriented bureaucratic corporation), the company reorganized the club. "We called it a Study Group," said T. G. Protheroe, a company officer. It was a voluntary organization, composed mostly of foremen. Even so, Cluett, Peabody was wary of an independent organization. "We are looking forward to an organization of only foremen," said Protheroe, "but it will be called a Committee of our Club." There was some doubt in management circles about whether even this committee should be given over entirely to foremen.[76]

The managerial objectives of the NAF changed little in the two decades after 1925. The account of the organization written by the NAF's first president, Thomas B. Fordham, is nothing less than a managerial rationale.

For Fordham, the foreman — no matter what his origins — was part of management, and his essential function was "to interpret to the group from which he came [i.e., labor] the economic side of the business, so that he can logically represent Management in an important phase in their efforts to make profit." According to Fordham, class need not — perhaps *did* not would be more accurate — exist. Most workers wanted to be "successful" (i.e., to help the company make profit), but many did not understand how to go about it. These men, Fordham argued, "need to be taught, calmly and coldly, the facts of right living." Fordham believed that foremen's clubs would, on the one hand, carry on these teaching and educative functions and, on the other hand, demonstrate to timid business leaders that the organization of foremen in clubs did not necessarily entail unionization or radicalism.[77]

Management also looked to the clubs for what they might contribute to improved intracompany communications. The massive supercorporations of the twentieth century could not be operated efficiently using nineteenth-century mechanisms of communication. One response, captured in the 1921 Sloan Report for General Motors, was the reorganization and decentralization of management in many of the nation's largest businesses.[78] Another was to increase the flow of communication within the organization, between upper-level management and foremen and between foremen in different departments or divisions. This accounts for the emphasis in the foremen's club movement on communication, and it partially explains corporate efforts to bring management and foremen together in one club, for only in these "mixed" clubs could management benefit from direct communication with foremen.[79] Inadequate communication between departments — attributed in part to independent, narrow-minded, and isolated foremen — could, however, be approached through clubs composed only of foremen. Employers hoped foremen would use these club opportunities to exchange ideas, promote "team work," improve "coordination," and develop feelings of "interdependence."[80] Both remedies required people talking to each other. The failure to do so jeopardized the whole scheme. Hence the frequent comments in club literature on the necessity for foremen to express themselves.[81]

Managerial objectives remained prominent in the NAF into the 1940s. The organization was still essentially educational, and it was no less dedicated to articulating management goals and to convincing the foreman that "he is a definite part of management . . ."[82] A 1937 assessment of the revived foremen's club movement by J. W. Reinhardt, vice-president of the Canton (Ohio) Development Corporation and a past president of the NAF, makes it clear that the clubs were business vehicles. Reinhardt emhasized the role of a foremen's club in preventing labor "dissension" and avoiding costly strikes, providing, as he put it, "a stabilizer for today and insurance for the future."[83]

But twenty years had brought two important changes in methods. First, the educative process had become much more refined and sophisticated. The NAF provided foremen with the most elaborate meeting and discussion outlines. Second, foremanship was now conceptualized as a profession. Those who had pioneered the foremen's clubs of the 1920s had recognized the ambivalent, boss/worker role of the foreman and the urgency of linking the foreman to management; but they had no consistent idea of how to go about accomplishing this objective, save that foremen could be moved and inspired to appreciate management's position through contact with upper-level supervisors in the clubs. A later generation, however, forcefully appealed to the status needs of foremen by describing foremanship as a profession, and not just any profession at that. According to an NAF manual, foremanship was no less a profession than medicine. NAF leaders hoped to market a foremen's "code of ethics" (in this context, ethics meant understanding and communicating the business point of view) by convincing foremen that they should imitate the medical profession. Just as physicians followed "rules or guiding principles," so should foremen. The manual even implied that foremen should replicate a rational, middle-class model of career behavior. "If you were a doctor," stated the manual, "you would first of all want to be successful and you would select the field of medicine and the community for your practice according to your estimate of your ability and background."[84]

The YMCA — whose foremen's classes had led directly to the clubs — was apparently less interested in corporate profit than in reestablishing what a 1938 foremen's club manual would call a "social sense of responsibility."[85] According to a four-volume manual for foremanship written for the YMCA in 1921, workers no longer felt themselves a part of their communities. Conditions of work and life had been corrupted by modernization. Because the "'working life' is divided," so was the "town" divided. Local citizens had somehow lost their sense of "responsibility toward the general body," casting votes for labor, or business, or some other interest group that represented only a segment of the community rather than the general welfare. The authors of this YMCA study sought to restore some unity to community life by restoring a group spirit within the factory. This restoration would begin with the workers under the foreman, the "oldest and smallest industrial cooperative unit." The foreman would become their teacher, and it would be his special task to make these ordinary workers understand (or appreciate anew) their duties in the shop. When foremen had learned to "subordinate themselves to the good of the team," and to communicate this need for subordination to those beneath them, workers would also come to understand their responsibilities in the larger community. The end product would be not only social harmony (i.e., the internalization of, and agreement on, capitalist values) but increased profits. Community and productivity went hand in hand. Anticipating the conclusions of industrial psychologist Mayo later in the decade, the YMCA's study of foremanship argued that efficiency was a product of group spirit: "A group of men working together, in the companionship which comes with common working problems, can swing work through with a capacity that is impossible in the lone individual."[86]

Some of the objectives of the foremen's clubs — improved efficiency and productivity, work-force education — were age-old goals that were now simply being pursued under a new format. Others — better bureaucratic communication, the binding of foremen to the company — were essentially twentieth-century objectives. But what makes the foremen's club movement significant — indeed, what gives it definition as a twentieth-century experience — is a matter of means, not ends. The foremen's club methodology was "democratic." Corporate objectives were to be attained through persuasion rather than coercion, and through a process that involved, rather than acted upon, the participants.

The word "democratic" consistently referred to a style of leadership, to the way authority was exercised in the clubs and in the factories. The YMCA drew the distinction between an old, "driving" style of leadership and a "democratic" style. The demise of the "driver" and the emergence of the leader was also a theme broached by Albert Sobey, a Flint, Michigan, businessman involved in the club movement. And Fordham's account of foremanship suggested "workers' participation" in decisions that might once have been made solely by the supervisor. The foreman could "either make the worker angry and depressed and resentful, or interested in doing what you suggest — suggest, mind you, not 'order' . . . the *clever* foreman *suggests* rather than orders."[87]

By the mid-1930s, coincident with the growing threat of fascism and Nazism in Europe, analysis of American mechanisms of authority had become even more pointed. As in World War I, "democracy" was raised to mythic status, and it became important to differentiate American ways of getting things done from the authoritarian methods of the European dictatorships. "Do you suppose it could be possible," said a foremen's club manual, "that a man could believe in democracy, have a son fighting for it, and still be a dictator in his own home or on his job? Could we be overlooking the promotion of democracy here at home while fighting for it abroad?"[88] Still, it would be incorrect to conclude that the fascist threat *created* this new democratic structure of authority, even in foremanship. When the Nazi armies crossed into Poland, democratic foremanship was more than two decades old. What the specter of European dictatorship accomplished was to heighten awareness of democratic methodology at all levels of social organization and to provide a convenient rationale for pushing forward with the development and refinement of a "democratic" system that had many functions completely unrelated to international politics.

The elements of a democratic system were derived from progressive education, philosophy, and the new social psychology. They included the small group, group discussion, and trained leadership. The foremen's clubs and related institutions were based on the premise that social groups were unique and powerful institutions that could be used to accomplish specific goals. Groups encouraged self-expression (essential, as we have seen, to bureaucratic communication), stimulated participants to think creatively, checked the development of unacceptable ideas, and increased productivity.[89]

Most important, groups — conferences, meetings, and clubs — were forums in which democratic methods like leadership and group discussion could be practiced. Foremen were educated through group discussion techniques, and they were taught to use such techniques in their own capacities as teachers. At Standard Oil of New Jersey, small-group discussion was utilized at foremen's conferences to present the problem of oil industry standardization. Group discussion was also practiced at the Works Progress Administration, which carried out a program of foremanship training in the late 1930s. NAF instructional materials were consistently couched in the language of group discussion; teachers (i.e., foremen and other supervisors) were enjoined to elicit discussion as part of the teaching process.[90]

The term "group discussion" labels, but does not describe, the substantive processes carried out in foremen's clubs and similar groups. Group discussion was always to take place under the observation and guidance of trained leaders. The YMCA's 1921 foreman's manual, while stressing the importance of a "democratic" style of leadership and a democratic model of factory organization, was a paean to leadership. According to the YMCA manual, most men, disturbed by responsibility, were content to be led and instructed. "Confidence [in the leader]," the study concluded, "is the greatest motive force for efficiency in industry." A 1929 employers' guide to conducting foremen's meetings advocated group discussion techniques, but again, only under the guidance of a competent leader — described as the key ingredient in a productive meeting.[91]

Were viable democratic processes possible under such conditions? Perhaps. But the likelihood of genuine democracy was considerably reduced by the prerogatives granted to leadership. In a foremen's handbook published in 1943, leadership was defined as "the ability to get other people to work willingly through the leader's influence or example." To accomplish this, the leader/foreman was to use noncoercive group discussion tactics. "The real leader," according to the handbook, "does not try to give them [the employees] any answers. Rather, by discussion he helps the man to analyze his own problem and to develop the right answer after the man has weighed all the facts." The good leader assists employees in problem solving "by being approachable, by listening, by drawing out the story, by suggesting various alternates, by always making the man think through his own situations until the answer is clear." Who was this leader/foreman? Was he an agent of the corporation or a friend of the workers? Could the methods outlined here have produced more than one "right answer"? Perhaps the author had some of the same questions, for the handbook contains a statement so baldly two-headed as to betray an awkward ambivalence. "A leader of men," it reads, "enjoys seeing others develop and grow under his guidance and direction, but *he never makes his pleasure obvious.* He has *a directness, a forthrightness* in all his acts."[92]

Other materials also cast doubt on the extent and legitimacy of the democracy operative in the clubs and similar groups. A 1929 employers' guide for foremen's meetings cautioned group leaders not to dominate meetings but instead to create the impression of a conference to exchange ideas. As if to confirm that the "exchange" was not really intended to be one, the second volume of the manual contained elaborate instructions for the discussion of specific issues. Many of the questions harbor an obvious corporate bias. On the subject of "Maintaining Discipline," for example, the leader should ask, "What are the qualifications of a good disciplinarian?"[93]

The NAF—the parent body of the foremen's clubs—advocated similar methods for its conference leaders. An NAF manual, prepared to help leader-foremen instruct fellow supervisors on a code of ethics, guides leader/foremen trainees through a series of purportedly democratic meetings. At one such meeting, the assembled foremen are informed that the NAF has developed a code of ethics. The leader then says: "It seemed to us this might be a good spring board from which to dive into this analysis of our guiding principles. What do you think? Do you think it would be helpful first to examine what the National Association of Foremen has already done in this field? It seems to me that it should be helpful for us to spend about the first four of these six sessions analyzing these guiding principles of the profession of foremanship, checking their validity, revising them if necessary . . ."[94]

But how much revising could be tolerated? Very little, since, according to NAF procedures, the final code would be a composite of the suggestions of each foremen's club, and all foremen would vote on the final result. Thus the efforts of the conference leaders had to be directed at unity, not diversity, and at hewing close to the existing code. Although participating foremen are asked to suggest changes, the only offered example of such a change is remarkably minor. Much of the manual, in fact, amounts to instructions for the discussion leader in the defense of key ideas in the existing code, like professionalism, social responsibility, and an "open mind." The manual makes it apparent that the end result of each discussion should be not only to confirm something very close to the language of the original code section, but to achieve a new level of commitment to the section itself. The first session ends in this manner: "All right, if you have agreed that this first principle is fair, that it is sound, and that it is practical, are you willing to accept it as part of your guiding principles? Are you willing to try to put it into practice? How many are thoroughly convinced that it is a good principle and are ready to accept it? (Call for a show of hands — try to get unanimous agreement.)"[95]

Genuine group discussion — in the sense of open-ended exchange and real options — could hardly have taken place in this atmosphere. What paraded as discussion is apparent in a section of the manual which offers instructions for discussing the possible results of the ethics program. "The Conference Leader," according to the manual, "should try to draw from the group what they might think would result from this Code of Ethics program. It may be necessary to ask some *leading questions* to elicit and get on the blackboard the following [seven] items."[96] In another sequence, the group is asked to analyze the attitude of a clothing store owner. The instructions are put this way: "By discussion get men to see that the attitude portrayed is 'closed-mindedness' and that the desired attitude is 'open-mindedness.'" The anticipated result of a lengthy "discussion" of this notion of an open mind was the collective realization that an open mind is defined by Owen D. Young's dictum, that "difficulties between worker and employer arise almost entirely from failure of each to see the other's side."[97] The exercise, in short, was designed to inculcate a consensus view of the relationship between capital and labor. Here, as elsewhere, the goal was less to promote meaningful discussion and exchange than to use the discussion method, whenever possible, to reinforce corporate values. Democratic methods — including the foremen's club — were a facade for the preconceived goals of business leaders in the NAF.

On the basis of membership alone, it would seem difficult to claim any transcendent importance for the foremen's club movement. At its peak in 1930, the NAF had perhaps 30,000 members. Yet these members were supervisors and foremen, each with his own substantial dominion and influence. And even if relatively few American workers came under the influence of club foremen, the movement cannot be easily dismissed. It demonstrates that for all the attention Elton Mayo has received for his experiments at Western Electric, the practical application of small groups and participatory techniques in the American factory preceded his investigations by more than a decade. More important, the foremen's club movement, in concert with the contributions of Mayo, Follett, Tead, Fitch, and others, establishes that American managers were seriously interested in democratic social engineering.

A COLLECTIVE BIOGRAPHY

This chapter has been organized into the two basic functional areas of demand and supply, consumption and production. Although this division was made for the sake of convenience and clarity, it also has an analytical purpose. The democratic social engineers who pursued careers on the consumption side of the system may be distinguished from those on the production side not just by what they did, but by where they came from.

On the consumption side, one characteristic is common to several persons, including three major figures in the history of American public relations: wartime service, with an obligation to sell a program or move people to action. Herbert Hoover had his food program. Edward Bernays worked with the Committee on Public Information. Ivey Lee served as publicity director for the American Red Cross. Others, of course, had no comparable experience. Dale Carnegie apparently spent eighteen months as an ordinary soldier, and Clarence Hicks missed the war altogether. But the experience of Hoover, Bernays, and Lee is enough to suggest that the war was a catalytic event for many who were beginning to see the possibilities in the new field of mass communications.[98]

On the production side, a clearer link exists. Most of those who practiced or wrote about some facet of industrial and labor relations in the 1920s had been active in the social settlements. Of five leading authorities in industrial relations — three discussed in this chapter — only Australian-born Mayo apparently had no settlement experience, and Mayo did not immigrate to the United States until 1923, when the settlement was no longer at the cutting edge of the American experience. The career paths of two — Follett and Meyer Bloomfield (whose work is not treated in this chapter) indicate a two-step process: from the settlements, through vocational guidance, to industrial relations. Follett spent a number of years at the Roxbury Neighborhood House, took up vocational guidance for the Boston public schools, and by 1925 was beginning to earn a reputation in business management.[99] Bloomfield is considered by some scholars to be the founder of the "science" of industrial relations. Like Follett, he spent most of the first decade of the century in settlement work, including a stint as director of the Civic Service House in Boston's North End. In 1910, he became director of the Vocational Bureau of Boston and in 1913 helped organize the National Vocational Guidance Association. After wartime service with the Emergency Fleet Corporation, Bloomfield and his brother established an industrial relations firm. The journal *Industrial Relations* was his creation.[100]

Of the others, Tead spent the two years after 1912 at South End House in Boston.[101] Bruno Lasker, whose organization, The Inquiry, was deeply involved in the development of small-group discussion techniques for the resolution of industrial conflict,[102] had strong roots in the settlement movement.[103] Among industrial relations figures with settlement backgrounds one might also include John A. Fitch and B. Seebohm Rowntree. Rowntree's interest in poverty early in the century had by 1921 become translated into the terms of industrial relations with the publication of *The Human Factor in Business*. Fitch, a contributing editor to the socially oriented *Survey* magazine, made several contributions to the literature of industrial relations, including *The Causes of Industrial Unrest* (1924).[104]

What accounts for the link — at this point only a correlation — between the settlements and industrial relations? One possibility is that settlement workers and specialists in industrial relations were practicing similar disciplines, requiring similar skills. Lasker is a case in point. His organization, The Inquiry, had its center of gravity in new problem-solving mechanisms of communication, especially small-group discussions under trained leaders. Lasker acquired these communications skills in the settlements. He later described the settlement movement as essentially an interpersonal phenomenon, one that "accomplishes its ends simply by becoming friends of people and drawing them on to higher achievements."[105] It takes no great effort to imagine that same statement coming from Mayo or a foreman's manual.

Moreover, settlement workers and the industrial relations experts shared the basic goal of finding solutions for social conflict. For settlement workers, these were conflicts between ethnic groups, between first- and second-generation immigrants, between immigrants and native Americans.[106] In industrial relations, the conflicts were between labor and management, between foremen and management, and between foremen and ordinary workers. Tead, Lasker, and Follett not only sought to resolve these conflicts, they virtually defined them out of existence.

Given these shared goals and methods, why did our subjects move from one occupation to another? The answer, I think, is that by 1920 the settlements had ceased to be the compelling vehicle for social reform and social control that they were a decade or two earlier. An earlier generation had located the source of most social problems and conflicts in the "new" immigrant. The "labor problem," as the nineteenth century called it, was so confounded with immigration in the public mind that most Americans had difficulty separating the two issues. Alexander Berkman's attempted assassination of Henry Clay Frick, for example, was seen essentially as the work of an immigrant anarchist, rather than an act springing from the relations between capital and labor. Something of this view held up through the Progressive Era, but as the peak of immigration passed, and as the flow of foreigners was restricted first by the war, and then by the national origin legislation of 1921 and 1924, some of this generalized fear of the immigrant was dissipated. It was still there, of course, especially in the specter of Communism, but the days of looking at the nation's problems as immigrant problems were over.

At the same time, a new problem appeared to take the place of the old. The problem was work. Work had been changing, for more than a century. But the changes of the first two decades of the twentieth century seemed to many Americans to go well beyond those of the past. Two events symbolized those changes. The first was the publication, in 1911, of Frederick W. Taylor's *The Principles of Scientific Management.* The second was the introduction of the moving assembly line at Henry Ford's Highland Park factory in 1913. Neither the assembly line nor scientific management would sweep the nation's production facilities; but together they represented the future of industrial labor. And it was not much of a future.[107]

Some settlement workers recognized the transformation of work as it was taking place and sought to do something about it. Jane Addams, for example, developed programs at Hull House so that workers might come to understand, and thus appreciate, their place in the new industrial order.[108] But the more perceptive among them realized that the settlements were inadequate mechanisms for dealing with strikes, boycotts, and the monotony of the work place. Bloomfield and Follett believed for a time in the 1910s that vocational guidance was the answer; ultimately they, too, took the next step and became directly involved in work-place issues.

CONCLUSION

The history of democratic social engineering in business is replete with contradictions and ironies. American industry was democratized in the midst of a decade justifiably infamous for the open-shop campaigns that devastated the union movement. As workers lost the ability to bargain collectively, they were increasingly drawn into the new democratized structures set up for them by employers. At the very moment when the stultifying and monotonous future of twentieth-century work became clear to almost everyone, and when factory managers were busily engaged in stripping control of the work process from ordinary workers, workers were for the first time offered the chance to participate in decisions about their work. In the decade after the Great War, when the power of propaganda was grasped fully for the first time, the advertisers and public relations counsels who used the new tools of persuasion talked the language of democracy, of the public's right to the "facts." When consumers became helpless, consumption became a democratic art. Just as a new and massive literature pointed to the growth of widespread distrust of ordinary people (the "masses"), these same ordinary people were brought into participatory roles. At a time when conflict seemed everywhere — when war refused to go away, when revolution seemed a possibility, when a general strike shook Seattle and Boston's police challenged the public order — the democratic social engineers told the American people that conflict was unnecessary. In short, at a moment when the realities of power and class had been revealed, social engineering became democratic.

The contradictions melt away only if we understand that a democratic approach was completely consistent with social control. Companies using democratic methods did not give up control over production; they solidified it. Nor did salesmen using Carnegie's democratic techniques surrender control to the "prospect." In democracy itself, American business had found a tool that increased productivity and sales and brought a new stability to labor relations. And it was all accomplished with groups, clubs, conferences, and discussions — devices so ostensibly innocent and so much a part of the mainstream of American thought and practice that few Americans could understand or appreciate that their content was political and, in its own way, coercive.

4

Depression, War, and the State

Few generalizations on the contours of modern American history have been as universally accepted as that which asserts the growing importance of the state. Certain elements of the argument – the rise of the welfare state, especially during the 1930s and 1960s; the militarization of the economy in the Second World War and the Cold War; the increasing responsibility of government for the nation's economic fortunes; the spread of government "regulation" of industry – are now part of the way most Americans think about their history.

Although there have been no genuine challenges to the basic argument, there has been disagreement about its implications. One group of economic historians has reexamined the history of nineteenth-century railroads and canals, and found that these "internal improvements" often owed their existence to the active participation of local, state, and national governments; laissez-faire, they concluded, was an inadequate description of the role of government even in the nineteenth century.[1] Other historians, focusing their research efforts on the Progressive Era, have questioned whether government "regulation" of business – in workmen's compensation, industrial safety, conservation, and antitrust, for example – was designed to control business or to serve its need for an economic environment that was predictable, efficient, and noncompetitive.[2] In the two decades after 1960, even Franklin Roosevelt's New Deal came under attack. A new generation of scholars now saw it as racist; unconcerned with the distribution of income; inadequate in scope; and grounded in hard-edged economic theories and ideas of social control that seemed far removed from the needs and welfare of the great masses of Americans.[3]

It was the seminal contribution of those scholars focusing on the twentieth century to demonstrate that the state was no neutral or even sepa-

rate entity, with some existence of its own, nor even a meaningful counterweight to the power of big business. It was, instead, an expression of
arrangements existing outside it, a device by which the nation's most
powerful constituents — and that *usually* meant business — could achieve
what had been denied them in nongovernmental channels. If, in practice,
things were a good deal more complex, still this view of the state was more
convincing than the one it had replaced.

This chapter takes this New Left approach a step further, into the
realm of *process*. Previous studies have argued that government and business existed in a symbiotic relationship on the basis of what the state *did*.
This one argues that no matter what the state did, it accomplished its purposes using the same methodology of democratic participation at work
in the private sector. The methodology had not always seemed so adapt-
able. In the 1920s, democratic social engineering often had special appeal
for those who were looking for a vehicle of social change superior to the
state. Herbert Croly's attraction to The Inquiry was one manifestation of
his disaffection from the nation-state, national political leadership, and
centralized vehicles of social reform.[4]

Yet in another sense, democratic social engineering was perfectly compatible with politics and a strong state, and for those who had no revulsion
to the use of government, the expansion of its functions in the 1930s made
available a powerful new instrument for the spread of the methodology.
The state could utilize, and make available, a whole range of small-group
experiences.

This was, in fact, what happened. Between 1935 and 1940, several
major New Deal agencies — including the Civilian Conservation Corps and
the Works Progress Administration — began to use democratic methods.
In addition, American involvement in the Second World War created new
opportunities for the dissemination of group-work ideas. Two characteristics of the war effort — the totalitarian nature of the enemy, and the need
for regimentation to defeat that enemy — combined to deepen the nation's
historic ambivalence over how power should be exercised. How, asked
America's social analysts, could the nation destroy fascism, an act which
seemed to require tearing down the state and stressing antiauthoritarianism, and at the same time teach Americans to accept the authority of the
state in a time of crisis? They found the answer in democratic social engineering. During the war, group process was practiced by agencies as
diverse in their functions as the War Relocation Authority, the Works Progress Administration, the Federal Agricultural Extension Service, and the
United Service Organizations, Inc. (USO), a private agency working in
cooperation with government. Democratic methods helped Americans

resettle the Japanese, quiet opposition to the draft, stimulate farm production, and recycle soldiers back to the front.

Democratic social engineering came to the New Deal as early as 1935, when Congress created the Works Progress Administration (WPA). Roosevelt turned the new agency over to former social worker Harry Hopkins, and Hopkins, seeking an administrator for the WPA's recreation division, found one in his friend Eduard C. Lindeman. A professor at the New York School of Social Work, Lindeman's research on rural youth and adult education had contributed to a growing body of recreational theory. Like many other New Yorkers with an interest in group methods in the early 1920s, Lindeman had participated in the activities of Bruno Lasker's Inquiry.[5]

For Lindeman, the central philosophical problem throughout the interwar years was that which Ralph Waldo Emerson had posed a century earlier: balancing the needs of the individual with those of the society or, put another way, achieving pure individualism outside a social context.[6] Lindeman's enemies were, on the one hand, excessive individualism; and, on the other hand, suffocating social organization and planning. Among the causes of the former were laissez-faire, "naive democracy," "quantity education," "external morality," "impersonal science," and "atomic specialization." Citizens had lost interest in government, workers had become apathetic. The year Roosevelt took office, Lindeman wrote in his notebook that the nation had lost its "sense of security"; the culture was "disintegrating."[7]

In the 1920s, Lindeman had advocated a new collectivity. But it was a collectivity of "small beginnings in the realm of the manageable," one separate from the massive units of government and industry. Like Mary Parker Follett, Lindeman looked to smaller collective units—to the home, the neighborhood, and the community—as sources of social regeneration and cohesion.[8]

The Great Depression did not change the problem, which remained that of finding a suitable reconciliation between society and individual; but it did lead Lindeman to define the point of reconciliation somewhat differently than he had a decade earlier. Between 1932 and 1935, he became an advocate of planning. While he retained a strong faith in the power of groups to solve social problems, the language he used to describe his goals—a language that insisted on "social organization" implemented by "social education" — implied a new willingness to experiment with something beyond the "smaller collective units." In 1934 and 1935, Lindeman remained distressed at the extent to which individualism and even "autarchy" prevented Americans from achieving a necessary level of unity and cooperation.[9]

Even as he was reaching a peak as an advocate of planning, Lindeman was beginning to question his new commitment to the "social" end of the individual/society continuum. By 1936 and 1937, Lindeman's notebooks reveal a growing discomfort with collectivism and social control. The collective era, he wrote, threatened "personal responsibility"; social control (a term he apparently used to summarize the Social Security Act) jeopardized "liberties." By the spring of 1937, Lindeman was deeply critical of the manipulation of the masses by "trained experts" and — very much aware of the European experience with fascism and Nazism — doubtful of the ability of ordinary people to resist authority. In his speeches he now spoke of a "democratic crisis."[10]

Lindeman's tenure at the WPA coincided with his growing feeling of discomfort with centralized authority. The simple fact that he had taken the position, and with it responsibility for recreation projects employing some forty thousand persons in five hundred cities, was enough to satisfy any lingering proclivity toward state planning; his efforts as recreation director would be aimed at generating a program of activities consistent with his lifelong interest in decentralized, participatory group experience.[11] To solve the crisis of democracy, Lindeman turned to a variety of small groups — play centers, drama clubs, forums, luncheon clubs, unions, women's groups, and sports teams, for example — and to discussion, "the laboratory of dem[ocracy]," as Lindeman put it. He was not without his doubts about the efficacy of this group approach; group life, as he analyzed it in 1937, was "now shot thru and thru with latent and overt pathological elements," and thus no longer offered the easy avenue to social change that it once had.[12]

Pathological or not, the small group remained Lindeman's vehicle of reform, the one mechanism capable of modifying behavior while preserving individual freedom.[13] "Democracy," he wrote in a WPA internal memorandum, "is the only system of control in which freedom is a basic foundation as well as a necessary element in its operations."[14] In practice, this meant WPA play centers, in which "children not yet of school age learn the first principles of group living in supervised play." It meant sports programs in which "team-mindedness" and "team-action" could contribute to a solution to "juvenile delinquency" ("a trained athlete," said Lindeman in a 1936 address, "does learn something about behaviour toward others and toward society even though he may not be highly intelligent"). It meant utilizing small group discussions and trained leaders at every age level. It meant community drama programs offering "an opportunity for cooperation in creating something which is a part of and belongs to each one in the group." Lindeman's regional director for the South, reporting on a Georgia drama workshop, emphasized process over content. "We are concerned," he wrote, "not so much with finished plays as with what happens to the people of the community who participate in dramatic activity."[15]

Although Lindeman resigned from the WPA in late 1937, when Aubrey Williams fired his lieutenants, Dorothy Cline and Howard White, there is evidence that his recreational philosophy would not be easily rooted out. WPA programs for children and juveniles, for example, continued to emphasize self-governing group activity.[16]

A second WPA unit to employ democratic methods was the Workers Service Program (WSP). Created in 1933 under the Federal Emergency Relief Administration, the WSP was originally part of a larger program in adult education aimed at unemployed teachers. By the late 1930s the program had been broadened to include all workers, employed and unemployed and, led by director Hilda W. Smith, the WSP had become an aggressive advocate of a variety of group techniques. Smith solicited information and advice on group discussion from social-group-work educator Grace Coyle, from the American Discussion League, Inc. (a New York City organization whose members included Alfred D. Sheffield), and from the Carnegie Endowment for International Peace, which had prepared a handbook for discussion leaders.[17]

Democratic techniques were not just a part of the WSP. They *defined* it. Had the discussion groups, conferences, and forums, and the facilities for communicating and teaching the techniques of group process, been eliminated from the program, not much would have remained. Whether the object of this "service" effort was trade union workers or an aggregation of over-fifty unemployables, the methodology was the same.

This methodology appealed to WPA administrators because of the way they defined the problems of unemployed and employed workers. Workers were "often socially isolated and lacking in group experience," and this isolation and lack of group experience were believed to be of great immediate and potential social danger. Costly and disruptive industrial disputes occurred because workers and their representatives lacked an "intimate knowledge of the issues involved and of the ultimate results of any policy adopted," and because representatives of organized labor, lacking experience in community organizations, came to these organizations feeling "alone" and "rather aggressive." One group of WPA teachers submitted an anonymous report in which it argued that "public unrest" was a function of an "illiterate and unenlightened public . . . that was mentally ill . . ."

WSP officials also believed that unemployed workers — a "drag on society" — understood neither why they were unemployed nor what they could do about it through their own groups.[18]

Group methods would alleviate these problems. Groups would provide the educational forums in which the ignorant masses would learn how recreation and self-expression could provide an "escape from a living monotony" and in which the unenlightened unemployed would learn "group responsibility" and "initiative." (Exactly what they would *do* with these newly acquired qualities was never clear; it was enough that they have them.) Although some critics charged that WSP activities were promoting class consciousness, such an effect would have been alien to WSP goals. As the economy geared up for war, WSP leaders sought to avoid industrial conflict by educating workers in the subtleties of their contracts through discussion groups and by integrating workers and their representatives into their communities (workers so integrated would, presumably, understand the peripheral nature of their personal needs). What precise purpose lay behind the WSP emphasis on democracy — on conducting classes and activities in "a democratic way, not as an authority whose word must be accepted" — is not obvious. One may surmise that WSP officials expected these democratic tactics to result in a high level of commitment to the above ideas and policies; this, at least, was what William Kilpatrick had in mind when he described his "project method" more than two decades before.[19]

A third agency that engineered its constituency with the tools of democracy was the Civilian Conservation Corps. Created in 1933 to provide an outlet for unemployed youth and to relieve pressure on the labor market, the CCC was not dismantled until 1942. Its longevity was largely due to an unemployment problem that persisted through 1941, but it also had something to do with the continued relevance of CCC methods to a society on the verge of war against a "totalitarian" enemy. Of primary importance in this regard was the Corps's military structure. Of lesser significance, perhaps, was the Corps's use of a small-group democratic methodology, a methodology that at first glance seems entirely out of place in a protomilitary organization.

Democratic methods appeared in the camps as early as 1935, apparently as part of a Corps campaign to promote "citizenship" (socially responsible [i.e., orderly] behavior). Although individual camps were free to experiment with a variety of programs and techniques with democratic content, the use of democratic methods was Corps policy. At a 3d Corps conference in the summer of 1935, CCC educational director Howard W. Oxley told Corps advisers (those in charge of camp educational projects) that "formal methods of instruction must give way to informal methods.

The adviser is afforded a rare opportunity to teach principles of living. Social understanding and social adjustments made necessary by camp life," Oxley added, "constitute an important phase of the learning that goes on, perhaps unconsciously, in the life of the enrollee at camp." That August, a district adviser notified camp advisers in the 1st Corps Area to "encourage group activities for the promotion of good citizenship and co-operative behavior." Some camp supervisors journeyed to Purdue University for training in group-process techniques originally developed for industrial foremen.[20]

According to an editorial appearing in the Corps newspaper, *Happy Days*, Corps officials envisioned the camps, and democratic procedures, as a bulwark against social revolution. The editorial began with the distinction between a "mob" and an "organization," the former moved by emotions, the latter by "intelligent discipline." The difference between the two was leadership. Leaders rewarded proper conduct and discouraged that which was improper. But not every kind of leadership was equally appropriate or productive. Physical force was inadequate and even counterproductive, because "individuals chafe under and resent discipline which they do not understand." The best leaders exercised their authority through groups, educating group members in "the consequences of wrong conduct, the reasons for right conduct," and using the power of the group to offer or withhold social approval and to secure general compliance.[21]

What happened to these directives and ideas at the camp level is another question altogether, but a cursory examination of *Happy Days* and official camp reports indicates that democratic methods reached into many camps and did so over much of the life of the CCC. Oxley's directive on informal education found concrete expression in class discussions and group meetings at a Paintsville, Kentucky, camp. At Solomonsville, Arizona, officers helped enrollees create elaborate models of democratic self-government, complete with primary and general elections, a congress, and trial by jury.[22] CCC officials also encouraged the growth of a national CCC fraternity. The fraternity was organized in February 1935 and by mid-year had six thousand members. Its original purpose had something to do with morale; CCC officials liked it because it served as an informal and democratically structured agency for the enforcement of camp regulations.[23]

By the late 1930s and early 1940s, group methods and an awareness of what could be accomplished through groups were more common than ever in the CCC. The American Youth Commission (AYC), a privately financed agency whose members included progressive educator William F. Russell of Teachers College, Columbia, reported the existence of current events discussion groups in many camps in 1939, apparently the product of an AYC experimental program. These discussions — according to the report, "above party lines" and not propagandistic — were designed to make CCC enrollees "know what has happened to the economic system and the attempts that are being made to rebuild it."[24] One Oklahoma camp conducted many of its academic, vocational, and on-the-job classes in a discussion format.[25] As late as March 1942, the 2d Corps Area Education Committee was still insisting on the use of group methods, especially in camps experiencing acute problems of discipline and morale. Enrollees would "acquire socially desirable attitudes" through "living" (it is frightening to think that "living" had become a means to some greater end). The committee had, however, grown impatient with the results attained through voluntarily organized groups and was recommending an approach weighted toward leadership and utilizing guides such as Ordway Tead's *Art of Leadership.*[26]

What little is known of the use of democratic methods in other agencies suggests that these techniques were widely disseminated. Like the CCC, the National Youth Administration carried on a program of leader-guided current events discussions. Dust-bowl refugees found organized group activities in the Farm Security Administration camps in California. Tenants in New Deal public housing projects — defined, like unemployed workers, as socially isolated — seemed ideal subjects for U.S. Housing Authority experiments with forums, discussion groups, and tenant-created community activities.[27] Even the middle-class residents of the New Deal community of Greenbelt, Maryland, found themselves knee-deep in cooperation, self-government, educational forums, and leaderless clubs ("There are no officers in the Camera Club!", wrote the Greenbelt *Cooperator.* "The photo fiends don't want any").[28] Wherever social workers, educators, or recreational theorists had a presence — and in the 1930s that was virtually everywhere — one finds the idea and practice of democratic social engineering.

THE TOTALITARIAN CHALLENGE

As the preceding chapters of this book demonstrate, such methods were neither unique to the decade of the 1930s nor limited to government programs. Democratic social engineering was so much a part of the twentieth-century American experience that traditional chronologies (e.g., the 1930s, the Great Depression) and traditional categories (e.g., government, the private sector) are of limited relevance. Nonetheless, at certain points in our history, the democratic approach has assumed special significance, and its growth has been especially rapid, because of the existence of historical circumstances that heightened awareness and consciousness of the methodology.

The decade after 1935 was such a time. Until then, democratic methods had been used heavily only in areas — late-nineteenth-century churches, Progressive Era schools and social settlements, and factories in the 1920s — that were either in crisis or defined as essential to the preservation of existing social relations. When, in the late 1930s, the entire nation appeared about to fall victim to social upheaval, and when the danger was widely defined as "totalitarian," democratic social engineering seemed to many the only solution. Indeed, it would be difficult to find an area of American life that remained untouched by democratic social engineering in this decade in which depression ended and war began.

The enthusiasm for democratic methods was related to what historian Edward Purcell, Jr., has labeled the "crisis of democratic theory." According to Purcell, democratic theory was underpinned with certain critical assumptions and principles, including the idea of a "higher law" and the rationality of human behavior. Between 1910 and 1935, Purcell argues, these assumptions and principles were exposed by psychologists, political theorists, and other advocates of relativist thinking. "By the early thirties," Purcell concludes, "traditional democratic theory seemed largely untenable." That is, it no longer seemed possible or reasonable to justify democracy as a function of values or moral assumptions. Methods, on the other hand, seemed somehow value-free. "Gradually," therefore, "methodology replaced moralism in the minds of many younger reformers and social scientists." Some took to statistics, others to psychology, in attempts to fashion systems that were unadulterated by moralism.[29]

The actual "crisis" in democratic theory, however, took place only in the late 1930s, when events in Europe and America conspired to make principles, values, a priori truths, and moral absolutes once again attractive and respectable. "Conditions that made a dictator seem possible," writes Purcell, "helped rekindle the belief of most Americans in the worth of popular government. As the depression shattered the complacent confidence of conservatives and the New Deal overcame the political helplessness of liberals, they began to cling to democracy with a new conviction." University of Chicago president Robert Maynard Hutchins called for a new social unity based on a "hierarchy of truths." Walter Lippmann turned to laissez-faire economic theory. Many social scientists discovered in moral relativism something akin to totalitarianism, and insisted on the need for direct, moral commitments. Others — a majority, Purcell argues — remained committed to the presumed objectivity of science yet also believed that ultimately science would substantiate and validate democratic assumptions.[30]

It remained for John Dewey to resolve the crisis and establish the basic postwar frameworks of understanding. What Dewey did was to firmly establish an identification between philosophical absolutism and political authoritarianism and between scientific experimentalism and democracy. There were two critical steps in arriving at these identities. First, Dewey had to establish that democracy, like authoritarianism, was a system of action, one that could actually produce results; second, he had to demonstrate that science need not be elitist. He did both by defining the discovery of truth as a process that began with a "democracy of individual facts" in which "all men could freely make up their own minds about the nature of truth." Dewey thus succeeded in combining relativism (individuals would choose their own truth) with absolutism (from a stock of existing "facts").[31] There were unanswered questions, of course. How did one recognize a "fact"? And what would happen if the process of freedom of choice resulted in no general social agreement? The first led straight back to elitism; the second to manipulation, propaganda, and other ways of achieving social consensus. But these were questions—and answers—that most Americans had always sought to avoid, and especially so in the egalitarian zeitgeist of the Great Depression and while they were attempting to define themselves as somehow different from the fascist propaganda experts. More than ever, Americans needed a way of deciding what was true and acting on it, and Dewey's gift could not easily be rejected.

The search for a resolution of the crisis was limited neither to theory nor to the academic disciplines. It took place in concrete ways at every point at which social control seemed a possibility. And wherever it took place, the goals were essentially the same: to find ways of moving people to action that were socially efficient and yet as removed as possible from authoritarianism. It became common to define what one wanted in contradistinction to the institutions of Hitler's Germany. The educational director of the International Ladies Garment Workers Union called for workers'-education projects in CCC camps and the military "if we are going to have the men with guns having the right ideas and not degenerating into Hitlerism while they are trying to destroy it." Lindeman evoked the ethos of fascism in a 1938 speech criticizing "intuitive leaders." A staff-management manual published for Boy Scout leaders in 1941 was very much taken up with the question of authority; a chapter on staff meetings carefully differentiated the concept of leadership from "coercion" and cited Paul Pigors' suggestively titled book, *Leadership or Domination*.[32]

Some commentators defended democratic methods on the grounds that the alternative was an American fascism. Kilpatrick, for example, found possible precursors of fascism in Huey Long, the Tampa Ku Klux Klan, and the vigilantes involved in San Francisco's waterfront strike. The solution, he believed, was social planning to eliminate poverty and insecurity—but planning through education, not indoctrination. LeRoy Bowman, director of leadership training for the United Parents Association, expressed the same fears in a 1935 essay on dictatorship and social group work. Bowman argued that participation in groups could help youth and adults achieve the habits of "judgment and concerted volition" inimical to mob conviction and dictatorship. And Lindeman warned that fascism and dictatorship would be the result of the failure to develop "habits of critical participation."[33]

As the nation made the transition from depression to war in the late 1930s and 1940s, social engineers broadened their search for democratic methods to include large public forums and radio. This effort was encouraged by Franklin D. Roosevelt, the progressive educator as president. According to historian Barry Karl, Roosevelt created a new system of White House communications, with himself in the role of "a teacher in a classroom of students," guiding the press and managing the news. Behind the facade of openness was the most precise orchestration of the communications process. "He answered the questions he chose to answer," observes Karl, "posed the questions he needed to answer, refused permission for quotation when that seemed appropriate to him, talked only for background at times, and, when necessary, introduced subjects he wanted the public to hear about."[34]

Roosevelt's now legendary fireside chats had a mass counterpart in radio-listening discussion groups. First used in England in the late 1920s, they numbered an estimated fifteen thousand in the United States in 1941, with a total membership of three hundred thousand persons. In *Democracy by Discussion* (1942), Emory Bogardus suggested that these radio groups might become a "nation-wide educational vehicle," a "sounding board of public opinion" for the president and Congress. "The whole nation," wrote Bogardus, "could participate in national affairs in a truly intelligent manner. Democracy could come into its own in a new and vitalized way."[35]

The federal government also sought to promote "truth-seeking under competent guidance" through a program of public forums sponsored by educational and civic groups. Although forums had been part of American life since at least the turn of the century, the forum program that would serve as a model for a national forum craze was developed in Iowa in 1931 by the Des Moines superintendent of schools, John W. Studebaker. It must have attracted Roosevelt's attention, for in 1934 Studebaker went to Washington as commissioner of education. With the support of his superior, Secretary of the Interior Harold Ickes, and Roosevelt, Studebaker created and administered the Public Forum Project. By 1937 this demonstration program had spawned, or been joined by, some fifteen hundred forum projects, including the San Diego Church Forum, the Harlem Economic Forum, the Dallas Open Forum, and the Hartford Lecture Series. The WPA also had a forum division. Using emergency funds provided by the Office of Education, by 1939 almost six hundred local communities had conducted public-forum feasibility demonstrations.[36]

There was in all of this a consciousness of how American democratic social engineering differed from its European brand. A 1936 *Bulletin* of the Office of Education placed the forum idea in the framework of Dewey's concept of scientific inquiry. Just as scientists needed freedom to inquire into the physical universe, so did the public welfare require freedom of inquiry in the public sphere. "Democracy," it asserted, "is the political expression of the scientific method."[37] Roosevelt had always supported the forum idea, and when, in 1941, he again put the weight of his office firmly behind the program, Chester W. Williams, director of adult and civic education for the U.S. Office of Education, praised the president for appreciating the unique character of American democratic social engineering. "This is the language of a great leader of democracy," Williams wrote, "a leader who is conscious of the creative powers of the people at the grass roots. He didn't ask that citizens be herded into mass meetings to be told what to believe and how to act. Rather, he asked for 'an appropriate *educational* program designed to help students and adults in understanding the complicated problems of these critical times.'"[38]

It may have been a distinction without a difference. It is not clear that Roosevelt had much interest in what Williams referred to as the "creative powers of the people." The fullest exposition of what the forum program was meant to accomplish is contained in Studebaker's *The American Way* (1935). For Studebaker, the "people" were an ignorant, uneducated, confused, and discouraged mass that understood little about "the complex problems of social and governmental policy" or "the essential aspects of the intricacies of associated living." Most of all, the people had failed to achieve an "insight, at once far-reaching and subtle," into the "concept of capitalism in democracy." Although Studebaker asserted that the projected forums were places where capitalism and democracy would enter into debate with other ideas "which stand in direct opposition," the game was fixed. Through "expertly managed discussion," the masses would come to understand that the existing system was superior to any alternative, and to support those who had the "soundest solutions" to some admittedly troubling problems.[39] Democratic social engineering was, at bottom, engineering.

WORLD WAR II

The approach of war accentuated the tensions already existing around the methodology of democratic social engineering. On the one hand, the totalitarian nature of the enemy, especially Hitler's Germany, made the American democratic self-image all the more important and thus intensified the demand for participatory group procedures. On the other hand, the war had to be won, and for many Americans the need for victory justified the most extreme forms of coercion. Few would have argued that the nation's manpower needs should be established in small group discussions, or that public forums were the place to allocate strategic war materials. Yet so strong was the desire to distinguish democracy from totalitarianism, and so confident were Americans in the power and utility of their own techniques of social engineering, that participatory methods found a place even in areas of the war effort that might easily have been made exempt.

Only ten days after German troops entered Paris, the American Association for the Study of Group Work met in the Columbia Men's Faculty Club to consider the impact of defense activity and war on group work. Although the United States was not yet a belligerent, those present recognized that even the climate of preparedness created an awkward situation for the association and for group work itself. There was much discussion of a possible group-work presence in the inevitable military training camps. Some believed it was "unreal" to expect that group work could function in the camps; others argued that while military leadership was fundamentally a leadership of "command," many officers recognized the "value of discussion before the command is given"; still others emphasized how group work could function in the camps at the level of "morale." Participants also discussed whether, and how, the association and individual group-work organizations ought to fit into any wartime structure. One speaker argued that the association must have a presence at the level of planning and talked about the necessity of having persons interested in group work in strategic positions. Another, representing the Boy Scouts, was resigned to cooperation with the war effort. The Boy Scouts, he said, "will identify with [the] government effort. If we stand for something else we will be subject to pressure."[40]

Those present at the meeting knew that a full-scale war would place civil liberties in jeopardy and possibly undermine voluntary and democratic systems of authority. Yet they also believed that if it came, war would be justified, and that group-work agencies could play a role in its prosecution, perhaps benefiting in the process. In a statement drafted in August 1940, the association's Committee on an Emergency Program cast off this ambivalence in favor of a bald proclamation on the contribution of group work to the defense effort. Group workers would contribute to morale — that is, to a "unified nation, strong in spirit, earnestly believing in the worthwhileness of the American way of life and willing to make sacrifices to preserve it"; they would help people "deal with the inevitable," that is, to "accept the necessities of action within the realm of the majority decision";[41] they would teach their constituent groups that "war is wrong, and constitutes a condition to which one submits only as a means to the end of preserving the democratic way of life"; they would keep the nation physically fit; they would help provide a release for the "feelings of frustration" common in emergencies among those unable to relieve human suffering; and they would "assist their communities in arousing loyalties to the country." This draft report also contained references to the need for vigilance in the protection of the individual; but this was not its thrust.[42]

During the war, much of the economy was regulated by law. But the federal government did experiment with democratic methods of increasing productivity and modifying patterns of consumption. The Department of Agriculture, apparently convinced that farmers were insufficiently dedicated to the war effort, suggested group discussions to "clarify their thinking as to what we are fighting for . . ." In March 1942, the Federal Agricultural Extension Service began working with the National Conference on Voluntary Local Leadership in order to mobilize neighborhood discussion groups "to overcome barriers to maximum production."[43]

M. L. Wilson, who headed the Extension Service, was convinced of the need to apply social science methods even in wartime. He supervised a nutrition program built around a committee on food habits chaired by anthropologist Margaret Mead and linked to a graduate research program at the University of Iowa under the supervision of social psychologist Kurt Lewin. The upshot was an important experiment in which Lewin sought to convince American women to serve heart, kidney, and brains — portions of the animal anatomy not normally consumed with gusto by middle-class families. Lewin concluded that a straight lecture method was significantly inferior to one employing a group, a group leader, and an expert. He described the latter method:

The group-discussion leader starts with a very short introduction linking the problem of nutrition with the war effort, and with general health. He points to the difficulties the government has met in trying to change food habits, and asks the opinion of the women, as a representative group of housewives, how successful a direct appeal to groups of housewives like themselves would be. From here on, the group is led step-by-step to seeing the problem more concretely, and, at the same time, to taking over the responsibility "to do something about it." This point is reached through a free group discussion which also brings out the specific reasons why the meats have been rejected by the housewife herself or by her family. These specific objections are the cue for the introduction of the expert, who discusses the various methods of getting around the difficulties.[44]

Lewin's work had little bearing on the outcome of the war. But the episode, and especially Wilson's commitment to group methods, reveals the continued lure of a democratic methodology grounded in the social sciences. Moreover, Lewin's paper proved a landmark. "This alone," Gardner Murphy offered a quarter century later, "would warrant a prominent and permanent place for Kurt Lewin in American social psychology."[45]

No wartime program has been so severely criticized for being subversive of democratic ideals as the concentration of West Coast Japanese in interior camps from 1942 through 1946. Yet even these Japanese, living in what were essentially prisons, were subject to the group-work projects of social engineers. Under the War Relocation Authority's Community Activities Section, first-generation (Issei) and second generation (Nisei) Japanese were offered a full program of group activities, including children's play groups, team sports, clubs, discussion groups and forums, and adult education. Some of this was accomplished with camp resources; but often the camps were opened to the YMCA, the YWCA, Boy Scouts, Girl Scouts, and other organizations historically interested in democratic group process.

Whether created within the camp or imported from outside, groups were administered in the best tradition of progressive education; camp activities directors were advised neither to attempt to take the initiative from the "evacuees" nor to control groups that had arisen spontaneously. Group workers might serve as a "catalyst" to the discussion process. Adult education was to be of "the self-sustaining, self-motivating type."[46]

The community activities program had several purposes. A minor one was to curb behavior in the camps then labeled "juvenile delinquency." At other times, community activities supervisors described the function of "American type activities" as that of demonstrating to young Japanese that "we do fully appreciate their position, and the fact that, they are real American citizens," or — by late 1944 — "securing evacuee participation in a program which will bring to the evacuees a clearer picture of the war and changes effected in the United States during the past two years."[47] Whether the Japanese were "real American citizens," or whether their understanding of the war was likely to be that of the average non-Japanese American, is irrelevant here; the point is that informally structured groups were to be used as vehicles for the transmission of the ideology of those operating the camps.

By far the most important purpose of the community activities program — a purpose which in some sense subsumes those described above — was to ensure that the Japanese in the camps retained, or developed, qualities considered essential to a proper "adjustment" to "life on the outside." From the beginning of the relocation program, WRA authorities and camp supervisors feared that isolation from the mainstream of American life would only encourage in the Japanese a tendency to insularity and cause them to withdraw into indigenous institutions. By mid-1943, American officials had concluded that interned Japanese were insufficiently schooled in "independence and leadership," inexperienced in "planning democratically with others," and — most disturbing — unaware of, or hostile to, the necessity of being involved in the community and part of social group activity outside the home and family. The camps had exacerbated these characteristics, but they had not created them. According to one community activities report, Japanese attitudes were a product of a lack of club experience during early childhood and of "natural family ties" which bound the Japanese until they were well past the age when they should (by American standards) have been independent.[48] The Japanese, in short, were antisocial, and they were antisocial because they were Japanese.

Democratic social engineering was, therefore, assimilationist. Clubs, discussions, team sports, and other group activities would draw the Nisei out of the Japanese community and — given the definition of the Japanese family as a socially dysfunctional social slavery — facilitate "the emancipation from the parent person." Some Nisei believed that these programs were designed to separate the generations, and they came to "distrust" camp leisure activities. By 1944, one function of WRA leadership-training institutes was to show the Japanese what was untrue: that children's play groups and adolescent clubs were harmless group functions deserving of their support.[49]

The United Service Organizations, Inc., or USO, was legally a private agency, incorporated in New York State and made up of six constituent organizations: the National Catholic Community Service, the Salvation Army, the Jewish Welfare Board, the National Travelers Aid, the Young Men's Christian Association, and the Young Women's Christian Association. Of 536 USO operations in late 1941, 150 were under the YMCA, 138 under Catholic services, and 91 under the YWCA, with the remainder divided among the other member organizations. Because it was the function of the USO to provide services for the military, USO programs were carried out with the cooperation, assistance, and guidance of the Joint Army and Navy Committee on Welfare and Recreation.[50]

It would be difficult to imagine an agency more committed to democratic social engineering than the USO. Virtually all its member organizations were prominent in the field of social group work, and this was especially true of the Protestant Christian associations, which had responsibility for more than forty percent of the USO's operations.[51] The importance of a democratic, group-work approach was a prominent theme of a USO field staff conference held in November 1942. Staff member Robert M. Heininger began with a description and analysis of soldiers and soldiering that led directly to group work. Military life was an unsettling, absorbing, and limiting experience: "Personal anxieties and uncertainties tend to discourage rational thinking. The necessarily highly-organized military life seems to dull intellectual curiosity. Many members of the armed forces and many war workers do not seem particularly eager to fulfill citizen obligations." Like the concentrated Japanese, the soldiers had turned inward, shunning political responsibilities and neglecting the ordinary round of social contacts that for group-work advocates defined the healthy personality. Soldiers needed opportunities for creative expression, recognition (from some source other than the military), and a feeling of belonging (to something other than the army).[52]

For Heininger and other staffers, USO programs were little more than a vehicle for fashioning a better-adjusted, more responsible soldier. Arts and crafts, dramatics, photography — the content of an activity program — were of "little significance" compared with the "human relationships involved in such activities. . . . Mass activities and small group activities are then conceived of not as an end in themselves nor as a part of an organizational scheme, but become opportunities for group life and self-expression for the individual." Arguing from the analogy of child-centered progressive education, Heininger claimed that USO clubs must be "constituent-centered," not "activity-centered." Only if soldiers helped plan and carry out programs and assisted in the policing of the clubs would they come to appreciate their democratic obligations.[53]

How much of this theory was practiced in the clubs? At the November staff conference, even those who insisted on the necessity of group work also lamented its frequent absence. Some clubs were "self-directed," some were not. Grace Coyle sent her students to USO centers, and it is difficult to imagine how anyone trained by this leading educator and theorist of social group work could have resisted the temptation to experiment with the newly acquired skills.[54]

Even the simplest and most innocent of activities could be orchestrated in the service of democratic methods. Consider the hallowed Hollywood image of the tired but dedicated wartime pilot, escaping from the strain of a mission just flown or soon to come, joining his comrades in song around the club piano. More likely, our flyboys have been gathered there by the club social worker, who only the day before had been informed by Captain U. K. Reese, music director of the 3d Service Command, that "it was the thinking of the leaders of the Armed Forces that our men do not 'sing' enough."[55] (Although Captain Reese understands the value of singing only intuitively, group psychotherapists, impressed by the success of revivalists like Billy Sunday, had long understood the power of song.)[56] This injunction does not find our social worker unprepared. Down from the bookshelf comes "Music: USO," a publication of the USO National Program Committee. "Singing," she learns, is "primarily a weapon, a medium through which men march straighter, give better commands, fight harder, work longer and move coordinately." Reading on, she discovers that little of this will occur spontaneously. Soldiers may want to sing, but it is up to the "right leader . . . [to] help to develop the habit of group singing. His primary job is to remove inhibitions and restraints, and to encourage general participation." By carefully gauging the feelings of the singers, and by choosing his songs accordingly, the leader could "influence the mood of a group."[57]

Those war movies will never be the same. And that is as it should be. Directives calling for more singing, instructional materials on song leading — here is evidence that social science had entered what we thought was a realm of privacy, informality, and spontaneity. We knew the USOs would be staffed with program-developing social workers; after all, someone had to purchase the sheet music and keep the piano in tune. Less predictable was that group singing would have a purpose that so clearly transcended simple entertainment. And we did not expect that such remote and ordinary aspects of the human experience would come under the influence of social engineers.[58]

CONCLUSION

The use of group-work methods in New Deal agencies like the WPA and the CCC demonstrates that democratic social engineering could function in a bureaucratic context. The growth of the state only added to the resources and the influence of the social engineers. The war confirmed these lessons, and added another: that democratic methods, far from disappearing under the challenge of totalitarianism, survived and prospered in a variety of agencies and institutions related to the war effort. The decade's experience with group process, outside as well as inside government, suggests that Americans responded to Nazism and fascism with a heightened sense of what it meant to be a democratic nation. In the most self-conscious way, Americans asked themselves how efficiency could be achieved — democratically; how children might be raised and juvenile delinquency prevented — democratically; how — democratically — all citizens, but especially the skeptical and doubting, might come to understand the Depression, the draft, the war, and the camps for Japanese. The answers came easily, for they were by now a part of the American experience: bring the farmers together to talk about productivity; assemble wayward youth in boys' clubs; hold public forums on the draft. Make sure that every club, every discussion, and every singing group had all the "facts" and a proper leader who understood what was at stake. Some will argue that such devices were so much naiveté, at best poor substitutes for coercion.[59] Kurt Lewin, who had apparently found a way to get housewives to put brains next to the mashed potatoes, knew better.

5

Social Engineering through Recreation: The Golden Age Clubs

In the winter of 1940, a charismatic German emigré could be found knocking on doors in a Chicago neighborhood, trying to persuade suspicious older persons to join an old-age club at the city's Olivet Institute, a settlement interested in recreation for the elderly. Oskar Schulze's successful effort in Chicago took him to Cleveland, where his enthusiasm would be joined with social-group-work methods and local philanthropy to create what would become known as the Golden Age Clubs. A single club established at Cleveland's Goodrich House Settlement in June 1940 became fifteen clubs with some five hundred members by late 1944. In 1952 there were thirty-five clubs in greater Cleveland, serving about two thousand older persons. By 1950 the Golden Age Clubs had taken root in Philadelphia, St. Louis, Chicago, Cincinnati, Pittsburgh, New York, Detroit, and other cities.[1]

The Golden Age Clubs were one product of efforts by social workers, educators, corporations, municipalities, federal agencies, and others to bring free time under control. These efforts had created a new profession of supervised leisure, or recreation. The movement had begun in the nineteenth century, as cities such as New York and Buffalo built parks and parkways to shape the attitudes of urban industrial and middle classes. During the Progressive Era, social reformers opened the schools for community meetings and carved playgrounds out of vacant lots. By the 1920s, many of the larger industrial corporations had established formal recreation programs for their employees, and adult education had entered the first of several decades of rapid growth.[2]

The link between the recreation movement and social group work – a new form of social work based on the group as opposed to the individual "case" — would be of special significance in the founding of the Golden Age Clubs two decades in the future. Recreation and social group work grew in stature simultaneously, and usually among the same people within the social work profession. In 1920, the School of Civics and Philanthropy at the University of Chicago offered a course in recreation training which focused on groups and their social functioning. Western Reserve University in Cleveland created its first course in recreation in 1916 and a more complete program of study after 1923. As interest in leisure and recreation expanded with the technological explosion of the late 1920s and the unemployment of the 1930s, social group work was institutionalized, first in local group-work organizations like that founded in Cleveland; then, following a major national conference on group work at Ligonier, Pennsylvania, in November 1934, in the American Association for the Study of Group Work, founded in 1936.[3]

The peculiar set of circumstances brought about by the worldwide depression of the 1930s made recreation even more central to the American way of life. Unemployment, the progenitor of the new leisure, created ample opportunity for shaping the free time now enjoyed in abundance by the old and the young. Social workers trained in recreation in the 1920s found convenient vehicles for their newly acquired expertise in the Works Progress Administration, the Civilian Conservation Corps, and the other New Deal agencies.

The growth of Nazism and fascism added another dimension to recreation. Because these systems or forms of government were often analyzed as the product of an inadequate primary-group life and insufficient citizen participation, it seemed reasonable to believe that an American fascism could be prevented by encouraging group formation and participation. One result was the boom in forums, described in the preceding chapter. Another, more suitable to the methods of the recreationists, was the club.

CLUBS

The club was by this date a time-honored method of social engineering. The Protestant Sunday schools, the settlements, the Christian associations, the scouts, the business corporations, and dozens of other agencies and organizations had by 1920 — in some cases much earlier — utilized clubs or clublike forms and recognized them as something more than simple play groups.[4] Yet the post-1935 club movement was unique in its magnitude and for its focus on the preservation of democracy.

Youth encountered club-centered recreation with special intensity in the public schools.[5] No less than other Americans, school administrators feared that democracy itself might be overwhelmed by totalitarianism (a convenient catchword for what was going on in Germany) and that the nation might ultimately find itself the victim of a demagogue. Many educators believed that democracy could not survive unless it were practiced, and it could be practiced in clubs and clublike activities.

Life magazine described and summarized the club movement in the schools in a January 1941 article. One of three schools featured was Benjamin Franklin High School in Rochester, New York. A photograph (see page 174) of Benjamin Franklin's Student Activities Committee showed a dozen students, marching into a classroom, led by a student playing a snare drum. Others carried neatly lettered signs: "Don't Be a Dub / Join a Club"; "Flower Arrangement is An Art / Learn It In a Club!" School officials urged students to join a club and to engage in other protodemocratic functions, such as conducting assemblies, maintaining the lunchroom and library, and leading classes. These activities were supported so that students would "learn to exercise the kind of restraint which a democratic society imposes on individuals." The clubs were also seen as minidemocracies, where students could learn the rudiments of responsible self-government — to lead, follow, administer, vote, hold office, and participate in group decision making.[6]

As the *Life* photograph suggests, students absorbed this democratic ideology and became active proponents of it. At Buffalo, New York's, Kensington High School, the 1941 yearbook reveals that participatory ideas affected the way students described their activities (if not the specific club experience). "The past year," stated the yearbook, "found Kensington students taking a more active part in the preparation and presentation of assembly programs. . . . For the second year, the Freshman boys planned the Armistice Day program. . . . Everyone participated in the St. Patrick's Day program and joined in singing the lovely ballads of old Ireland."[7]

By the mid-1930s, local social service agencies had begun to realize that recreational theory — and the club itself — had as much relevance for the retired as for jobless youth and students. That brings us to Cleveland, and to the Golden Age Clubs.

GOLDEN AGE CLUBS

The story of the Golden Age Clubs can be told through the lives of three persons who played crucial roles in their creation. Margaret Wagner, executive director of the Benjamin Rose Institute, succeeded in securing financial support for the clubs from the institute and other city foundations. Grace Coyle, a social work professor at Western Reserve University, gave the clubs an intellectual rationale. Her social-group-work theories, largely derived from her contacts at Columbia, forged the links between the foundations and Cleveland's numerous and active social welfare agencies. Schulze (pronounced Schultz-ze), was the city's inspirational club organizer and leader. Like Coyle, he believed in social group work as a way of buttressing democratic institutions.

Wagner, Coyle, and Schulze were successful in this joint venture in social entrepreneurship in large measure because they had a common understanding of the impact of history on the elderly. According to this shared understanding — in effect, an ideology — older persons were among the first and most tragic victims of a half century of social disintegration. Isolated by the collapse of community in an industrial, urban society, and economically deprived by the economic dislocation of the 1920s (in Germany, where Schulze was living) and the 1930s, older people had, they believed, sought refuge in the comforting but fantastic schemes of demagogic politicians. The Golden Age Clubs were designed to reintegrate an embittered and isolated older generation into American group life and to promote a new attitude of social responsibility conducive to more reasonable political behavior.

Margaret Wagner and the Townsend Movement

Margaret Wagner retired in 1959 after twenty-nine years' service as executive director of the Rose Institute. She had been educated, like others of her social class, at private schools, including the School of Applied Social Sciences (SASS) at Western Reserve. In her first job in social welfare — with the City Hospital, a teaching institution where she established a social service department — she became convinced, and with good reason, that old people were suffering from inactivity. Her later interest in old-age clubs would arise in part from this early experience in the late 1920s as a medical social worker.[8]

The foundation where Wagner would spend most of her working life was established by the will of Cleveland meat packer Benjamin Rose. Under its provisions, the Benjamin Rose Institute administered a system of grants for "respectable and deserving needy, aged people . . . mostly of the Anglo-Saxon race . . ." By 1930, when Wagner joined the Rose Institute staff, this pension system was inadequate to the needs of Cleveland's aged, a group, Wagner recalled in 1955, "too small to make an impression on a negligent society and . . . lost in a vigorous country, busily concentrating on its youth."[9]

Cleveland's growing population of older citizens had responded to the Great Depression and to the inadequacy of private charity by actively participating in the political system. With their help, Ohio became the first state to pass an old-age pension law by a direct vote of its citizens.[10] Wagner recalled the circumstances surrounding the initial grant made under the law, in November 1934:

The [International Order of] Eagles officiated. There was a parade, the band played, the Governor was present. The master of the Eagles, with drums rolling, presented the first assistance check to an old gentleman who stood up in the mass of citizens to receive great applause. It was apparent that this was going to be used for political effect. It disturbed us at the Rose Institute very much.[11]

Chagrined as first the Eagles and then the American Legion controlled distribution of the state's old-age relief funds, Wagner sought to bring the political nature of the process to the attention of state and national governments.[12] Wagner could expect no assistance from neopopulist Ohio governor Martin L. Davey, who bid often and directly for the votes of the state's pensioners. In spite of the additional aid it produced for old people, Wagner resented Davey's personal style as unnecessarily manipulative and as corrosive of the political system.[13]

Lacking confidence in older voters, Wagner must have been distressed at the enthusiasm for pension advocate Francis Townsend among Cleveland's older citizens. Throughout the 1930s, the Long Beach, California, physician drew large crowds in the city's public arenas. When Townsend brought his national convention to Cleveland in 1936, the *Plain Dealer* found fervent but deluded old people, many of them poor, "seeking the rainbow's end so long as their leader bids them," and predicted a backlash of bitterness when the dream of large pensions dissolved and the defrauded victims awoke. In Townsend's refusal to allow his organization to be run through a representative system, the *Plain Dealer* found a microcosm of the European experience: "The doctor is the dictator. What he says goes."[14]

This anti-Townsend attitude was also apparent in Cleveland's settlements, where social workers sought to contain the Townsend impulse while maintaining free-speech policies that allowed the Townsend Clubs access to facilities.[15] One solution was to guide free speech in appropriate directions. At Hiram House, for example, social workers produced a Christmas operetta, "Timely Townsend Times," in which Townsend and Huey Long were presented as vote-buying charlatans and the Townsend Clubs (which, according to one verse, made up "quite half this town") were pictured as a combination of silliness and graft. Also of some concern were the "self-respecting aged men" who, because of retirement provisions in the Townsend pension system, "will never work a day again." The poor taxpayer, who would have to shoulder the expense of this extravagance, was the production's beleaguered hero.[16]

Under Wagner's guidance, the Rose Institute broadened its approach to the aged in the early and mid-1930s, adopting an improved medical program and seeking to raise standards of care within the city's nursing homes. Wagner was less successful in convincing the settlement houses that problems of loneliness and political irresponsibility could be treated through regular social activity — i.e., recreation. Local officials shared the priorities of the national New Deal and its "conscience," Eleanor Roosevelt; the young, because of their potential for militancy and radicalism, were the focus of settlement social programs. Recreation, though a growing field of popular and academic interest, was seldom interpreted with the needs of the elderly in mind. And wherever she went, Wagner was told — in blatant contradiction to the evidence generated by the Townsend experience — that old people did not want to be grouped together.[17]

Grace Coyle and Social Work

The ultimate emergence of the Golden Age Clubs in Cleveland rather than elsewhere owed much to the presence in that city of Grace Coyle, by 1940 one of the nation's foremost advocates of social group work. Coyle's personal history recapitulates key facets of the history of democratic social engineering. Inspired as a young girl by the writings of Jane Addams, Coyle volunteered at a Boston settlement house while earning a B.A. (1914) at Wellesley College. In 1918, after three years as a settlement worker in the coal regions of Pennsylvania, Coyle found a position in the Industrial Women's Department of the YWCA in New York City. There she designed leadership-training courses and nourished an interest in adult education and recreation. A few years later, Coyle found part-time work on the staff of The Inquiry and thus contact with John Dewey, William H. Kilpatrick, Eduard C. Lindeman, and Harrison Elliott — all influential in Coyle's intellectual development. Resuming her schooling in 1926, Coyle earned advanced degrees in economics and sociology from Columbia University. She joined the group-work faculty of the School of Applied Social Sciences at Western Reserve University in 1934.[18]

Coyle's arrival at SASS did not signal the beginning of that department's interest in social group work. Indeed, the school had been a leader in group work more than a decade before Coyle came on the scene. In response to requests from the Cleveland Girls Council and other prominent social agencies, SASS was one of the first schools to offer training in group work. At the SASS annual dinner in 1924, one speaker eloquently praised the new graduate training program. "We stand at the tension points of human society," he said. "We are scouts ahead of the shock troops. We are geniuses in the art of compromise. We are following the thin, red trail of causation back to its source. We are exercising personal leadership in the co-operative technique of conflict." SASS was to be applauded for establishing the professional standards and programs required to produce "intelligent, tactful and practical social engineers."[19] As early as 1932, the Committee of Eighteen, made up of SASS faculty and others interested in Cleveland social work, had gone on record in favor of group-work programs for adults. "It is very clearly the responsibility of social workers," the committee concluded, "through group work processes, to direct [the] thinking of dissatisfied groups." And in 1933, just the year before her faculty appointment, Coyle, settlement worker Alice Gannett, and others interested in promoting group work had established the Joint Committee of the Case Work and Group Work Councils of the Welfare Federation of Cleveland. By the spring of 1935, the group workers within this body had apparently been successful in persuading the case workers of the necessity for more group work. According to notes made in that year, "unemployment and its attendant problems of maladjustment brought to case workers a keen realization of [the] need of their clients for group contacts."[20]

Coyle's lifelong advocacy of group work was not just a new technique for an old profession; behind it was a new way of conceptualizing and managing social relationships, built on a foundation of history and social theory. With Mary Parker Follett, Elton Mayo, Kilpatrick, Dewey, and a whole school of Chicago sociologists dependent on the thought of Émile Durkheim, Coyle argued that science, technology, and urbanization had destroyed traditional sources of social cohesion — such as the neighborhood, the church, and the work place — threatening democracy itself. Filling the void were thousands of functional groups, serving the specific interests of their members. But for Coyle neither the existence of these groups, nor existing ways of eliminating differences between them, ensured a sufficient degree of social unity. She found the solution within the structure and process of the group — in fact, within the groups which made up the organizational revolution. Consensus could be achieved through informal, cooperative, group discussion, guided by a leader trained in "collective thinking" and the art of persuasion. Because it was participatory, the process itself would serve as an ongoing lesson in the habits of democracy and the meaning of life. More than most advocates of similar systems, Coyle appreciated the dangers inherent in them: guided discussion could easily degenerate into manipulation; the group might become an end in itself, resulting in neglect of the needs and feelings of individuals.[21]

Through the efforts of Coyle, W. I. Newstetter, Clara A. Kaiser, and others of similar persuasion on the SASS faculty, social-group-work principles gradually percolated down through Cleveland's philanthropic foundations and social settlements. One can see this happening, for example, at the Alta Social Settlement in 1937. Following a Coyle presentation on group work, social worker W. T. McCullough summarized Coyle's point of view for the annual report. "It is the aim of the group leader," McCullough wrote, "to help the group members re-evaluate their experiences in terms of social purposes — in other words, to lead group members to understand that they are part of a dynamic changing society in which they have some responsibility for exerting their influence toward making a better society in which to live. This . . . is . . . an objective which is essential and necessary to the continuation of democracy." A later proposal to the Alta board of trustees recognized an interesting distinction. "Case work," it said, "by and large deals with individuals who recognize that they have a problem and they desire its solution. Group work deals with people who may have problems but who do not recognize the problems or at least do not look upon the group work agency as a place to get help in solving their problems."[22] In short, group work recognized a problem that existed apart from its subjects; its purpose was social, as Coyle had always maintained.

Although group work continued to gain in stature as a technique of social control, until the late 1930s it was widely used only among those who dealt with youth (see the photograph on p. 169). A logical mechanism for harnessing the collective energy which youth normally channeled into gangs, and which in 1938 seemed so menacing, group work seemed inapplicable to an elderly population defined as passive and inactive.[23] It was Oskar Schulze who demonstrated the fallacy in this point of view.

Oskar Schulze, Club Organizer

Schulze was a man of importance in his native Germany. A 1908 graduate of Teachers Training College in Dresden, Schulze taught public school and did graduate work in social sciences and administration at Dresden's Polytechnicum. As a Dresden city councillor after the war, he had some measure of responsibility for old people in two large municipal homes, and in 1929, on becoming Leipzig's Third Mayor, he took charge of most of the city's social welfare activities. It was there, administering the richly endowed Johannes Hospital, that Schulze became convinced that mere provision of physical comforts would not suffice to make old people content; he grew committed to recreation as a form of treatment. Dismissed in the summer of 1933, apparently for political reasons, he spent the next three years in Istanbul.[24]

His years in Weimar and Nazi Germany left him with memories and conceptions of history that profoundly influenced his work in Cleveland.

According to Schulze, the agricultural Germany of the first half of the nineteenth century had emerged from the Franco-Prussian war of 1870–71 as an industrial nation. "In all cities," Schulze wrote, "the factories grew up like mushrooms on a muggy summer day . . ." Here is German history as Schulze recalled it: The boom of the early 1870s was followed by a severe depression, unemployment among industrial workers, and finally, in 1889, by social legislation, inspired by the biblical prescriptions of aid for the needy and old. The First World War left Germany in chaos, many of its people without adequate food, shelter, and clothing. The crushing blow, according to Schulze, was administered by the catastrophic inflation of 1923 (Schulze was, ironically, in charge of printing money in his district), when the middle class lost much of its property and wealth. Those who had managed to save for old age found their money worthless and had to resort to public relief. Although pensioners received substantial private aid and relief allowances higher than normal, they remained embittered and despairing, "easy prey for radical doctrines." Their demands became impossible to fulfill, and they "eagerly hearkened to Hitler's siren call." Making promises he would never keep, Adolf Hitler — Schulze concluded — came to power with the votes and support of the victims of the inflation, especially the aged.[25]

THEORY AND PRACTICE

Schulze's concern for the health of democratic institutions was, of course, especially conditioned by his experiences in Germany. But in different ways, it also affected Wagner, Coyle, and others involved in the Golden Age Club movement. According to Emil Lederer, the German writer whose book, *State of the Masses*, is cited in Coyle's later work, groups functioned to check, balance, and restrict the natural irrationality of people. When the Nazis destroyed organizational life in the German nation, they destroyed the institutions through which the individual was exposed to the "testing, stimulating and provoking influence of his fellow man" and created the preconditions for the totalitarian state.[26]

This emphasis on the destruction of group life was not universally accepted in the United States, where it was easier to defend the continued viability of group structures. Yet by 1935 it had become impossible to avoid analogies, however facile, between the rise of Adolf Hitler and the emergence of American mass politics under Charles Coughlin, Francis Townsend, Huey Long, and even (in his use of the radio) Franklin D. Roosevelt. Leadership theorist LeRoy E. Bowman argued that insufficient experience in rigorous group decision-making processes had left the nation vulnerable to an unthinking mass movement which could bring dictatorship in its wake.[27] The relationship between social group work and democracy was also a subject of intense concern within the social work profession in the late 1930s and throughout the 1940s. Coyle was not so willing to accept the premise of a decline in group life, yet her own emphasis on the perversion of genuine group life and the emergence of a variety of pressure groups, associations, classes, and movements was an American analogue to Lederer's focus on crowd and Bowman's on mob.[28]

The solution, exemplified in the Golden Age Clubs, was a rebirth of genuine and independent, primary-group life, with all that implied for those group processes and experiences considered essential to a healthy corporate and democratic social existence.[29] This is the context in which the regular exhortations by Schulze and others to conquer loneliness and insecurity among the aged must be interpreted. Security and self-worth were qualities believed to be socially as well as individually desirable; and they were achievable through group interaction.[30]

Schulze and his wife, Suzanne, arrived in Cleveland from Turkey in January 1937. She soon found a teaching position in SASS, Coyle's department, and rapidly achieved recognition as an authority on the institutional care of children. Because he spoke no English, Oskar Schulze had more difficulty securing meaningful employment. Following a series of odd jobs, he left in January 1940 for Chicago and a position at the Olivet Institute.[31]

Schulze began by inviting the old people in the neighborhood to attend a social gathering one afternoon a week. The settlement provided movies, lectures, music, and other entertainments. As he would often emphasize, Schulze found the old people suspicious, mistrustful, and reticent — even among themselves. He learned of great loneliness and "came across deplorable living conditions such as I had never before seen or imagined." "Many of these stories," Schulze concluded, "closely paralelled [sic] those of their kind in Germany; only it was the Depression rather [than] the inflation, which brought about their impoverishment." Within five months Schulze had created a viable old-age club with a stable nucleus of thirty club members, men and women, from sixty-five to ninety-seven years old. Schulze's democratic methods were apparent even in this first effort. He was especially pleased when the members elected a group to take charge of arrangements for future gatherings. "This action," he reported, "is in full accord with my aims to win over the old folks themselves toward a program of active participation in care for the needy aged."[32]

Schulze believed that he had seen the "shy and distrustful" individuals of earlier encounters become "a happy crowd of old folks, knit together by ties of friendship," a metamorphosis with political and social implications. During Chicago's primary elections, the old people had begun to come forward with problems and questions. The Institute brought in a speaker from a woman's club, who explained the workings of the primary system. "The situation that presented itself before the election," Schulze wrote, "afforded ample evidence of the devices employed by various politicians and candidates to ingratiate themselves with the older voters, and of how susceptible the latter are to the lure of the demagogue."[33]

Schulze returned to Cleveland in the summer of 1940 with this successful experience behind him. He had pieced together a philosophy of social action which would strike a responsive chord in Cleveland's welfare community, and he now had some facility with English. Schulze knew of Wagner's strong sympathy for his work, but for the moment the Rose Institute did not come forward with aid. Fortunately, Alice Gannett, an old friend who had sheltered the Schulzes in Goodrich House on their arrival in the city, requested a demonstration of the club concept in her facility.[34]

Unlike most of Cleveland's social settlements, Goodrich House had for some time taken a lively interest in the aged, and from a perspective that dovetailed with Schulze's. A strong exponent of the need for vigilance in the maintenance of democratic government, Gannett had moved her settlement into adult education as a way of ensuring an intelligent citizenship. She was also familiar with group-work concepts. As a participant in a 1937 radio forum, Gannett had been asked, "What would you do to maintain our democracy?" "I should insist," she had replied, "on education of men, women and children in their civic duties through forums, clubs, discussion groups and co-operative enterprises."[35] Gannett's aid proved all that Schulze needed. Although a disappointing eight persons came to the Goodrich club's first meeting in October 1940, within several months Schulze had duplicated his Olivet experience. Members included a number of Townsend followers.[36]

This initial success gave Schulze a vehicle for national publicity and allowed Wagner to overcome the inertia of her board of trustees. In June 1940 she asked the board's consideration of a broad recreational project for older people. According to the minutes of the meeting,

she pointed out that contact with beneficiaries over a period of several years had demonstrated their need for social activity, which in many instances had been provided by Townsend Clubs, and that there was a growing tendency to organize old people in small groups, to be used politically, by such groups as the Townsend Clubs, the Bigelow Plan or Martin L. Davey Clubs. There has been no effort to combat this insidious movement by anything constructive.[37]

When Schulze returned in 1941 from Atlantic City, where he had reported on his work to the National Conference of Social Work, Wagner and

Leyton Carter, director of the Cleveland Foundation, issued a joint invitation to Schulze to present his findings before a group of Cleveland's civic leaders. For two hours, Schulze told the heartrending and touching stories which had already emerged from the Goodrich club and demonstrated what Wagner and others who had worked with him had known for some time — that he was genial, persuasive, articulate, and compassionate — an excellent choice to head the club program. Rose Institute trustees emerged from the meeting convinced of the value of group work for the aged and committed to utilizing this "rare person," Oskar Schulze. Soon thereafter, the Rose Institute and the Cleveland Foundation agreed to provide funding for a program of Golden Age Clubs.[38]

The clubs reflected their complex origins. At the simplest level, they were social institutions. Members played checkers, rummy, and dominoes; they celebrated Christmas, Hanukkah, Easter, and a variety of other holidays; they sat through musical presentations, films, and lectures given by speakers from the Art Museum, the Garden Center, and the Natural History Museum. Despite Schulze's insistence that time not be wasted in idle gossip, simple talk was a common enough feature of the weekly meeting. Many functions were familial in concept and purpose. Members celebrated birthdays and anniversaries and helped one another in time of distress. When a member was ill or absent, others came to call; the women sometimes sewed for the men. Schulze was proud of the "family atmosphere" which developed in a number of the clubs. The clubs were in some measure an attempt to provide a substitute for the practical and emotional services traditionally provided by family and kinship groups and now in inadequate supply, especially in urban areas.[39]

On another level, the Golden Age Clubs were educational institutions in the progressive tradition. The theory which justified and explained them in this educational role derived from the work of recreational theorist Eduard C. Lindeman and educator William H. Kilpatrick, both members of The Inquiry. Lindeman had argued in *The Meaning of Adult Education* (1926) that the reconstruction of meaningful group life must begin in manageable form, with each individual working to bring some measure of intelligent influence to bear on available local groups and group situations (the neighborhood, the home) or small units of larger groups (the trade union). Adult education was designed to train individuals for participation in collective experiences, the mainstays of "contributory personalities."[40] As we have seen, for Lindeman, Kilpatrick, and others, the purpose of education, including adult education, was not so much the absorption of a given body of knowledge, but the process by which instruction took place. Thus, the classroom (and the Golden Age Club) was designed to replicate an ideal larger society; the school (and the club) would itself function as "an ideal community in which pupils get practice in co-operation, in self-government, and in the application of intelligence to difficulties or problems as they may arise."[41] The child or adult would emerge with increased awareness of his/her relationship to the larger group and with the problem-solving habits and skills necessary to resist the temptation to join "the mob."[42] In 1932, "the new era of social planning and social control" required preparation in the art of conference, a knowledge of "how to substitute for aggressiveness and power the satisfactions of shared experience, and shared responsibility."[43] The Golden Age Clubs were explicitly designed on this educational model.

Direct education was also attempted. Although there is no evidence that the clubs were employed to "indoctrinate" members in the sense in which that word is usually used, Schulze, who in the early years of the Golden Age movement handled much club activity personally, functioned as group leader for the discussions on issues considered especially important, including the Townsend movement and Negro slavery.[44]

Whether education was pursued directly or indirectly, the role of the club/group leader was crucial. Familiar with group-work precepts, Schulze believed that leaders should facilitate rather than control, encouraging participants to arrive at their own conclusions and assuming that if the process worked as it should, those conclusions would be politically acceptable and socially benign. In his frequent appearances as a public speaker, Schulze liked to tell the story of Mr. K, a club member who, having listened to heated club debate on a possible speaker from the Townsend movement, had denounced the very idea: "Who would want to listen to such nonsense, there are sounder programs of public assistance to whose improvement we should give our time rather than wasting it on a pipe dream." For Schulze this was evidence that democratic social engineering worked. Similarly, Wagner claimed that Golden Agers had helped block the Townsend movement's efforts to secure office space in Cleveland to headquarter the organization.[45]

THE POSTWAR YEARS

Many of the special historical circumstances that had spawned the Golden Age Clubs—the rise of Hitler, the Townsend movement, high rates of unemployment—disappeared after 1945. Perhaps because other circumstances did not change, the club movement continued to grow and to be rationalized in terms that evoked something of the spirit of the interwar years and yet reflected an altered postwar climate.

When Schulze resigned in 1948 as director of the Rose Institute's Rec-

reation Project for Older People, the Golden Age Club program was transferred to the Cleveland Welfare Federation and placed under the direction of James H. Woods. Though Woods and his colleagues carried on
Schulze's interest in the relationship between the aged and the political
system, they approached the subject from a somewhat different perspective. Whereas Schulze had at times despaired of the existence of the social
order should the old follow false prophets, Woods was skeptical of the
benefits to be derived from club programs designed "just to keep them
[the aged] quiet and to prevent the formation of an old-age pressure
group."[46] Although he did not deny that politicians sought the vote of
the old, Woods envisioned politics less as a battleground of ideologies
tugging at the elderly than as a field in which it was healthy for the aged,
who had given up so much else in life, to be involved. The clubs and the
new Golden Age Centers (structures exclusively for the use of the aged)
could help foster in the aged an appropriate set of values and responsible
voting behavior. Neither Woods nor Ralph Leavenworth, president of the
board of trustees of the Golden Age Center of Cleveland, was above raising
the specter of old-age politics to secure funds from the foundations; the
centers were justified, like the clubs, in part for their anticipated antiradical
impact. But the sense of crisis which was so much a part of Schulze's world
view was gone.[47]

A similar though less pronounced change in tone and emphasis took
place nationally between 1940 and 1965. During the 1930s, analyses of
right- and left-wing movements focused on unemployment, considered
destructive of morale, status, self-confidence, security, and other qualities believed conducive to social stability. The aged, though seen as of
less potential danger to the social fabric than unemployed men in their
thirties, were part of this analysis. Pensioners constituted a unique group,
one especially vulnerable to irrational appeals, prone to ignorant voting
behavior, and capable of appropriating the public revenue for class purposes.[48] Among the leading spokesmen for this point of view was Frank
G. Dickinson, professor of economics at the University of Illinois.
Throughout the 1940s, Dickinson forecast a new form of class warfare
emerging from pension politics: Karl Marx's version of the class struggle
had been overcome by prosperity and replaced by a new and equally bitter
conflict. Heavy pension taxes would bring workers and employers together
against an alliance of senior citizens and politicians. "Townsendism," said
Dickinson, "may be as important in the next fifty years as were the doctrines of Karl Marx during the last half-century."[49]

Others found grounds for apprehension in the high level of unemployment in the late 1940s (with its disproportionate impact on the older
worker), the rise of Joseph McCarthy, and particularly the continued spec-

tacle of California, where George McLain was thought to be taking advantage of the state's ample population of old people and controlling the Department of Social Welfare.[50] The California experience and its Florida counterpart were the subject of a number of studies, most of them by sociologists, which traced the disposition to authoritarian movements and pressure-group politics to isolation from mainstream institutions of family, occupation, and community. "It is far less the financial hardships of the position of elderly people," wrote Talcott Parsons, "than their social isolation which makes old age a problem."[51]

Older Americans experienced this viewpoint in the watered-down form of political advice, dispensed in Golden Age Clubs and in the rapidly multiplying magazines marketed to the middle-aged and retired. The advice resembled that which might have been offered in a high school civics class: gather the facts, study the issues, develop constructive alternatives, have patience with the political process, recognize that everything — including welfare legislation — has an economic cost, and that someone must pay for the benefits. These instructions assumed that proper political behavior was a matter of mechanics, of knowing what was correct and doing it. This not only diminished what the aged had attempted to accomplish through their own methods; it also ignored the participation/isolation analysis upon which it had been premised.[52]

The remedies which emerged from this analysis necessarily involved reintegration of the aged into primary institutions (e.g., providing the retired with advisory functions in public relations, production, labor relations, and other facets of the business from which they had been separated); encouraging participation in voluntary associations, like the Golden Age Clubs; even limiting or eliminating retirement as it had developed historically and somehow reincorporating the aged into the workforce.[53] A society which had once seen retirement as a relatively risk-free way of handling a variety of problems, including the central one of aging in an age of "leisure," must have wondered if it had not underestimated the aged and their willingness to organize, as Lindeman put it, "for an appropriate revenge for the debasement of their role in society."[54] The problem, after all, was not so much that the aged had no group life as that they had the wrong kind; not so much that they had rejected or ceased to participate in all institutions as that they had come together in threatening mass movements.

Yet by the early 1960s, McCarthy was a fading memory and even California had proved incapable of sustaining old-age politics in the teeth of regular additions to social security. The vision of "gerontocracy" was apparently a thing of the past.[55]

CONCLUSION

The Golden Age Clubs were only one manifestation of a body of social analysis which profoundly influenced a number of areas of American life over a period of several decades. Linked to the clubs through the person of Coyle and, perhaps, through Schulze's wife, Suzanne, this social analysis, and the methodology of democratic social engineering that it generated, can be traced back to the social settlement movement of the late nineteenth century and the efforts of Jane Addams, who conceived of her work as a counterweight to social disorganization. Coyle absorbed elements of it from Addams, Follett, Mayo, Kilpatrick, Dewey, Lindeman, and others, translating what she found into the language of social work and finally, in Cleveland, presiding over the first consistent attempt to apply social-group-work precepts to the elderly.

What is perhaps more surprising is that the intellectual superstructure of the Golden Age Clubs was not Coyle's possession alone. Others understood parts of it. Margaret Wagner would have been more than receptive to Coyle's notion that group life had somehow been perverted; she could see it happening with the Eagles and in the Townsend movement. She also understood that "bad" groups could be countered with "good" groups. Wagner apparently knew little of what was supposed to go on in these groups, but she knew enough to realize that whatever it was, Schulze was perfect for it. Schulze, for his part, had Wagner's vision of the fragility of democratic institutions and a knowledge of the mechanics of social-group work and leadership that Coyle could only have admired. Coyle, Wagner, and Schulze more or less agreed on the problem and its solution; that they did says much about how familiar democratic social engineering had become.

The Golden Age Clubs can also be understood as the result of a societal "decision" to turn unemployment into the "new leisure." That decision consigned the elderly to a workless future (or, if you will, to a special place on the frontier of leisure). Most accepted this status but turned to politics to secure the pensions that would make it tolerable. Others withdrew from politics or avoided it. Either way, they acted in ways that Wagner, Coyle, Schulze, and the Cleveland establishment found threatening. Those who took to the Townsend program for companionship or political clout were denounced as irresponsible or as unfortunate victims of a forbidden kind of leadership called demagoguery. Those who withdrew were described as fodder for demagogues — potential victims, potentially irresponsible. Both groups — those who participated improperly and those who did not participate enough — had to be brought back into a proper relationship to society and to politics. The Townsendites had to be weaned (yes, like babies) from the sugary milk of the Townsend movement to the more wholesome formula of Roosevelt's New Deal. The isolates had to be made to realize that it was wrong not to belong and participate. By the late 1930s, there were agreed-upon mechanisms for achieving these goals: a way of solving problems and controlling behavior through group processes, known as social-group work; a discipline created to treat those with leisure time, called recreation; and an institution, at once suited to social-group work and recreation and designed to reach Cleveland's recalcitrant older people. That, of course, was the Golden Age Club.

6

Invading the Family: Benjamin Spock and American Child Rearing

Between 1943 and 1945, Benjamin Spock dictated what would become *The Common Sense Book of Baby and Child Care.* Published in 1946, *Baby and Child Care*[1] expresses the accumulated wisdom and experience of an important segment of the generation that grew to adulthood between World War I and World War II. Spock could produce such a document, and articulate widely held values, because he was preeminently an eclectic, adept at picking up fragments of the cultural fabric from a variety of friends and acquaintances and from a broad-based career that involved private practice, consulting for child-guidance clinics, and participation in interdisciplinary conferences. Spock's "circle" — that is, the personal and professional acquaintances from whom he took, or with whom he shared, a way of looking at the world — included anthropologist Margaret Mead, psychologists Erik Erikson and Kurt Lewin, child-development administrator and theorist Lawrence K. Frank, and progressive educator Caroline Zachry. Many others, whose paths never crossed Spock's applied compatible ideas in their own spheres of influence. They included industrial psychologist Elton Mayo and social-group-work theorists Mary Parker Follett and Grace Coyle.

Baby and Child Care, therefore, must be read as an analysis of American civilization in the interwar years — an analysis that was shared by contemporaries in many fields. As such, it is a document in cultural disintegration. Spock had no small feeling of discomfort with the world in which he lived. He found economic institutions too competitive, social institutions insufficiently grounded in history and tradition. The Great Depression, the threat of totalitarianism, and the actual experience of war were basic ingredients in his world view. At the center of this unstable world

was an unstable infant and child — fearful, frustrated, insecure, and potentially destructive in his aggressive tendencies.[2] Through control over the
child-rearing process, Spock sought to create adults who would be more
cooperative, more consensus oriented, more group-conscious, and a society
that would be more knowable, more consistent, and more comforting.
He wrote to prevent chaos and to achieve discipline rather than license.
His search for a method, necessarily a troubled one at a time when all
forms of control were viewed as potentially dangerous, led him to a "democratic" model of child rearing which featured the family as a small group,
the parent as a group leader, and the child as occasional participant in
a group decision-making process. This model of child rearing would later
be labeled "permissive," but its content belies the word's laissez-faire connotation. Spock should be understood not as someone who stripped away
or eliminated authority, but as an advocate of a new system of authority,
as powerful and effective in its way as John B. Watson's behaviorism. Spock
was a democratic social engineer.

AN UNSTABLE WORLD

Before we can appreciate Spock's solution — his social-engineering methods,
his reform program — we must first understand what Spock perceived as
the problem. In the largest sense, the problem lay in the disordered state
of world affairs in the late 1930s and during World War II. *Baby and Child
Care* was conceptualized against a background of European dictatorship;
it was written during the world war. For Spock, the child could all too
easily come to participate in this tragedy, whether as a timid follower or
as a charismatic leader-dictator. Spock's child, therefore, is unstable — a
potential tyrant, an incipient demagogue. It is not so much that the child
can be irreparably injured by parental error as that the child is *prone* to
such injury. If the infant is not born a barbarian, the potential for a twentieth-century version of savagery is never far below the surface. Though
Spock does his best to assure parents that "discipline, good behavior, and
pleasant manners" are "part of the unfolding of [the child's] nature," that
process of unfolding is liable to disruption, with serious, even permanent,
consequences at every step in the child-rearing process. Overfeeding will
make a child "rebel and become more balky." More important, "he's apt
to lose some of his active, positive feeling about life." In weaning, a baby
may want more nursing, "when life looks dark." "If mealtime becomes a
struggle," concludes Spock, the baby "goes on the defensive and builds
up a balky, suspicious attitude toward life and toward people."And if meals

become "agonizing," "the problem may last for years" and will have other behavior ramifications.[3]

The child is father of the man. Conflict between mother and child over toilet training, for example, will injure the child's "personality," producing not only an obstinate child but a recalcitrant adult. "We all know grownups," suggests Spock parenthetically, "who are still automatically saying 'no' to every request." "Worrisomeness" over toilet habits, if "deeply implanted at an early age," is "apt to turn him into a fussy, finicky person."[4]

Nor is Spock's newborn a tabula rasa. From birth, the child has aggressive, hostile feelings. Because the adult will need his aggressive instincts in the business world, they are never eliminated, only "refined," "civilized," and tamed. (They also serve a useful purpose in a world at war.) However, the child's aggressive core is also the source of concern, for it may be enlarged as well as limited. Shamed, insecure, frustrated (the latter is a common word in the Spockian vocabulary), a child will become *more* aggressive, not less. In 1969, basing his ideas of aggression on the work of anthropologists Konrad Lorenz and Robert Ardrey, Spock wrote: "Man raised himself from barbarism by visualizing higher values and by inhibiting and sublimating his cruder drives. . . . Man is distinctly more aggressive, cruel, and relentless than any of the other apes."[5]

Spock's aggressive child was part of a widespread interest in aggression and in the relationship between individual neuroses and social disorganization. After 1935, in response to European and world war, a number of social theorists came to focus their efforts on aggression and its causes. John Dollard published his famous study linking frustration and aggression in 1939. The following year, S. R. Slavson, a well-known group psychotherapist who, through his work at the Jewish Board of Guardians in New York City, was familiar to Spock, labeled aggression "the foundation of all life."[6] At Sarah Lawrence, Lois B. Murphy was carrying on child-development research, with Spock in a consulting role. "There was considerable preoccupation with aggression and hostility," she later recalled. "Personalities were being described in terms of aggressive drives and so forth, out of context of the total personality."[7]

Social psychologist Lewin described similar pitfalls. Although Lewin's work was adult centered, he believed that in the absence of a sense of security children would become frustrated. His particular contribution to this strain of thought was a 1941 article in which he argued that frustrated children became more aggressive in play and regressed to "babyish" behavior. Not only was Lewin's work implicitly based on world politics, but he often made this relationship explicit. "We still live," he wrote in 1939 with reference to the relations between nation-states, "essentially in a state of anarchy similar to that of the rule of the sword during medieval times."[8]

The person most responsible for conceptualizing the relationship between the child and authoritarian politics was Frank. Perhaps the most influential figure in the child-development movement, Frank brought foundation monies into the field in the 1920s and later chaired the Macy Foundation in the years when it financed child-rearing research (including Murphy's work at Sarah Lawrence). Although Spock later remembered Frank as something of an egghead and disavowed any influence, there is no doubt that the two men had substantial contact, personal and professional, over a period of years. One need not challenge Spock's recollections to suggest that Frank expressed Spock's views, albeit in somewhat more explicit and more political prose.[9] Frank, who characterized American culture as "sick, mentally disordered, and in need of treatment," found the source of authoritarianism in "individuals who have been warped and distorted by their nurture and rearing." "Dictators of today," he wrote in 1941, "are the most recent of a long line of destructive power-seeking personalities." Those who followed dictators were also engaged in working out repressed anxieties and resentments, even at the expense of self-interest. Frustrations from childhood, particularly over coercive toilet training and weaning, colored the "private idiomatic world" constructed by the child and produced adults hostile to all authority.[10]

Not only was Spock directly influenced by many of these scholars; he also shared their values and assumptions. His world view was something of an interwar composite: insecure and/or frustrated, an unstable generation of infants and children became aggressive or submissive, fodder for demagoguery and totalitarianism, inadequate citizens given to violent outbursts against the social fabric.

THE SECURE CHILD

Because insecurity in the infant and child had been isolated and defined as the first element in a complex train of causation leading to social chaos, remedies for insecurity promised considerable cultural leverage. The search for such remedies was a central task for the author of *Baby and Child Care*. Spock sought to deal with the child's need for security: first, by insisting on the natural and historical qualities of the child-rearing process, second, by fashioning a system of discipline and guidance designed to induce security in the child.

Spock believed that life in the United States in 1940 was too competitive, too modern, too lacking in history and tradition. Therefore, *Baby and Child Care* consistently evokes a simpler, older, less complex culture. "In civilizations that are simpler than ours," writes Spock, "children and grownups too go to sleep curled up together. It's not surprising that a child, particularly an only one, should feel a little lonesome going to sleep in a room by himself." As evidence that a flexible schedule is "natural," Spock asks his reader to "think of a mother, far away in an 'uncivilized' land, who has never heard of a schedule, or a pediatrician, or a cow. . . . The rhythm of the baby's digestive system is what sets the schedule."[11]

Spock and his circle thus sought to return to child rearing and child development some feeling for these processes as natural, historical, and inherently meaningful. "Each child as he develops," writes Spock in *Baby and Child Care*, "is retracing the whole past history of mankind, physically and spiritually, step by step." When the child learns to walk, he is "celebrating" the moment in prehistory when man ceased to walk on four feet. Parents are advised that child rearing is also a natural process, best delegated to "instincts" and "common sense." Spock's analysis of crying unites the understanding of parent and child. The child cries "for a good reason"; the mother's feeling of uneasiness, her desire to comfort, is "meant to be part of your nature too."[12]

Spock shared this analysis with influential contemporaries in anthropology, psychology, and child development, including Mead, Erikson, and Frank. Both Mead and Spock were interested, in the same years, in the phenomenon of competitive and cooperative societies and in child rearing in each of these environments. Much of Mead's work was premised on the assumption that there was something unnatural in the process of child rearing in a culture in which the child was, as she put it, "jerked toward adulthood as rapidly as possible."[13] The high value Spock placed on large families was paralleled by Mead's affinity for child rearing among large numbers of relatives — a condition she found in "primitive" societies. Like Spock, she was a disciple of Zachry, a prominent figure in child-development and psychoanalytic circles in New York City.[14]

Erikson articulated what Spock, who was much less conscious in his social analysis, could only imply. Like Spock, Erikson was deeply concerned whether individuals could survive, as complete, emotionally healthy, and confident human beings, while their cultures moved from the simple to the complex, from the agrarian to the industrial. Although Erikson was interested primarily in adolescence, and Spock in infancy and early childhood, they shared the belief that problems of personality adjustment — that is, neurosis — could be explained with reference to basic social patterns, and they agreed on the central role of the loss of ego identity or confusion of identities in producing such neurosis. For Erikson, the primary problems of the age were the difficulties that infants, youth, and especially adolescents encountered in maintaining a well-defined sense of self. Identity, "inherited from primitive, agrarian, feudal, and patrician cultures," was now threatened by "industrial revolution, world-wide communication, standardization, centralization, and mechanization."[15]

Erikson's discussion of the Sioux Indians contains elements of nostalgia for a simpler civilization not unlike the occasional reference in *Baby and Child Care*. Erikson quotes heavily from poet Carl Sandburg and describes the Sioux as a "once proud people" whose traditions of combat and the hunt could now be evoked only in ceremonies and celebrations. The Sioux, in promoting "free release" rather than "rigid retention" of body waste and property, encouraged autonomy and status in the peer community. The Westerner, by contrast, "pursues ambitious strivings, but compulsively remains within standardized careers. . . . The specialization thus developed has led this Western civilization to the mastery of machinery, but also to an undercurrent of boundless discontent and of individual disorientation." The Sioux, on the other hand, maintain a powerful "conscience" in the face of historical change.[16] Erikson all but concludes that the Sioux child-rearing pattern remains viable, in spite of the destruction of the economic and spiritual life it supported and in spite of the denigration of Sioux culture. Just as Spock tried to counter the destructive process of modernization by encouraging mothers to minister to the unstable child in "natural" ways, so Erikson could not help but applaud a Sioux culture which had not yet allowed modernization to strip it of child-rearing practices perhaps better suited to a preindustrial world.[17]

Consistent with this emphasis on naturalism, Spock joined other child-rearing experts in advocating comforting stage theories of child development. Jean Piaget, the French psychologist, emphasized in his learning theory the necessity of the child's passing through one conceptual stage before he could enter the next. The timing of the movement between stages was generally predictable according to age, and it could not be rushed. Piaget's work strongly implied that learning was a natural process which inhered in the child and over which parents would exercise only the most basic supervision. Here was a conception of learning that was timeless in an era of rapid change, stable in a period of cultural disintegration.[18]

Arnold Gesell and Frances L. Ilg of the Yale University Child Development Clinic brought an entirely new level of comfort to upper-middle-class parents with the publication in 1943 of *Infant and Child in the Culture of Today*, a book that described in exquisite detail how a "typical" child might be expected to behave at each stage of development. For parents with backgrounds similar to those of parents whose children had participated in the Yale study, this catalogue of predicted behaviors brought new confidence that their child was normal.[19]

Spock's major contribution to this developmental approach came in his discussion of children over the age of six. From his own middle childhood, Spock fondly remembered secret clubs and small friendship groups; during the 1930s, he was impressed by the ability of six- to eight-year-old children to take leadership of a class away from their teacher, and he also came into contact with the work of two persons — Erikson and Susan Isaacs — which rationalized child independence in these years. For Isaacs, children's groups were a vital mechanism for deflecting some of the emotional intensity that ordinarily built up between parents and children. For Erikson and Spock, the central end was identity, requiring, as Spock would have it, that "a youth must largely outgrow his dependence and emulation of his parents." Thus, Spock came to advocate, for reasons at once personal and social, the efficacy of the gang. Here was an institution in which children could assert their independence from adults and exercise "the instinct to get community life organized." All of this was part of the natural process of growing up, a minor element in the larger developmental framework, perhaps, but an important one to Spock.[20]

Although Spock is not known as an advocate of discipline, his second mechanism for ensuring secure (and therefore, nonaggressive) children involved just that: a system of discipline and guidance. At its heart was parental authority — to be exercised as clearly, unequivocally, evenly, and regularly as possible. In *Baby and Child Care*, mothers are cautioned to avoid "choices, arguments, cross looks, scoldings." Those who regularly provide their children with explanations will not produce more cooperative offspring; indeed, the child "would be happier and get more security from [the mother] if she had an air of self-confidence and steered him in a friendly, automatic way through the routines of the day." Stay in charge, Spock suggests, "as a friendly boss." At bedtime, and during other routines, maintain an "air of cheerful certainty" and utilize the desire of children for "a certain amount of ritual." A child "needs to feel that his mother and father, however agreeable, still have their own rights, know how to be firm, won't let him be unreasonable or rude. He likes them better that way."[21]

This conception of authority was congenial to Spock as an individual and yet characteristic of social theory in the late 1930s. For his biographer, Spock discussed his early days in the New Haven schools:

Psychologically, most school-age children love to conform to the class, and love routine tasks. At Worthington Hooker the monitors would pass out oak leaves and each of us would trace an oak leaf. Then they would pass out readers and everybody would open his reader to page fourteen and take turns reading a couple of sentences. Then the readers would all be called in and they'd pass out the arithmetic books. I *loved* it. I *loved* being a cog in a machine in a regular class.

In 1915, at the age of twelve, Spock attended a day school for boys. "There were no choices," Spock remembers with affection, "and there was nobody different to make fun of me."[22]

Spock's predisposition to routine, to clear-cut lines of authority, and to freedom from decision-making responsibility found sustenance in the environment of the late 1930s and early 1940s. Freudians Isaacs and David Levy advocated a firm, consistent approach to the discipline of infants and children. Isaacs found the typical middle-class home characterized by a "general lack of positive and informed guidance, relieved only by exasperated threats or bribings or actual whippings." Ilg called for "discerning guidance" in infant care, and pediatricians Ruth Morris Bakwin and Harry Bakwin, perhaps drawing on Levy, found the overprotective parent guilty of disciplinary "inconsistencies." They considered consistent authority essential to a child's sense of security.[23]

Erikson's studies of the Sioux highlighted the relationship between an absence of equivocation and mental health. So committed was Erikson to this analysis that in *Childhood and Society* he claimed that American Indian policy had failed when it proved unable "to arrive at a clear design of either conquering or colonizing, converting or liberating . . . thus demonstrating an inconsistency which the Indians interpreted as insecurity and bad conscience."[24] By analogy, the problem with American parenting was neither too much discipline nor too little, but a dearth of clarity and standards.

DEMOCRATIC CHILD REARING

At this point, Spock had analyzed the child as unstable, and he had suggested two solutions to the problem, one emphasizing natural techniques of child rearing, the other focusing on discipline. It was the second solution that threatened to unbalance this amalgam of views. For if the child was unstable, and the parent too diligent in her discipline, the child's delicate adjustment might be impaired, with dire consequences to follow.

Spock was not alone in coming up against this problem. In the late 1930s, when Spock's views were percolating, Frank struggled with the need to reconcile his concern about authoritarianism with the apparent need for authority. The social order — his social order — was threatening to collapse. Bootlegging, industrial violence, gangsters, war — for Frank these amounted to the disintegration of "respect for law and order." How, then, to destroy fascism, an act that seemed to require tearing down the state and inculcating a new antiauthoritarian impulse, and at the same time teach Americans to accept the authority of the state, "which, to be really effective, must function, not in physical coercion and police supervision, but within the individual himself"?[25]

This was Spock's dilemma as well. *Baby and Child Care* was designed to produce responsible and disciplined children — children of generally good humor who went to bed when asked, ate a variety of foods at regular mealtimes, and avoided dangerous and destructive behavior. The potential for good behavior existed in every child, but its fulfillment was jeopardized at every turn. The unstable child's potential for aggression (or submission) might be irrevocably released by incorrect parenting. To achieve discipline without risking an authoritarian response, Spock developed what might be called a "democratic" model of child rearing. Its components were firm yet friendly leadership of the child by the adult, avoidance of obvious confrontation and conflict, and limited, but conceptually important, participation by the child in its own upbringing.

"Stay in control as a friendly leader," advises Spock. If the child, for example, insists on tugging at the cord of a favorite lamp (see photograph, p. 175), he is to be distracted, not scolded or confronted, least of all threatened. Actions a child *must* take are to be treated as positively as possible. Thus, the change to a new room on the birth of a baby is to be accomplished so that the child "feels that he is graduating because he is a big boy."[26] The clever parent deflects the child's grievances.

Discipline must be internalized. A properly led child, argues Spock, will want to go to bed on time, to sit down at a meal when it is ready, and to eat nutritious food.[27] What Spock expects from the parent-child relationship is what he expects from proper schooling. "A good teacher," he writes in *Baby and Child Care*, "knows that she can't teach democracy out of a book if she's acting like a dictator in person." Encouraged to participate in choosing and planning projects and to work together in carrying them out, students develop the ability to work productively even in the absence of the teacher. "Each one wants to do his share, because he is proud to be a respected member of the group and feels a sense of responsibility to the others." "This," claims Spock, "is the very highest kind of discipline."[28]

Because this method was so widely shared, Spock might well have come to it from any number of sources. Nonetheless, Spock's bloodlines as a progressive educator and advocate of group theory can be traced with some precision, a process that not only makes possible improved understanding of Spock's approach in *Baby and Child Care*, but also confirms that Spock and his methodology were central to the interwar generation.

Spock was introduced to progressive educational theory by Zachry, by Spock's own estimate a person who was to have enormous influence on his ideas of child rearing. Zachry had learned her trade in the heady atmosphere of Columbia University in the 1920s. There, at Teachers College, she earned a doctorate in educational psychology in 1928 under William Kilpatrick. Between 1934 and 1939, with Rockefeller money and within the Progressive Education Association, she conducted a major study of adolescence, ultimately ascribing authoritarian youth to authoritarian maternal influence.[29]

In about 1940, on the rebound from an unsettling and disappointing experience with psychotherapy as a tool for treating maladjustment in children, Spock was drawn to Zachry's emphasis, prominent in the sessions she offered at her Institute on Human Development in New York City, on more practical methods of treatment which could be carried out within the family. Through Zachry, Spock came to see child rearing through the prism of progressive education. The *process* of child rearing took on new importance for him, and he grew convinced of the need to allow the child an opportunity to participate in his own upbringing.[30] The Spock-Zachry link makes it possible to see that Spock's ideas about groups, group decision making, leadership, and social control were directly descended from the Columbia/New York City intellectuals who played such an important formative role in the development of democratic social engineering.

Spock was present at a session of Zachry's institute when Lewin presented his theory of leadership styles, articulating a perspective on small groups and group leadership that would, presumably, surface in *Baby and Child Care*. Lewin was single-minded in his attempts to discover the psychological and sociological conditions conducive to modal forms of government — laissez-faire, democratic, and autocratic.[31] "So revealing," was Lewin's concept of democracy at the psychological level, Spock recalled, that he later shared it with parents.[32]

What was it that Spock responded to with such enthusiasm? Any Lewin presentation after 1939 would likely have included several constructs. Lewin believed that a sense of belonging was essential to human beings, including children, and that belonging was a function of participation in groups. The family was the most important of all groups, and leadership was the primary element in the "atmosphere" of the group. On the basis of experiments he supervised at the University of Iowa in the mid-1930s, Lewin developed a typology of democratic, autocratic, and laissez-faire groups, each dependent for its definition on the style of the group leader. In the "democratic" group, policies were a product of "group determination, encouraged and drawn out by the leader." Leaders suggested alternatives on "technical" matters, but remained apart from much of the actual work undertaken by the group. By 1940, Lewin was convinced that a democratic group could be an efficient institution. Participation in the decision-making process had a significant impact on members. "A process like decision making," he wrote, "is able to affect conduct for many months to come. The decision seems to have a 'freezing' effect which is partly due . . . to the 'commitment to a group.'"[33]

What Kilpatrick had done for education, and Lewin for psychology, Spock would accomplish in child rearing.[34] Spock's family was meant to be a decision-making organization on Lewin's model. The mother leads, avoiding confrontation, if possible allowing the child to determine the course of action, but on her own terms. In the process, the child is not so much liberated as committed to some course of action whose essential limits are determined by the leader-parent.

The idea of the family as a small group was not original with Spock. It was perhaps first given forceful expression by turn-of-the-century religious educator George Albert Coe. A pioneer in democratic methods, Coe argued as early as 1904 against the then-traditional command/obey relationship between parent and child. Compulsion brought changed behavior, but not changed "character" (i.e., no internalization). "Not through mere conformity," he wrote, "but through exercising the functions of a member of the family community, does the character of the child grow."[35]

More than two decades later, teachers frustrated by the continued absence of textbooks in child rearing that reflected this viewpoint turned to the work of Follett. Although Follett never wrote a word explicitly about child rearing, her second book, *Creative Experience* (1924), was curiously influential within the child-development movement. Harold Anderson, who would chair the Department of Psychology at the University of Illinois for nine years in the 1930s, took a position in 1929 as instructor at the Iowa Child Welfare Research Station. He recalled: "When I started this course on mental hygiene of the school child, I took Follett, and asked my graduate students to buy that book and read it, and every time Follett said 'employer,' write in 'parent,' and every time it said 'employee,' write 'child,' and then write your own book on creative experience of children and parents." Attempting to explain the book's appeal (he was not the only teacher to use it in this way), Anderson said:

Now there are different ways of influencing or direct[ing] the behavior of O's [others] . . . by suggestion, persuasion, or command. Now suggestion . . . means that the other person has an opportunity to participate in the decision . . . he can use his decision to take a suggestion or to leave it. . . . He makes the decision as to whether he's going to be persuaded.

Anderson saw in Follett's work new and subtle mechanisms of persuasion. The notebooks of recreational theorist Eduard C. Lindeman (also part of the Columbia environment) reveal that as early as 1932–33, Lindeman had defined personalities as "patterns of response learned primarily in family life" and had conceptualized the pediatrician as someone whose real concern was personality.[36]

While Anderson translated Follett into the realm of child rearing, others developed and elaborated her ideas in terms Spock would have appreciated. With intellectual debts to Follett, Dewey, and Gardner Murphy (Lois' spouse), Frank Walser lamented the assault on democracy, the passing of "the old reverence for authority," and rising levels of conflict between the races, between parents and children, and between teachers and pupils. Walser called for a new "art of conference," to be characterized by "democratic grouping" and the substitution of cooperation for competition in all areas of social conflict. The art of conference, he predicted, would prefigure the spread of "the new habit of pause and calm reasoning" in the home.[37]

When Talcott Parsons and other sociologists founded the Department of Social Relations at Harvard in 1950 and proceeded to proclaim the role of the family as a small group with therapeutic potential, they were only ratifying what American mothers, *Baby and Child Care* in hand, had been doing since 1946. Neither Henry A. Murray's call for a "regenerated system of morality" to be achieved through the family, nor Edward Shils's application of the industrial sociology of Elton Mayo to the family group, nor Parsons' conclusion that personal interaction was the "crucial element in socialization" was really original.[38] Spock had said all of this in *Baby and Child Care*, and he had taken it from Freud, the progressive educators, S. R. Slavson and the group psychotherapists, Lewin, and, intuitively perhaps, from industrial relations. The Parsonians invested family small-group theory with the imprimatur of Harvard and the University of Chicago, but they were essentially latecomers in an invasion of the family that had begun much earlier.

In May of 1968, during protests against the Vietnam War, Columbia University vice-president David Truman charged Spock with having raised an entire generation of youth on an inadequate and harmful diet of permissiveness.[39] In his defense, Spock has argued that moderate strictness and moderate permissiveness are both viable child-rearing methods and that the success of each is dependent upon the "spirit" with which the parent manages the child and the attitude this spirit engenders. Poor results stem from "strictness that comes from harsh feelings" or "permissiveness that is timid or vacillating."[40]

Permissiveness was not laissez-faire.[41] Fearing the development of insecurity in the child, Spock anticipated that parents who allowed their children new levels of "freedom" would obviate potential anxiety by applying such freedom evenly, regularly, routinely, and (paradoxically) with authority. It was essential that the child feel secure, whatever the mode of discipline in which he or she was raised. What Spock had done, in effect, was to enlarge the playpen and put the parent inside — not as boss, but as a leader.

CONCLUSION

The importance of Spock as an interpreter of American culture lies in the degree to which his ideas and methodology of child rearing were common to other aspects of that culture. By this measure, Spock spoke clearly, if not always explicitly, for a generation that had come to maturity in the traumatic decades after 1917. For this generation, what came to be known as permissiveness in child rearing was part of a new democratic authority structure also being tailored for education, industrial relations, even the handling of the aged. Permissiveness was becoming a central characteristic of American life. Spock's infants and children — like the students in progressive education classes, like the old people in the Golden Age Clubs, like the workers in Mayo's factories — would be granted new levels of participation in their own subworld. Always, however, those who offered such freedom expected to achieve through it a heightened obedience to constituted authority. The illusion of independence and the fact of participation in a group decision-making process would encourage commitment to goals that were, in fact, arrived at outside of the group process and to decisions that were, in fact, the product of the calculation and skill of the group leader. Threatened by mass movements, dictators, and what they perceived as the destruction of community life, a significant contingent of American reformers had turned to social psychology, and ultimately to group processes that they defined as democratic, to create a potent new mechanism of social engineering.

7

Declension:
The Postwar Years

The years between 1917 and 1945 might well be understood as the "golden age" of democratic social engineering. In this period, group-process methods penetrated the business system and the federal bureaucracy, came to prominence in recreation and social work, and shaped the operations of Presidents Wilson, Hoover, and Roosevelt. Two world wars, each presented to the American people as a struggle between democracy and some alien ideology, gave democratic methods a special strength.

The postwar history of democratic social engineering is much less unified. I have divided it into three loosely drawn and overlapping periods, each with its own emphasis. The first period, between 1945 and 1960, resembles the "golden age." Democratic social engineering remained the province of educators, child-rearing experts, and others traditionally responsible for social control, and the Cold War provided American democracy with a suitable "totalitarian" enemy. Although democratic social engineering was under attack in certain areas — most notably, in business — its influence expanded in child rearing, the high school, and elsewhere.[1] The second period, from the mid-1950s through the early 1970s, encompasses the beginnings of significant resistance to democratic social engineering as well as the growing use of nondirective or democratic methods by the New Left, the counterculture, and others outside the power structure. In the third period, since 1970, two disparate tendencies have become evident. On the one hand, intellectuals have once again become a dominant force in the history of democratic social engineering, this time as part of a major effort to demystify the origins and operation of social authority. On the other hand, the small, local, and voluntary organizations that have traditionally provided the locus of democratic social engineering have in the

1970s and 1980s been held out by some scholars and social activists as the best hope for a revival of genuine democratic populism.

In the first half of the century, democratic social engineering achieved special prominence in business, education, social work, and recreation, and made some inroads into child rearing and the family. In all of these areas except, perhaps, business, democratic methods remained a significant force in the immediate postwar years.

For family life, Benjamin Spock led the way, conceptualizing the family as a small group and the parent as a group leader, setting down the terms of democratic discipline that later generations would label "permissive." In the thirty years following the appearance of *Baby and Child Care* in 1946, the manual sold 28 million copies in 208 printings,[2] attesting to Spock's enormous influence among parents and children. Entire generations of Americans were introduced to democratic ways of achieving control and consent. Had Spock been an isolated figure, his influence on authority patterns would still have been great. But Spock was not alone. By 1950, academic sociologists had realized the potential of the family as a therapeutic device, reachable through small-group techniques; and in the 1960s and 1970s, family psychotherapy, a discipline saturated with ideas about small groups and leadership that were inseparable from democratic social engineering, took on an importance that pioneer S. R. Slavson could hardly have imagined in the mid-1930s.[3]

Within the social work profession, social group work enjoyed continued influence after 1945, shedding some characteristics and taking on others. As late as the 1950s, there were social-work theorists such as Grace Coyle and Alan Klein for whom the development of democratic habits of participation and decision making remained the primary justification for any social-group-work program. Coyle's continued interest in democratic goals sprang from her belief that social group work was a bulwark against totalitarianism, and that America remained, long after Hitler's defeat, vulnerable to some kind of totalitarian challenge.[4] Gradually, however, the interwar emphasis on using groups to produce a democratic and socially responsible citizenry became less prominent. We have seen how, in the 1950s, those who administered the Golden Age Clubs that Coyle had helped create did so with a much diminished sense of anxiety about what the elderly might do or not do with the vote. As group work moved into mental hospitals, child guidance clinics, and other settings that were narrowly therapeutic, it became more attuned to problems of individual mal-adjustment and less concerned with the social activity of entire groups. Although social group work remained a strong force in a rapidly growing profession, it never regained the conscious, articulated concern with citizenship that had propelled the field in the 1930s and 1940s. Indeed, by 1960 social group workers were in intellectual disarray, unsure about what it was that defined their specialization and lacking the kind of moral purposefulness that had informed the work and thought of an earlier generation.[5]

The word "democracy" continued to have considerable authority for postwar Americans. In the context of the public schools, for example, democracy stood for the hoped-for Americanization and assimilation of a large group of new, working-class students.[6] Nonetheless, the use of democratic methods in education remained uneven. The latest version of Dewey's progressive educational theory, a curriculum package known since the 1930s as the "core curriculum," incorporated teacher-pupil planning, cooperative group planning, and other mechanisms familiar to progressive educators, all toward the goal of producing democratic citizens. Efforts of the United States Office of Education to market the core curriculum to local school districts in the 1940s and 1950s met with limited success. In 1952, only about 3.5 percent of the nation's 24,000 secondary schools had adopted the core curriculum, increasing to some 25 percent in 1960.[7]

The level of acceptance of the core curriculum provides only one measure of the degree to which democratic methods had penetrated the public schools. At the extracurricular level, the participatory method of democratic social engineering grew dramatically in the postwar years (see the photographs on pp. 168–180). In Buffalo, New York, school administrators encouraged the development of school clubs and facilitated the creation of student councils and student courts, even in vocational schools where the core curriculum would have been seen as unsuitable or unworkable. The Buffalo public school system also was the scene of an unusual but influential effort to control student dress — and thus control the spread of juvenile delinquency — through democratic methods. Dress was regulated on a school-by-school basis until 1955, when the Inter-High Council, a student organization representing the Buffalo high schools, developed a voluntary dress code at the suggestion and under the guidance of the associate superintendent. Called Dress-Right, the code was installed with considerable fanfare and by 1957 had become a model for similar programs across the nation. Although the code was always presented as a "democratic enterprise" — indeed, students did draft its specific provisions — it was also clearly an attempt to bypass the unwritten dress code of the peer group and to replace that informal peer-group process of control with a regulatory framework designed and "enforced" by the well-behaved students active in the Inter-High Council.[8]

The application of democratic social engineering was not limited to the schools. In the struggle to contain juvenile delinquency — perhaps the most discussed social problem of the postwar decade — democratic methods played a significant, even vital role. In Buffalo, the tone for local efforts against delinquency was established by popular Children's Court judge Victor Wylegala. "We are entering a critical period," Wylegala wrote in the local newspaper, "a period which could bring disaster to the community's young people."[9] Because juvenile delinquency could "crop up anywhere, under any circumstances," a "constant vigilance" was required. For Wylegala, the most crucial agency of vigilance was the democratic family. "The wise parent," Wylegala wrote, "will let youngsters make decisions in small matters on their own. For more important questions, a child can be made to believe he is making the decision while his parents have in reality already set out his course at his subconscious level. He gets his direction in a less blunt way and, most important, he gets it with the feeling of responsibility."[10] Nor was the judge unmindful of the therapeutic role of community institutions, including the schools, the churches, the scouts, and the Boys Clubs. Thousands of cases of juvenile delinquency had been solved, he claimed, "by active participation in some community group activity."[11]

While it is difficult to know whether parents followed Wylegala's advice in their homes, there is little doubt of adults' commitment to democratic social engineering in a community context. New York State's postwar teen center program brought youth into the planning process and provided for youth-selected representatives in governance. The local YMCA had a junior leadership club in which boys learned to "participate in group thinking and group decisions" and helped conduct gym and swim classes, while the diocesan youth director urged Catholic Youth Council leaders to allow youths to plan and run their own activities. In conjunction with city government, Buffalo's Catholic and Christian youth councils arranged for youth to "take over" the mayor's office and the City Council for a day.[12]

Democratic social engineering was also applied as a solution to another postwar problem of some magnitude: discrimination. Race riots in Harlem and Detroit, the zoot-suit riots in Los Angeles, and, of course, the virulent anti-Semitism of the Nazis had revealed deep currents of racial, ethnic, and religious hostility. Throughout the late 1940s, Americans sought to eliminate social conflict and discrimination and to understand themselves as a unified people. The word "democracy" represented these goals.

One result of these efforts was the research program of the Commission on Community Interrelations (CCI) of the American Jewish Congress, created to find ways of reducing discrimination directed against minorities and, especially, Jews. In origin and conception, it mirrored the work of The Inquiry, the now-defunct organization established in the wake of World War I to combat discrimination against ethnic and racial minorities. The CCI was established as the research arm of the Congress in September 1944, under the direction of German Jew and Gestalt psychologist Kurt Lewin. Lewin approached this task with the social scientist's faith that an "enduring scientific solution" of social-group conflict could be found, and with the conviction that this enduring solution lay in some form of group management. Although aware of the moral and philosophical implications of "engineering" an end to discrimination in a democratic society, he stopped short of concluding that engineering and democracy were antithetical. In the spirit of B. F. Skinner's *Beyond Freedom and Dignity* (1971), Lewin boldly announced that democracy and social control were compatible. "We do not want group manipulation," he wrote in a statement on the philosophy and goals of the CCI. "But we do need that amount of management of groups which is necessary for harmonious living together. We want this group management to be done 'by the people, for the people.'"[13]

Building on this premise, the CCI sought to carry out a program that was, on the one hand, based on scientific studies of discrimination and, on the other, accessible to the average citizen. The CCI's major research projects included a study of the most effective method of dealing with public anti-Semitic remarks, called the Incident Control Project; several studies analyzing how Jews identified with, and participated in, the Jewish community and the community-at-large; another project surveying the impact of enforced segregation; and still another measuring the extent to which prejudice could be reduced through supervised play in interracial groups. The results of this research were made available to community relations workers, the staffs of organizations such as the YMCA and the Girl Scouts, and government agencies such as the New York State Commission against Discrimination. The findings of the Incident Control Project were distributed through church, women's, veterans', and student organizations.[14]

At home and abroad, the Cold War was prosecuted with methods that bore not the slightest relationship to democratic social engineering — with loyalty oaths and HUAC investigations, with the CIA in Guatemala, with dollars in Vietnam, and with real fighting, by soldiers, in Korea. Nonetheless, there is evidence — fragmentary, admittedly — that nondirective authority and its assumptions had become part of the language in which some Americans, at least, thought about and discussed postwar foreign policy.

In the early 1950s, for example, the State Department addressed the legendary problem of insecurity in an atomic age through a program called Group Conversation. Group Conversation involved assembling persons from different backgrounds to discuss "universals" — family customs, school days, the seasons of the year. Having learned to care for one another, jitters and fears would disappear.[15]

At about the same time, the American Friends Service Committee decided that the Communist "menace" could best be met using small discussion groups. Although the Friends insisted that the discussion group was a "seeking, learning experience and not a platform for the indoctrination of the 'right' ideas by the leader or anyone else," the literature the organization used in these discussions presupposed that some ideas were better than others. A list of questions in *The Enemy Redefined* contained the following gem: "If you lived in a country taken over by Communists, loss of which liberties would you fear most?"[16]

Ideas about participation, discussion, and openness were present in the rarefied atmosphere of international world order. The United Nations could be interpreted as an exercise in democratic social engineering. Although the commitment to democratic process was hardly complete (most foreign policy decisions were made elsewhere; the United States retained and used the Security Council veto), American participation in the United Nations affirmed that the ideology of the open forum had become applicable to foreign affairs. An earlier generation, though committed to domestic applications of democratic methods, had been unwilling to entrust the world of diplomacy to an untested system, and the League of Nations was lost. By 1945, policymakers had apparently become convinced that the national interest required the whole apparatus of the international forum. "Behind this conviction," write historians Norman and Emily Rosenberg and James Moore, "lay certain assumptions: that international conflict often stemmed from breakdowns in communication, that free debate would produce a consensus behind the most convincing argument, and that the American point of view would invariably triumph in an open forum."[17]

The Cold War also contributed to the postwar maturation of pluralism, a political theory in which competing interest groups operated to reduce the likelihood of dominance by extreme factions (e.g., Communism), and the *process* of interest group competition ensured against the emergence of potentially unhealthy fixed purposes.[18] Pluralism was a particular expression, at a particular time, of the broader method of democratic social engineering. The inspiration for this aspect of pluralist theory was John Dewey, who early in the century had argued the need to avoid a priori truth and abstract values. For Dewey this required the nurturing of institutions that would allow the rational, deliberate, and empirically scientific determination of appropriate courses of action. On the plane of political theory, this entailed a view of politics in which "truth" emerged naturally from an ongoing *process* of competition between an array of competing public and private interests.[19] In *The Process of Government* (1908), political scientist Arthur Bentley had contributed to the conflation of means and ends with his insistence that political scientists could profitably study men only as participants in some active relation to other men (and, by implication, influence them only by entering into these active relations).[20] What Dewey and Bentley had discovered was the utility of conceptualizing social and political life as consisting of ongoing processes and interactions.

A second characteristic of pluralist theory was its focus on the central role of interest groups in the political process. This focus had been present in several studies inspired by Bentley's work, including Pendleton Herring's *Group Representation before Congress* (1929) and Belle Zeller's *Pressure Politics in New York* (1937),[21] but it was made explicit in a seminal pluralist tract published in 1951, David Truman's *The Governmental Process*. The book was designed to demonstrate that political interest groups did not distort or endanger the process of government. Truman began with the idea of the group itself, arguing from Dewey and Elton Mayo, among others, that groups were natural constructs through which individuals came to understand and react to their society. A second reason interest groups were not to be feared was that in organizational structure, they had been "molded in conformity with the 'democratic' expectations of the community." That is, most political interest groups held periodic elections of officials and functioned through widespread membership participation in the formulation of policy. Truman identified a variety of ostensibly anti-democratic intragroup phenomena, all associated with leadership. These included internal propaganda, through which leaders could control the channels of communication within the group; secrecy; and off-the-record debate.[22]

But Truman remained unconcerned with these corruptions of democratic process. He believed, on the one hand, that in the long run groups would control their leaders. They would do so because the "democratic mold" in which these groups were cast was part of, and enforced by, a set of social "rules." These rules — essentially a code of democratic behavior — were acquired in the family, in the public schools, and in other basic groups: they were, therefore, sacrosanct. A group that violated the code would lose cohesion, status, and power. Truman believed, on the other hand, that if violations occurred (as he had admitted they did), they were functional. For example: although Truman understood that the referendum was a leadership "tactic," and hence latently undemocratic, the functions assigned to the referendum seemed reasonable enough. Like propaganda, Truman wrote, "it serves primarily to emphasize unity, to give sanction to a previously determined decision, and, by the appearance of wide rank-and-file participation in policy forming, to strengthen the group internally and make it more effective externally."[23] Since Truman did not impugn these functions, we can only conclude that he did not see them as antidemocratic, or at least not seriously so. What we have then, is a lawyer's argument: interest groups could not be structurally or operatively undemocratic, but *even if they were*, it made no difference.

A third reason for Truman's optimism involved his interpretation of how interest groups plugged into the process of government and linked up with other interest groups. In a section of the book bearing a strong relationship to classical economics, Truman argued that interest groups were only "a segment" of a system of influence characterized by a "protean complex of crisscrossing relationships" and a "multiplicity of points of access" to governmental decision-making processes. Because there were so many interest groups, and because interest groups were only part of a much larger system, such groups did not represent a threat to the system's proper functioning. Moreover, because groups had overlapping memberships, interest groups were constantly subject to "the competing claims of other groups *within* a given interest group" and vulnerable to the challenge of potential interest groups that might at any moment coalesce to represent dissatisfied members of existing organizations.[24]

Certainly Truman was not a democratic social engineer in the sense that Coyle was, or Mayo. Internal group processes — the essential stuff of democratic social engineering — were for him secondary to questions of access. Unlike most theorists of group leadership, Truman was less concerned with controlling a potentially unstable democratic population or group membership than with explaining how undemocratic tactics would not upset the effective functioning of the political system. Nonetheless, Truman shared with democratic social engineers the conviction that groups were crucial social units, and he was hardly oblivious to their internal operations. Most important, the emphases in Truman's pluralism on the decision-making process and on open access to that process had their counterparts in earlier representations of group-process theory that bore no relationship to politics. It had long been an article of faith among group-process theorists that participation, whether apparent or actual, was essential to the modification of behavior. Truman's principle of access to this process is analogous to the group-process idea that within a given group, individuals must have their own kind of access — to discussion, to selection of leaders, to decision making. Truman's pluralism was a special brand of democratic social engineering, related to older forms but now applied to an entire political system.

A second classic of 1950s pluralism, Robert A. Dahl's *A Preface to Democratic Theory* (1956), is especially revealing of the contradictions inevitably generated by a political theory that claimed at once to be a mechanism of social control and a vehicle for popular governance. In the opening pages of the *Preface*, Dahl took up the central problem of just what "democracy" and "democratic theory" were. "I do not promise to define 'democracy' rigorously," he wrote, "but at a minimum . . . democratic theory is concerned with processes by which ordinary citizens exert a relatively high degree of control over leaders . . ." Dahl added to this conception with the claim that elections, while ineffective indicators of preference, were essential in "controlling leaders."[25] Elsewhere, however, Dahl described the evolution of American politics in language replete with images suggestive of social disorder:

It is not a static system. The normal American system has evolved, and by evolving it has survived. It has evolved and survived from aristocracy to mass democracy, through slavery, civil war, the tentative uneasy reconciliation of North and South, the repression of Negroes and their halting liberation; through two great wars of world-wide scope, mobilization, far-flung military enterprise, and return to hazardous peace; through numerous periods of economic instability and one prolonged depression with mass unemployment, farm "holidays," veterans' marches, tear gas, and even bullets; through two periods of postwar cynicism, demagogic excesses, invasions of traditional liberties, and the groping, awkward, often savage, attempt to cope with problems of subversion, fear, and civil tension.

Democracy, Dahl concluded, "appears to be a relatively efficient system for reinforcing agreement, encouraging moderation, and maintaining social peace in a restless and immoderate people operating a gigantic, powerful, diversified, and incredibly complex society."[26] What, then, was democracy? A kind of populism in which "ordinary citizens" managed to control their leaders? Or a system designed to bring order to a society perpetually on the verge of social excesses led by veterans, farmers, the unemployed, and other "ordinary" citizens? This choice — a choice, really, between the ideology of democracy and its intent — appears clearly in *A Preface to Democratic Theory*, but it is not peculiar to Dahl's work. Indeed, it is a dichotomy present in the writings of Mayo, Coyle, William H. Kilpatrick, and other theorists and, in fact, inherent in the very idea of a system of social control operating through a democratic method.

To this catalogue of arenas in which democratic social engineering either penetrated or grew in strength in the immediate postwar years, one must append a possible exception. In business, participatory management techniques appear to have only held their own in the postwar decade. Although "soft" methods of labor control remained important to companies with liberal management, the thrust of managerial ideology was toward the recovery and defense of "management prerogatives." Convinced that managerial control had eroded during the war, that there was no middle democratic way between managed mass production and "mob production," and that the future of free-enterprise capitalism was at stake, the typical postwar firm was combative rather than "cooperative" in its labor relations policies.[27]

THE AGE OF REVOLT, 1955–1975

The turbulent 1960s brought two developments of significance for the history of democratic social engineering. The first was a surge of new interest in democratic, participatory forms. The second, cutting at cross-purposes to the first, was the equally rapid development of an intense cynicism about certain aspects of authority in a democracy.

A distinguishing characteristic of the 1960s interest in participation was its apparent distance from the social-control establishment. In *Social Control* (1901), Edward A. Ross had pointed out that the business of keeping order was in modern society given over to "professionals" — to rulers, priests, schoolmasters, and magistrates — as well as to less specialized lawmakers, editors, and educators.[28] In contrast, many 1960s advocates of participation were students and social activists who seemed to be less interested in maintaining order than in disrupting it.

Students for a Democratic Society (SDS) called for an open and democratic society, one allowing for full public participation in policymaking through a restructured system of political parties and voluntary associations.[29] Although saddled with its own bureaucracy, SDS also managed to practice participatory democracy, often at the cost of "long, formless mass meetings."[30] Tom Hayden, responsible for articulating an SDS program and ideology, was aware of the sterility of student government and of the coercive power of "group unity." He advocated "critical, freewheeling discussion" and praised Dewey as the source of a persistent, restless, and penetrating social radicalism built on inquiry.[31] Women activists would later raise the possibility that SDS's unstructured forms of participatory democracy created the likelihood of male dominance. "Women were excluded," writes Sara Evans, "not necessarily by design, but thoroughly nonetheless."[32]

If the counterculture differed from the New Left in its attitude toward politics and social reform, there is evidence of certain shared attitudes toward authority. Take, for example, Ken Kesey's Merry Pranksters, described by Tom Wolfe in *The Electric Kool-Aid Acid Test* (1968). The Pranksters seemed to operate on the brink of anarchy. They made decisions spontaneously and organically, rather than deliberately. They rejected the guidance of the past for the nonguidance of the present, and, in some sense, refused to acknowledge the function of leadership. Kesey, whose influence over the group was actually profound, was nonetheless called the "non-navigator" and the "non-teacher."[33]

The contested terrain of education produced some of the most interesting literature on participation. And every important statement on the subject, including Jerry Farber's "The Student as Nigger" (1967), Neil Postman and Charles Weingartner's *Teaching as a Subversive Activity* (1969), and Charles E. Silberman's *Crisis in the Classroom* (1971), had Dewey's emphases on process and participation in central roles.[34]

Originally published in the Los Angeles *Free Press*, "The Student as Nigger" had a large informal circulation. Brief yet compelling, it was made for the blue ditto, and it was in that form that it became something like folklore for millions of students. "Students are niggers," Farber began. Like plantation slaves, they were denied a voice in decisions that affected them. Instead, they were "allowed to have a toy government run for the most part by Uncle Toms and concerned principally with trivia." According to Farber, a master-slave relationship defined the educational process in American colleges. Faculty told the student what courses to take, what to read, what to believe, and "where to set the margins on his typewriter." Worse still, students went along with it:

They haven't gone through twelve years of public school for nothing. They've learned one thing and perhaps only one thing during those twelve years. They've forgotten their algebra. They've grown to fear and resent literature. They write like they've been lobotomized. But, Jesus, can they follow orders! Freshmen come up to me with an essay and ask if I want it folded, and whether their name should be in the upper right hand corner. And I want to cry and kiss them and caress their poor tortured heads.[35]

Although Farber attempted to explain *why* education had become trapped in this authoritarian mold, "The Student as Nigger" was less successful here, focusing on the psychological needs of teachers. Two years later, Farber offered a more complex explanation as well as a way out. In language that rang of Dewey and Marshall McLuhan, Farber affirmed that "the medium in school truly is the message. And the medium is, above all, coercive." Farber raised the specter of an American fascism, grounded in an authoritarian school environment that was itself composed of hundreds of petty authoritarian acts. And behind it all was a class-based economic and business system, churning out "good little Americans. . . . We learn how to take the crap that's going to be shoveled on us all our lives." Running the show were "the power centers," the big corporations and government agencies that had the most to gain from maintaining the status quo and from restricting the range of options that seemed real and possible to ordinary people. The product of this authoritarian system, wrote Faber, "doesn't expect a wide range to choose from in politics. His chief arena of choice is the marketplace, where he can choose enthusiastically among forty or fifty varieties of cigarette, without, incidentally, ever being tempted to choose the one variety that will turn him on."

If the medium was the message, the solution was to change the medium. As if he had copied it from Dewey, Farber went on to assert the importance of "democracy" (which he defined as "power in the hands of the people") and to insist that the achievement of this ideal lay in revamping the educational process. "The way to educate children for democracy," wrote Farber, "is to let them do it — that doesn't mean allowing them to practice empty forms, to make pretend decisions or to vote on trivia; it means that they participate in the real decisions that affect them. You learn democracy in school not by defining it or by simulating it but by doing it."[36]

These sanguine, Populist reinventions of the nation's tradition of democratic, participatory authority were rendered in the midst of a dawning consciousness that authority was exercised in harmful ways that had not been previously understood. With that consciousness came rebellion against portions of the framework of democratic authority — against, for example, the sacred cow of participation or the act of assisting in the process of authority. By the mid-1960s, elements of both right and left had lost faith in democratic methods and taken up more authoritarian ones.

Advocates of democratic authority had long understood that its practice required the participation of those who were to be subdued, controlled, reformed, socialized, or otherwise affected. It was not simply that persons had to be gathered in groups in order to be efficiently reached, although this was certainly part of it. More important was the belief that the act of participation — of planning a project, of entering into a discussion, of helping make a decision — was a major ingredient in the larger act of social education that was taking place.

Therefore, when reaction came, it was a reaction characterized by nonparticipation and withdrawal. As a movement, nonparticipation began in the aftermath of the Second World War, with what became known, in 1952, as the "beat generation." The "beats," or "beatniks" as they would soon be called, were a subculture, for whom involvement was fleeting and personal, rather than committed and social. The beats withdrew physically, into the darkened recesses of coffee houses, into the world of marijuana, into the distancing enclosure of the automobile, into the protection of being in transit. Although not without political opinions, they withdrew from politics. More important for our purposes, they withdrew from the matrix of organizations, from which generations of social engineers had fashioned mechanisms of control; one can search long and hard in Jack Kerouac's 1957 classic *On the Road* without finding any evidence of families, clubs, businesses, schools, churches, and forums. Kerouac and his friends understood that they were safe from organized socialization only in small, unstructured, and transitory groups of close friends. Kerouac's search for an authority-free environment led ultimately to a vision of life-in-motion.[37]

Evidence of withdrawal also emerges from the voting statistics. Between 1948 and 1980, the percent of the civilian resident voting-age population casting ballots for president declined consistently — virtually every four years — to a thirty-two-year low in 1980. Accurately enough, the Port Huron Statement, the manifesto drawn up in 1962 by the first convention of the SDS, described Americans as being "in withdrawal from public life, from any collective effort at directing their own affairs."[38]

Although the Port Huron Statement was ultimately an optimistic document, full of faith in the possibilities of democratic participation, it never strayed far from the conclusion that a corrupted democracy was itself the core of the American rebellion against participation. Hayden located the source of apathy (i.e., nonparticipation) in "social institutions," in higher education itself. He understood that the university and other institutions operated through democratic forms; he understood democratic social engineering. He attacked student government for establishing the limits and style of controversy, for discouraging initiative, and for training "those who want to spend their lives in political pretense." Voters were victimized by "pseudo-problems," by banal political campaigns, and by a party system that failed to produce genuine alternatives.[39]

As the nation deepened its involvement in Vietnam and took up the problems of race and the cities, Americans became more conscious of the issue of authority and more knowledgeable about the uses, abuses, and limitations of democratic methods. The Free Speech Movement at the University of California at Berkeley in 1964 occurred, in part, over the question of democracy, and especially over the university's claim to neutrality. Although the university had by its own admission become politically involved — linked, for example, to the national defense program — it continued to insist on its neutrality. By the fall of 1964, the issue had come to a head over a series of university regulations governing the rights of students to engage in political activity on and off the campus. The regulations were framed in the language of democracy. One set aside a "free speech" area, where students could distribute political literature. Another limited distributed materials to those that were "informative" rather than "advocative" or "persuasive." The students soon discovered that behind the rhetoric of freedom and evenhandedness were political intentions quite at cross-purposes to those of the students. The original "free speech" area was outside the main campus traffic pattern. The prohibition of advocacy was a way of preventing students from engaging in off-campus political activity that might endanger the ties between the university and the conservative local community.[40] The Berkeley revolt took place in the context of the students' growing understanding that beneath the administration's discourse of democracy was a thinly disguised partisanship. The university had not gone the whole way and brought students into the regulatory process; it had used democracy as a mechanism of control.

Much the same perception was responsible for the teach-ins that came to the college campuses in 1965. They were inspired, at first, by Lyndon Johnson's announcement of the first sustained bombing raids on North Vietnam. Like the Free Speech Movement, however, they were also part of a growing conviction that the democratic process was not really democratic. Protesting students and faculty first directed their ire at a clumsy and inadequate State Department White Paper justifying the bombing, then at State Department "truth teams" that arrived on college campuses to defend the White Paper, explain the war, and counter the teach-ins.[41] On one level, the issues were substantive: why were we in Vietnam? why were we bombing North Vietnam? But on another level, they were procedural, wrapped up in the Johnson administration's efforts to monopolize the channels of communication and information and to indoctrinate the American population through processes that were ostensibly educative.

So acute was the mid-1960s consciousness of authority that even the most free-spirited elements of the counterculture were discovered to have an interest in control. In *The Electric Kool-Aid Acid Test,* Tom Wolfe claimed that Kesey's Pranksters had adopted their anarchic style not to transcend society but to push it along. They sought control. The Pranksters had brought the Hell's Angels to their Bay Area retreat and, benefiting from Kesey's mountain-man leadership, controlled them (i.e., the Pranksters survived). The Beatles could not be so easily subdued; they could not be made to participate in a film the Pranksters were producing. "But we can," Wolfe paraphrased, "imagine them into the movie and work them into the great flow of acausal connection and then it will happen of its own accord."[42] Even within the Pranksters' group, Wolfe found that informal processes had taken the place of traditional rules. In the selection of members, for example, the Pranksters had renounced blackballing, probationary periods, and other devices characteristic of college fraternities. "And yet," Wolfe wrote, "there was a period of proving yourself, and everyone knew it was going on and no one ever said a word about it."[43] In short, Wolfe was arguing that in governing themselves and in relating to the outside world, the Pranksters practiced an anarchic form of democratic social engineering.[44]

While Hayden, Wolfe, and others found too much power in places where it ought not to have been, a well-known behavioral psychologist wrote contemptuously of the weakness of the democracy approach. In *Beyond Freedom and Dignity,* Harvard University's B. F. Skinner looked squarely at existing democratic methods of control and found them all either ineffective or intellectually fraudulent. Progressive educational methods were ineffective. "Guidance" — for example, in the education of small children — was little more than a myth of individualism. "One who merely guides a natural development," Skinner argued, "cannot easily be accused of trying to control it. Growth remains an achievement of the individual, testifying to his freedom and worth . . ."[45] Interviewed at the American Psychological Association meeting in Washington, D.C., Skinner said: "We're all controlled all the time. Parents control children and employers control employees — and they do it badly." For Skinner, guidance, persuasion, and permissiveness were not, as many Americans believed, neutral techniques that magically preserved freedom and dignity, self-reliance and individualism. To the extent that they worked, they were, indeed, techniques of control; to the extent that they did not work, they simply left room for other forms of control. As Skinner wrote, "the fundamental mistake made by all those who choose weak methods of control is to assume that the balance of control is left to the individual, when in fact it is left to other conditions."[46] The alternative to ineffective systems of control, Skinner suggested, was a more elaborate and more effective system of operant conditioning.[47]

THE DEMYSTIFICATION OF AUTHORITY, 1960 —

The sensitivity toward authority that characterized politics, education, generational rebellion, campus protest, and other areas of American life in the postwar era had an intellectual component as well. In political science, sociology, English, history, and other disciplines, a new generation of American, British, and French scholars began to probe the foundations of authority in the twentieth-century Western democracies. An earlier generation had framed the subject in terms of elections, dictatorship, overt conflicts, the media, the "people," military might, and other "visible" contestants in, or manifestations of, the struggle for power. This one began from the assumption that what was visible, legible, and overt might be less significant than authority that was invisible, illegible, or covert. Many scholars have penetrated one or more of the mechanisms of democratic authority, including participation, inquiry, the group, or the concept of a circumscribed choice. And two — David Riesman and Christopher Lasch — have, albeit elliptically and in their own frameworks of the "lonely crowd" and the "culture of narcissism," written about the system that I have labeled democratic social engineering.

Most of the scholars that were part of this movement were children of Vietnam or Watergate. They had heard a complex Asian civil war described as Communist aggression, the bombing of North Vietnam called "protective reaction," a corrupt and dictatorial regime in the south propped up in the name of freedom, promises to end the war carried out half a decade after they were made. Watergate produced the simplest of lessons: even the president lied. So it was that this generation of intellectuals — pretty much, but not entirely, a left-wing bunch — became deeply suspicious of the visible and the obvious, and thus committed to creating a more readable world.

One sign of the increasing sensitivity to authority was the revival of interest in the work of Italian philosopher Antonio Gramsci.[48] In extensive notebooks kept while he was a prisoner of the fascists in the 1920s and 1930s, Gramsci developed a theory of social engineering that has come to be identified by the word "hegemony." Gramsci began with the assumption that society was composed of two classes. "There really are rulers and ruled, leaders and led," he emphasized. "The entire science and art of politics are based on this primordial and . . . irreducible fact." The dominance of one class over another — the dominance of the bourgeoisie over the working class — was maintained through politics. But politics for Gramsci meant much more than a system of elections, much more even than a democratic system of elections in which all men had the vote. Politics was "the art of governing men, of securing their permanent consent."[49]

Politics, then, was a process that encompassed all the institutions and mechanisms of class dominance. Gramsci divided politics into two distinct arenas: "political society," which consisted of public institutions — the courts, police, army, bureaucracy, and the electoral process — and "civil society," a matrix of public and private institutions and organizations, such as schools, churches, clubs, parties, and journals.[50] Civil society was the crucial apparatus of hegemony, the larger process by which the ruling class secured and maintained the consent of the governed.

Eugene D. Genovese and T. J. Jackson Lears are among those scholars who have claimed to find in Gramsci's hegemony evidence that the domination of the working class was considerably less than complete. Both rely on Gramsci's suggestion that "man-in-the-mass" had "two theoretical consciousnesses," one "implicit in his activity," the other "inherited from the past and uncritically absorbed."[51] While this would seem to allow the subordinate to grant his consent with one consciousness while withholding it with the other, Gramsci is explicit about the powerful hold of the second kind of consciousness: it "influences moral conduct and the direction of will, with varying efficacity but often powerfully enough to produce . . . a condition of moral and political passivity."[52] In addition, Lears interprets Gramsci's discussion of "spontaneous philosophy" as a defense of the existence of private and autonomous feelings with the potential for development into counterhegemonies. While Gramsci's language is perhaps sufficiently ambiguous to allow for this reading, Gramsci made clear his view that ideas and opinions were not "'spontaneously born' in each individual brain: they have had a centre of formation, of irradiation, of dissemination, of persuasion."[53] True, Gramsci acknowledged the "moments in history in which a class or group discovers its objective and subjective unity in action." But, he emphasized, in "normal times" its conduct was "not independent and autonomous, but submissive and [intellectually] subordinate."[54]

Gramsci understood that complete and permanent domination was never achieved through hegemony — the ruling class often had to resort to force and to continually renew its hegemonic efforts. Nonetheless, his hegemony was a powerful and insidious process. In language full of irony, Gramsci described hegemony as "turning necessity and coercion into 'freedom,'" and as perpetuating an ideal in which "the individual can govern himself without his self-government thereby entering into conflict with political society . . ." The institutions of hegemony were everywhere. The state, for example, might pursue an unpopular action by creating a public opinion to support it. The schools were hegemonic institutions (Gramsci feared the new student-centered education; "the more the new curricula nominally affirm and theorise the pupil's activity and working collaboration with the teacher, the more they are actually designed as if the pupil were purely passive"). Even the most loosely organized institutions served hegemonic purposes. The "popular assembly"-type political clubs of the French Revolution, for example, were for Gramsci only a medium of elite domination. "Certainly, among those who frequented the clubs," he wrote, "there must have existed tight, select groupings of people who knew each other, who met separately and prepared the climate of the meetings, in order to support one tendency or another."[55] The more elaborate political forms of parliamentary government and universal suffrage were also inseparable from the hegemonic apparatus. The act of voting was not a grant of consent in any meaningful sense; it was an expression of a consent that had been carefully prepared and educated. Thus the counting of votes was but "the final ceremony of a long process." Democracy was a myth, an "ideological bluff." Anticipating an argument made in 1960 by Sheldon Wolin, Gramsci sought to demonstrate that sociology, and even science itself, were varieties of political activity and political thought, and hence elements of the hegemonic order.[56]

Modern theorists of authority have been especially interested in a phenomenon implicit in Gramsci's conceptualization of hegemony: the disappearance — or apparent disappearance — of conflict in authority relations. Wolin, and more recently John Kenneth Galbraith, traced this disappearance in part to the classical liberal economics of Adam Smith. "What was truly radical in liberalism," wrote Wolin, "was its conception of society as a network of activities carried on by actors who knew no principle of authority. Society represented not only a spontaneous and self-adjusting order, but a condition untroubled by the presence of authority."[57]

Christopher Lasch noted a similar absence of conflict, especially within what Gramsci called hegemonic institutions. Through an explication of the work of French scholar Jacques Ellul, Lasch explained his own belief in the importance of conflict: "For Ellul, the most serious moral and social issues revolve around relationships — parent and child, man and woman, teacher and pupil, man and God — in which there is an irreducible element of tension. In modern society, however, tensions are banished from all realms but the political." Thus parenting had become a process of bargaining and negotiating, and teaching an agreeable game in which students "learn without pain" from a "permissive leader." By abdicating legitimate "moral and intellectual authority," parents and teachers, Lasch believed, had deprived their charges of the reasonable conflict necessary to the development of the healthy personality.[58]

Most writers engaged in demystifying authority believed that the plane of politics, once considered the beginning and the end of authority relations, had receded in importance and had been replaced by some other system of authority. Wolin developed the idea in *Politics and Vision* (1960). Responding, implicitly, to ideologues who were proclaiming the emergence of a grand social consensus that subsumed all ideology and conflict, Wolin insisted that the "political" had not declined. It had, instead, been diffused, "transferred to another plane," absorbed into nonpolitical private institutions. Put another way, personal authority — "authority whose power was visible and traceable to a specific person" — had by the late eighteenth century been displaced by a new source of authority called "society." The power of society, Wolin wrote, was "impersonal and was directed against all of the members indifferently. Society was no single individual: it was none of it, yet it was all of us." The nineteenth-century positivists, with their emphasis on the existence of natural, discoverable "laws" of human conduct and social organization, were for Wolin the theorists of the new social authority, for these laws "carried prescriptive injunctions to which men ought to conform." By 1900, what once had been clearly political had been buried under the "quest for community" and the "adoration of organization."[59]

The tendency to depreciate the role of the state was also present in the work of French social theorist Michel Foucault. "Power," wrote Foucault, "isn't localised in the State apparatus . . . nothing in society will be changed if the mechanisms of power that function outside, below and alongside the State apparatuses, on a much more minute and everyday level, are not also changed." Like Wolin, Foucault described a modern system of authority (power, as he called it) that emerged in the seventeenth and eighteenth centuries, when the question of "obtaining productive service from individuals in their concrete lives" became paramount. Repressive power — the power of violence and coercion — was insufficient and unworkable in this context. "What makes power hold good," he wrote, "is simply the fact that it doesn't only weigh on us as a force that says no, but that it traverses and produces things, it induces pleasure, forms knowledge, produces discourse. It needs to be considered as a productive network which runs through the whole social body." Thus Foucault sought to understand power at levels beneath the obviously political: at the level of gesture, discourse, and learning process. The idea of "inquiry," for example, usually understood as a neutral, scientific search for objective truth, was for Foucault a process full of political import, carried out with conscious ideological purpose. Similarly, the institution of the people's court, a staple of the revolutionary situation, contained within it subtle mechanisms by which popular justice was strangled and controlled. This process was accomplished through institutions — "a table, a chairman, magistrates, confronting the two opponents" — that by their very presence confirmed the existence of certain penal categories (theft, fraud) and certain moral categories (honesty, dishonesty), as well as the assumption that the contending parties would abide by and submit to these categories.[60]

Richard Sennett's *Authority* (1980) contained a similar historical overview. Sennett wrote as if the state hardly mattered, and as if physical force were no longer an ingredient in authority. The problem, as Sennett defined it, was the nineteenth-century one of constructing a system of authority on the ruins of the French and Industrial Revolutions. In this context, authority became less a matter of physical violence or the threat of it, and more a function of "controls like shame . . . controls less palpable than physical pain but equal in their subduing effect."[61] Among these controls was paternalism, a system designed on the one hand to make authority palpable (i.e., to represent authority in a person) but on the other hand to disguise it (through a metaphor: a boss is a father). A second form of authority, developed in the nineteenth century and carried over into the twentieth, involved "autonomy," a word that for Sennett meant self-possession or self-discipline. Autonomous power "seems to come from nowhere, to be impersonal."[62] Sennett used the word "influence" to describe some of the specific mechanisms of autonomous power, including the participative and democratic tactics of the human relations school of labor relations. "The idea of influence," Sennett concluded, "is thus the ultimate expression of autonomy. Its effect is to mystify what the boss wants and what the boss stands for. Influence directed to making workers more content with their work denies them a similar freedom; the nature of the contentments is designed for them. Pleasure is expected to erase confrontation. However, the influencers do not say who they are, what they stand for, or what they expect; the influences are not rules but stimulations. It is up to the subordinate to find the design. This is the most extreme example of a saying of Hegel's: the injustice of society is that the subordinate must make sense of what power is."[63]

Increasing subtlety over time is also the dominant paradigm in John Kenneth Galbraith's schematic *The Anatomy of Power* (1983). Over two centuries, according to Galbraith, condign power (force) had yielded gradually to compensatory power (money) and finally, in the twentieth century, to conditioned power (persuasion). Under a system that operates by conditioned power — that is, by "changing belief" — power might be so subtly exercised that "the fact of submission is not recognized."[64] Galbraith also appreciated the role that democracy in its traditional political forms could play in obfuscating power. "Nothing better conceals the exercise of power in and through the state," he writes, "than the political litany, undertaken virtually as a form of religious office, that all men and women come equally in their sovereignty to the polling place and are subject to the result in accordance with the will of the majority."[65]

David Noble dealt no less perceptively with a more limited topic, the role of engineers and engineering in the half century after 1880. According to Noble, authority and domination were hidden within a profession, engineering, and a phenomenon, technology, that purported to be independent and autonomous. Noble defined technology as a "mode of organizing and perpetuating (or changing) social relationships . . . and an instrument for control and domination." He conceptualized engineers — the agents of technology — as advocates of corporate growth, stability, and control. Their labors in behalf of business have been difficult to observe and understand, argued Noble, because they were carried out under the banner of science.[66]

In a section of his book dealing with labor-management relations, Noble described the post-1915 transition from an authoritarian system of scientific management to a system of "human relations" that incorporated some of the methods of democratic social engineering. The new system of labor control was founded on the "consent" of the worker (Noble puts the word in quotation marks), who "had to be made to feel that he was participating in all management decisions that affected him."[67]

Political scientists have not been so willing to deny the viability of the political process, but some of them have managed to redefine that process in ways that sharpen the definition of authority. Peter Lyman has recently argued, for example, that American culture represses certain kinds of political speech. Women, blacks, and other groups that express their frustration at domination through "angry" speech risk having their anger labeled "irrational," "emotional," or "unstable," and their protest itself described as "mob behavior" or "riot." These descriptions — and reason itself — are thus elements of a code of behavior designed to "deny anger its political power" and to devalue the content of the speech or protest. This code exists, according to Lyman, because of the perceived need to deny the authenticity of a politics of anger. Angry speech must be ridiculed not only because the "culture" does not wish to see the goals of blacks and women realized, but also because angry speech itself "questions the rationality of social order and the fairness of the rules of participation in rational discourse."[68]

In *Power: A Radical View* (1974), Steven Lukes made a more general argument and developed it within the parameters of mainstream political science. Lukes divided analyses of power into what he called 1-dimensional, 2-dimensional, and 3-dimensional views. The 1-dimensional view corresponded to the "pluralist" view of power, and was represented by the work of Robert Dahl. Its focus was on concrete behavior, decision making, and "issue-areas" (including the assumption that struggles over concrete issues involved actual conflict). The 2-dimensional view, represented in the 1960s collaborations of Peter Bachrach and Morton Baratz, broadened the definition of power to include nondecisions that might prevent potential issues from becoming actual ones.[69]

Lukes found even the 2-dimensional view inadequate. Two-dimensional theory, he argued, assumed that non-decision-making power operated only when identifiable grievances existed which could be denied a place in the political process. According to Lukes, a lack of identifiable grievances did not demonstrate consensus. "Is it not the most supreme and most insidious exercise of power," he asked, "to prevent people, to whatever degree, from having grievances by shaping their perceptions, cognitions and preferences in such a way that they accept their role in the existing order of things. . . . To assume that the absence of grievance equals genuine consensus is simply to rule out the possibility of false or manipulated consensus."[70]

Several theorists of authority have been especially sensitive to the issue of participation and skeptical of participatory democracy as a reachable goal. This skepticism is summarized in a conjugation recalled by Bertram Gross and printed in his *Friendly Fascism* (1980):

I participate.	We participate.
You (singular) participate.	You (plural) participate.
He, she or it participates.	THEY decide.[71]

On the whole, Gross's framework for understanding power is not one that much concerns us here. He described a "new form of despotism" composed of "complexes" — the military-industrial complex, the nuclear-power complex, and the communications complex, for example. But within this framework, participatory democracy disguised and protected the dominance of business, sidetracked dissidents, and sometimes became an instrument of repression.[72] Gross was suspicious of teaching machines ("the programmed students are given the feeling of participation by their having to provide answers to carefully administered questions"), certain plebiscites (illusionary participation by TV viewers), and student government ("sidetracking the energy of activists and paving the way for a quick return to passivity"). On Huey Long's dictum "Sure, we'll have fascism, but it will come disguised as Americanism," Gross remarked, "if he were alive today, I am positive he would add the words, 'and democracy.'"[73]

Ellul also commented on the link between democracy and control. Although Ellul's subject was propaganda, what he described was something like Gramsci's hegemony, a system of social influence and persuasion that pervaded the behavior and thought of every individual. The relationship between propaganda and democracy was paradoxical. Propaganda corrupted democracy and made the "true exercise of it almost impossible." But if democracy and propaganda were incompatible, they were also, in the American context, inseparable. Propaganda emanated from the ideological center of the culture, reflecting its most important presuppositions and expressing its deepest currents.[74] In America, these presuppositions and currents had been closely associated with democracy, and democracy's propaganda — i.e., its hegemonic system — had, therefore, been closely tied to the democratic process. "Stalinist propaganda," as Ellul explained it, "was in great measure founded on Pavlov's theory of the conditioned reflex. Hitlerian propaganda was in great measure founded on Freud's theory of repression and libido. *American propaganda is founded in great measure on Dewey's theory of teaching.*"[75]

Certain aspects of Ellul's commentary are peculiarly relevant to the American experience. Ellul's book was almost entirely concerned with what he called "sociological propaganda." Like Gramsci's "civil society" and what I have labeled democratic social engineering, sociological propaganda operated through a culture's existing organizations and institutions, including, according to Ellul, the schools, the factories, the social service agencies, and the movies. Because Americans coveted a "uniform" society, their propaganda had emphasized integrative functions, including active participation in group life. This brought Ellul to what he called "horizontal propaganda," or propaganda made inside a group in which the propagandist was a discussion leader. The result was a propaganda uniquely American in its nondirective character. Sociological propaganda operated "imperceptibly," "spontaneously," and as "a sort of persuasion from within." Through a process of small-group dialectic characteristic of horizontal propaganda, it produced "voluntary" rather than "mechanical" adherence to desired norms.[76]

The postwar literature on authority also includes two books — Lasch's *The Culture of Narcissism* (1978), and David Riesman's *The Lonely Crowd* (1950) — that might be seen as direct antecedents of the current study. Written in the malaise of the late 1970s, *The Culture of Narcissism* described a "crisis of confidence" in Western, capitalist culture. The product of this long-developing crisis was the "new narcissist," an inadequate and dependent being capable of happiness only in a "therapeutic" climate. These therapeutic climates, according to Lasch, were dominated by experts, managerial and professional classes, and corporations that had their own ideas of what ought to be done and pursued them through bureaucracies that housed many of the narcissists. Within those bureaucracies — and within families, schools, and other institutions just as deeply affected by the culture of narcissism — a "body of therapeutic theory and practice," what Lasch also referred to as "therapeutic forms of social control," fed off the narcissist's hunger for security and self-esteem.[77]

Beneath this terminology is the world of democratic social engineering. Lasch's "body of therapeutic theory and practice" included progressive education and progressive child rearing, small groups, discussions, participatory modes of industrial relations, and "democratic" family practices. Administering the therapy were psychiatrists, child-development experts, juvenile court judges, human relations personnel, teachers, social workers and, it seems, parents — many of the same people who fill the pages above. As a class, the "new narcissists" were simply those who occupied the social environments — the clubs, small groups, and bureaucracies — that have been the primary vehicles of democratic social engineering.[78] Finally, there is a sense in which Lasch's use of the word "therapeutic" corresponds to my word "democratic." As Lasch uses the term, therapeutic implies the participation of the oppressed in his/her own oppression. Medical jurisprudence, for example, intentionally "implicates the offender in his own control"; in a psychiatric situation, the deviant's cooperation with the therapist marks the beginning of the healing process.[79]

The Lonely Crowd was written in another rather desperate era, the late 1940s, when a series of centralizing, bureaucratizing, and conformity-inducing events and impulses, including the war, the Red Scare, and growth of the mass media, seemed to have set individualism on a course to extinction. Riesman and his co-authors claimed to have observed a change in the "social character" of the American people, from the aggressive, independent, "inner-directed" type dominant in the nineteenth century, to an adjustment-oriented, "other-directed" type increasingly characteristic of the twentieth century. In most respects, Riesman's approach was very different from my own. He was in search of the "American character," and he was particularly concerned with discovering why modern Americans seemed so given to conformity and so willing to forego the entrepreneurial personality that a previous age had found so productive. Furthermore, Riesman had little interest in the notion of social engineering as a mechanism employed by one segment of the population against another. General changes in social character were for Riesman a function not of social engineering but of socialization, the broad process by which the social heritage was transmitted from one generation to another.[80]

Yet when it came to delineating the mechanisms and institutions of socialization responsible for other-direction, Riesman focused on groups (including the family, the classroom, and the peer group), group processes, leadership, and other elements of what I have called democratic social engineering. Lacking the roles and standards of their nineteenth-century counterparts, modern parents had resorted to "personnel" methods of manipulation and rationalizing. Teachers, for their part, had lost sight of a "curriculum" and had instead taken to giving lessons in cooperation. The adolescent peer group, too, rejected such values as independence in judgment and the acquisition of skills while rewarding adherence to fashion and other group-based but standardless norms. Although Riesman acknowledged the continued strength of the nineteenth-century ideology of free enterprise and individualism, the purpose of *The Lonely Crowd* was to alert the American people to "an enormous ideological shift favoring submission to the group" and to the debilitating consequences of that shift for personal autonomy.[81]

THE PARTICIPATORY IDEAL, REDIVIVUS

This new awareness of the perils of the group and participation has not, however, swept all opinion before it or even produced a profound cynicism about the possibilities or rationality of building a participatory democracy. The 1970s produced at least two nonleftist studies of authority, each committed in some way to the participatory ideal. Carole Pateman's *Participation and Democratic Theory* (1970) began with the argument that contemporary theorists of democracy had lost sight of the links between participatory structure and democratic character established by Rousseau, John Stuart Mill, Tocqueville, and G. D. H. Cole. Instead, recent theory had developed from the narrow political and pluralist vision of Joseph Schumpeter's *Capitalism, Socialism and Democracy* (1943).[82] Moved by a late-1960s mix of renewed interest in democratic participation and a declining sense of "political efficacy," Pateman argued for a new theoretical emphasis on participation. Convinced by an examination of the academic literature on human relations in industry that "an individual's (politically relevant) attitudes will depend to a large extent on the authority structure of his work environment," Pateman suggested a practical program centered on the democratization of the work place.[83] Pateman seems to have had no sense of, or interest in, the problems of cooptation and manipulation present in democratically organized environments.

Where Pateman's argument had been set forth in classic "objective" academic style, Robert Nisbet's similar statement in *Twilight of Authority* (1975) was unabashedly political. For Nisbet, recent American history was the story of the rise of a "new despotism," characterized by the repudiation of liberalism; the obsolescence of political society; the degradation of language, the university, science, and other mechanisms of social order and creativity; and the decline of kinship, neighborhood, voluntary association, and other humanizing and individualizing agencies. Nisbet lamented the gradual disappearance of "intermediate institutions" and the emergence of that "monolith of power," the state, with its commissions, bureaus, and regulatory agencies. Like most recent scholars of authority, he also understood that the penetration of the state into everyday lives had been accomplished through a change in the nature of authority. Applied and softened through social work, psychiatry, organizations, therapy, and other modern instruments, governmental power, wrote Nisbet, "is today blander, more indirect, engaged in the mobilization of the human mind when possible rather than in the infliction of corporal punishments." Though much concerned about the seepage of power into the "smallest details of human life," Nisbet advocated a return to the very neighborhoods, voluntary associations, and community centers that had been the focus of power-as-therapy (of democratic social engineering), and he remained enamored of the social sciences, through which this social engineering had been accomplished. Nisbet's ideal — of "the spontaneous, of untrammeled, unforced volition" — was admirable enough, and his solution seems the logical one.[84] But finding freedom in small groups would be more difficult than he realized.

Interestingly, Nisbet's libertarian argument had its mirror-image on the left. There, too, activists and academics remained convinced that primary groups and voluntary associations held the key to social reformism. David Moberg, a regular contributor to the national socialist weekly *In These Times*, in 1980 pleaded for a more democratic, participatory approach to home life, child rearing, work, and politics. The theoretical basis for Moberg's argument was derived explicitly from Pateman's doctrine of "political efficacy," and, like Pateman, Moberg was apparently unaware of the extent to which these arenas had been the object of social engineering.[85] More ironic was Bertram Gross's insistence that the avenue to "democratizing the social base" was to be found in the philosophy of Mary Parker Follett. Having once been part of the human-relations movement in industry, Gross was well versed in Follett and even aware, as we have seen, of the potentially antidemocratic uses of participatory arrangements. And yet Gross could see no other way out. "In retrospect," he wrote, "I have learned that much of this [democratic theory] has been absorbed into the rhetoric of nondemocratic elitism, the practice of co-optation, and the arts of protecting or expanding concentrated power. But still the question burns in my mind. Could not the best elements of the so-called 'scientific management' — perhaps blended with the 'scientific workmanship hinted at by Harry Braverman — be used in the unending struggle for true democracy?"[86]

Other elements of the left remained convinced that certain kinds of primary institutions could flourish apart from elite domination. In a recent essay on the origins of French socialism, historian David Hunt demonstrated the role of drinking clubs and simple "sociability" in the formation of political consciousness and organization in the years before the 1848 revolution, and he suggested the relevance of this "practice of association" for our own time.[87] Harry Boyte, the leading theorist of democratic organizing in the 1970s, was even more sanguine. Boyte, too, understood the problems of cooptation and manipulation, and even acknowledged the Marxist claim that work place, family, and neighborhood were "forces of production" and thus subject to capitalist influence. But Boyte believed that ordinary people had the right and the ability to control their own institutions, and that this goal could be achieved through what he called "free space," viz., space "relatively independent of elite control." For a model of free space, Boyte turned to the work of historian E. P. Thompson. "The countryside," wrote Thompson, "was ruled by the gentry, the towns by corrupt corporations, the nation by the corruptest corporation of all, but the chapel, the tavern and the home were their own. In the 'unsteepled' places of worship there was room for a free intellectual life and for democratic experiments." Boyte added that beauty parlors and barber shops provided "free space" for the American civil-rights movement of the 1950s, and that in the 1970s, free space existed in "a myriad of workplace, neighborhood, cooperative, and other protest groups."[88] Boyte's free space, in short, was dependent on a kind of physical distancing from elite control; democratic social engineers did not enter black barber shops.

Boyte may well be correct that the hope for a socialist renaissance rests on the effective utilization of existing free space. Doubtless there are places and institutions — fraternal organizations, secret societies, street gangs, social cliques, informal clubs, neighborhood associations, and Boyte's barber shops among them — that are highly resistant to even the subtlest forms of social engineering. But as earlier chapters in this book demonstrate, democratic social engineers have entered the chapel, the home, and the neighborhood. And some institutions — high school fraternities, the tavern, and street gangs, for example — have been subject to legal prohibition or police intimidation. There may be less free space than Boyte realized.

Even Foucault and Sennett, more theoreticians of authority than organizers of the working class, held onto a faith in the possibilities of finding a reasonable authority. Yet this faith was limited. Neither Foucault nor Sennett would go so far as to suggest the continued viability of voluntary associations or the continued independence of home and family. Both realized that authority operated at levels that encompassed these institutions and through the most intimate patterns of organization and discourse. Where, then, could one find a staging area for an assault on the modern structure of authority? What free space remained? Sennett and Foucault had an answer for these questions, and it is the same one: discussion. Sennett believed that authority could be remade through "an active, interpretative search for the meaning of power." If controls were treated as "propositions rather than axioms," authority would be made visible, and thus ripe for change. "For a master to discuss his power actively is for him to exert a real and admirable strength," wrote Sennett. "For a subject to enter into the discussion and contest the master is for the subject also a strength." Yet one wonders, short of writing books about authority, just how such discussions might be generated. How, and why, would masters agree to debate the source and nature of their authority? And how was the "subject" to bring about such an exchange in the first place?[89]

Foucault's world of possibilities was even more circumscribed. His *The Order of Things*, as one reviewer observed, "ends by prophesying a new era in which self-conscious discourse is not about Man or the think-

ing subject but about discourse alone. . . . as if there would be no reflec-
tive talk except talk about talk."[90] Foucault must have known, even as
he made this prophecy, that the very idea of pure talk, of talk without
authority, was a philosophical and historical fantasy. But he may also
have realized that it was all that remained of the democratic dream.

Coming of Age under Democratic Social Engineering: A Photo Essay

Youth were an early and regular object of democratic social engineering. In the Progressive Era, educators and social-settlement workers experimented with clubs that were to replace troublesome gangs and take wayward youth from the brink of delinquency to responsible citizenship. By 1950, millions of youth belonged to school clubs, participated in student courts and teen councils, were members of the YWCA or the Boys Clubs, or had in some other way opened themselves to social engineering through group process.

In an effort to redirect energy that might have gone into local gangs, the Buffalo Boys Clubs created an alternative network of clubs with names such as Amicus Club and Jokers Club, then integrated these clubs into a system of youth governance. Here, West Side youth examine a list of candidates and club affiliations. 1938. Courtesy of Butler-Mitchell Boys Club Alumni Association, Buffalo, New York, Paul R. Missana, Historian.

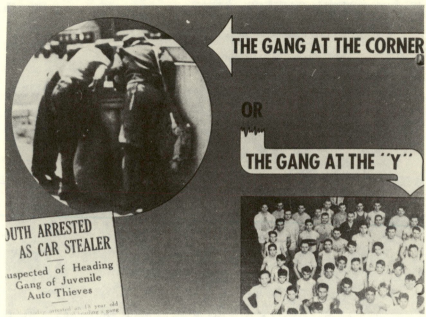

Before democratic methods could be effectively applied, it was necessary to bring youth under adult supervision. The "gang at the corner" must become the "gang at the 'Y'." c. 1940. Courtesy of YMCA of the USA.

Youth Forum on Delinquency, 1953. Original caption: "Four high school students last night said too much stress has been placed on present day juvenile delinquency. They defended, as well as advocated, reforms for the present younger generation, on the *Courier-Express* Press Table over Station WEBR, March 8, 1953." Photograph reproduced by permission of Buffalo and Erie County Historical Society, *Courier-Express* Collection.

The Dress Right code, posted on the cafeteria wall at Buffalo's Burgard Vocational High School, 1958. Concerned that youth would reject a code imposed from above, school officials turned the project over to the Inter-High [student] Council. Although adherence to Dress Right was supposed to be voluntary (i.e., dependent upon publicity, exhortation, and peer-group pressure), some school officials required obedience. Burgard Vocational High School, *Craftsman*, 1958.

The Student Court

THE Tribal Council Court was added to Seneca's fast-growing student government. The first sound of the gavel rang out shortly after the beginning of the second term.

With the hope of correcting any and all students who might be led astray, Judge Ryan, chief judge of the City Court, graciously taught the student judges some of Blackstone's rules of court procedure, so that all students might have a fair trial.

The court wishes to thank the students for their cooperation in obeying their obligations to it.

A meeting of the Student Court at Seneca Vocational High School, Buffalo, 1955. Private-school encouragement of student participation in governance and discipline dates to the Progressive Era. Student government did not become common in the public high schools until the 1940s. Seneca Vocational High School, *Chieftain*, 1955.

The Student Activities Committee at Benjamin Franklin High School, Rochester, New York, drumming up recruits for school clubs, 1940/41. School administrators had been favorably disposed toward using extracurricular activities to teach behavior and values since the mid-1920s. During World War II, enthusiasm for school clubs, where students would practice responsible self-government, reached a new high. Photograph by Eliot Elisofon, reproduced by permission of *Life Magazine*, © 1941, 1969, *Time, Inc.*

Better to remove and distract him than to say, "No, no!"

This Dorothea Fox drawing, from Benjamin Spock's *The Common Sense Book of Baby and Child Care* (1946), illustrates one facet of democratic social engineering: the use of indirect mechanisms of authority. Courtesy of Dorothea Fox.

GUIDANCE

GIRLS
COUNSELOR

GERTRUDE
ZIEMANN

To the Boys and Girls of Hutchinson-Central:

The counseling service at Hutchinson is relatively new and up to this date has been on a part time basis. Next year it will be on a full time basis and the door of Room 256 and Room 207 will be open to you at all times.

The purpose of this service is to assist you in learning to know yourself; to help you understand your abilities and aptitudes, your interests and accomplishments, and your failings and limitations. We can provide you with accurate information concerning educational and vocational requirements and opportunities suitable to your qualifications. We will try to help you in solving your personal problems.

Your educational problems may have to do with a change in your course of study, selection of a Major, especially in the General course, a choice of electives or credits for graduation. The answers to these problems are available if you will but ask for them. If you are failing in your subjects we can give you some hints on how to improve your study habits.

Perhaps you are uncertain about the choice of a college or school after graduation from high school. There are over two hundred college catalogs available and many interesting books of views of the various colleges. In addition we have pamphlets on the offerings of technical institutes, the armed forces, and private business and trade schools. These may be seen at any time. We shall be glad to give the seniors information on scholarships which are available and to assist them in filling out applications for college entrance.

Among your vocational problems, there is perhaps no one decision so important for you to make as the decision of which path you should follow in your life work. It is your life and what you do with it in great part rests on your choice of a career. In order to make intelligent decisions in planning your life career you need to understand yourself and your opportunities. Do not hesitate to seek aid from all possible sources in making this decision.

How can you learn about yourself—your strengths and weaknesses, your likes and dislikes? Your abilities, interests and personality traits are not hidden as a rule but reveal themselves in school records, in the use of your leisure time and in daily life contacts.

Your interests, that is, your likes and dislikes, should be taken into consideration in planning your future. If you do not know what your interests are, we can give you a simple test which will help you to recognize your interest pattern, or to eliminate those fields in which you are not interested. There

Girls' Guidance Counselor, Hutchinson-Central High School, Buffalo, 1949. The ideology of guidance was democratic; students would make career decisions on the basis of information provided by the counselor. However, the existence of gender-typed counselors suggests how limited the freedom of decision really was. Hutchinson-Central High School, *Calendar*, 1949, p. 8.

Cafeteria monitors at Girls' Vocational High School, Buffalo, 1948. In the postwar era, many schools used students to police the cafeteria, hallways, and locker areas. Students went along, in part because monitors often possessed a physical freedom not otherwise available. Girls' Vocational High School, *Herald*, 1948.

Teen Council, Buffalo, c. 1957. Local and state youth programs in the postwar period usually had a democratic component. Through teen councils such as this, youth helped make policy and plan youth-center activities. Buffalo Youth Board, *Report*, 1957.

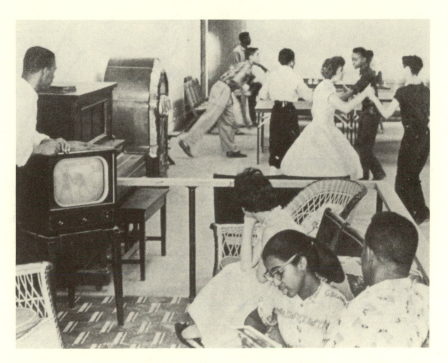

Drop-in Teen Lounge, Buffalo, c. 1957. Buffalo Youth Board, *Report*, 1957.

STUDENT COUNCIL ...

One view of the Student Council at Buffalo's Lafayette High School, 1953. Not all students accepted democratic methods at face value. Lafayette High School, *Oracle*, 1953.

8

Conclusion

For much of this century, Americans have understood themselves through the word "democracy." The term at once conveyed a system of governance, based on citizen participation; respect for the individual — a promise of control over one's own life; and the unity and loyalty of a heterogeneous people. In the Progressive Era, the word stood for the nation's desire to assimilate millions of immigrants; in 1918 and 1941, it captured Americans' sense of themselves as a special people with the unique ability to prosecute a war without damaging the fiber of individualism. In 1950, it called forth a healthy conformity to dominant values.

When democracy weakened as a social force in the decades after 1955, democratic social engineering suffered with it. The growing postwar skepticism of democracy, registered in the "beat" movement, in the declaration of a "credibility gap," in declining voter participation, in dozens of books that described the "selling of the president," the "selling of the Pentagon," or the "segmented society," and in countless other phenomena, gave notice that a system of authority founded on democracy was in troubled waters. Although the recent enthusiasm for Japanese management techniques is evidence that democratic social engineering is still with us (after all, so is democracy), the future of a system of authority with weakened ideological roots is problematical.

Prior to the postwar declension, a profound commitment to the system and ideological field of force known as democracy fueled, reinforced, underlay, and sanctioned the development of democratic social engineering. Because Americans understood themselves as participants in a democratic process, they were willing to administer — and, for the most part, to tolerate — authority that was encoded as democracy. The social workers, psychologists, sociologists, educators, and philosophers who at the turn of the century were responsible for this encoding might best be described as engaged in the act of translating the institutions and mechanisms of a democratic culture — the mass, the voluntary association, the act of participation, the notion of choice — into "society," the group, guided discussion, and other elements of a system of social engineering. In little more than half a century, democratic social engineering was operating in homes, factories, schools, churches, and clubs. Foremen and line workers, senior citizens, adolescents and small children, and many others came under the influence of groups, group leaders, and group methods. Even discourse — the forum, the conference, conversation itself — was shaped by democratic theory.

Yet questions remain, and they are not all questions that can be answered by historical method. The nature of one's response to and interpretation of democratic social engineering may depend less on history than on philosophy, ethics, and, in the broadest sense of the word, politics. The largest question, that which encompasses the others, is quite simple: is democratic social engineering a legitimate form of authority? To phrase the same question in polar terms, is democratic social engineering dangerous, or is it harmless? Is it a vehicle of class domination, or a mechanism of genuine social participation? Is it an especially repressive form of authority — something out of *1984*, perhaps — or is it a particularly mild and benign form of authority, the product of a progressive, historical evolution?

From the recent literature on authority and responses to drafts of this book, I have isolated three basic defenses, real or potential, of democratic social engineering — subarguments, really, of the general class for legitimacy. Each is presented below, with as much objectivity as I could muster, and each is followed by a rejoinder.

The first possible defense of democratic social engineering takes the form of a challenge to distinguish authority that is reasonable and natural in some very basic sense from authority that is unreasonable and unnatural. According to one side of this argument, democratic social engineering is really only socialization by another name (and hence not arguably "engineering"). Societies, even social classes, perpetuate themselves and hold themselves together by passing on values, mores, customs, traditions, and appropriate behaviors. This is not wrong but natural and reasonable. One can identify democratic social engineering as socialization because the mechanisms through which it operates lie deep within the system of social relations — in, for example, child-rearing patterns or conversation. To retain its usefulness as a concept, power (or social engineering) must, according to this argument, be cleanly separated from socialization, from general social processes. If diffuse controls with "unintended and unforeseen effects" are included within the concept of power, the latter becomes indistinguishable from language and other attributes of natural authority and loses its utility as an analytic device.[1]

The other side of this "reasonable and natural" defense shifts the argument away from socialization toward authority as the inevitable result of social needs. Wherever men pursue collective goals, authority is necessary. As R. G. Collingwood states, "command and obedience are found, not in all societies, but in all where the nature of the common task is such as to require them. Watch two men moving a piano; at a certain moment one says 'lift,' and the other lifts." According to political scientist Dennis Wrong, "only the most doctrinaire anarchist or proponent of direct democracy would maintain that authorizing some men to direct the activities of others is so corrupting and conflict-producing for all concerned that it should never be considered as a means of achieving collective goals."[2]

I am sympathetic to at least one aspect of this natural/reasonable argument. Because democratic social engineering resides at the intersection of authority (power) and socialization, it *is*, I agree, often difficult to distinguish the two. But this is precisely why democratic social engineering is so dangerous. It is power presented as socialization, social control parading as participation, choice, discussion, and other "democratic" processes. What we are beginning to understand about power is that it is most compelling when it is least distinguishable from socialization, for only at that level are dominance and the mechanics of dominance entirely, or almost entirely, obscured.[3] This is the message of Antonio Gramsci and Michel Foucault. "In thinking of the mechanisms of power," states Foucault, "I am thinking rather of its capillary form of existence, the point where power reaches into the very grain of individuals, touches their bodies and inserts itself into their actions and attitudes, their discourses, learning processes and everyday lives."[4]

The possibility broached in the natural/reasonable argument that democratic social engineering involves controls with "unintended and unforeseen" consequences raises the question of consciousness. Clearly, many practitioners of democratic social engineering were conscious of what they were doing. The late-nineteenth-century churches sought new members, employers tried to make their workers more productive and less inclined to radicalism, child-rearing experts wanted to produce children who would not be vulnerable to totalitarian appeals, and Golden Age Club leaders looked to democratic methods to educate the elderly into responsible patterns of political behavior. These consequences were "intended" and, to the extent that they could be, "foreseen." Supporting all these efforts, moreover, were people who called themselves social scientists and who worked in organized disciplines. From the highest level of theory to the lowest plane of practice, democratic social engineering was developed and carried out at a high level of consciousness.[5]

The second half of the natural/reasonable argument purports to make the case for authority as a natural function of human relations. Implicit in Collingwood's comment on piano lifting, however, is the assumption of the existence of collective goals. The legitimacy of democratic social engineering might, then, hinge on whether the participants in the relationship were pursuing goals that could reasonably be termed collective. The word "collective," however, suggests joint determination, a formulation that brings us back to the question of consciousness. If all parties to the process are not equally conscious, there can be no meaningful joint determination, and we cannot speak of collective goals. Wrong's notion that the populace grants some men the authority to direct others only begs the question; under democratic social engineering, what sort of authorization takes place?

A second set of three arguments around the issue of legitimacy accepts the processes and methods of democratic social engineering as a given — even grants the manipulative character of the system — and focuses instead on demonstrating why such a system, no matter how manipulative in its internal operations, would likely be socially harmless. The first argument in this "harmless" set finds democratic social engineering a minor weapon in the arsenal of authority — minor, say, in relationship to other mechanisms of authority such as the law, force, or the mass media; or minor in itself (viz., in terms of numbers and character of institutions penetrated, persons affected, intellectual figures involved, etc.). According to one rendering of the latter argument, democratic social engineering might best be understood not as a central expression of American culture, but as the product of a select, discrete, and limited "school" of democratic authority or group process.

The second of the "harmless" arguments holds intragroup mechanisms such as group process legitimate because the basic institutions in which such systems operate are so widely distributed. In contrast to forms of authority that are not widely available, such as the authority that derives from control of the mass media, from the ability to engage in surveillance, or from the possession of an army, the authority that emanates from the small group is accessible not just to the rich, the state, or a powerful bureaucrat such as J. Edgar Hoover, but to millions of ordinary people. Perhaps the most recent exponent of this view is John Kenneth Galbraith, for whom the dominant form of authority in twentieth-century America is a blend of belief-changing education and persuasion known as "conditioned power." In some measure, writes Galbraith, "conditioned power is available to all who can form an organization."[6]

Not only is organization available to all, but the tools of persuasion — argumentation, inquiry, leadership, etc. — are also, ostensibly, widely available. Americans' historical interest in town government, debate, argumentative journalism, public forums, and other instruments of democracy are evidence — so this argument goes — not of the existence of social engineers, but of a broad-based public preparation for, and interest in, persuasive methods. Therefore, the ultimate impact of the rise of conditioned power, operating through organizations, conferences, and committees, is to increase participation in the exercise of power and ultimately to diffuse power itself.[7]

The third argument in the set maintains that democratic social engineering is harmless because it is ineffective; democratic social engineering does not work. B. F. Skinner has forged a career around the principle that permissiveness, guidance, persuasion, and other variants or relatives of democratic social engineering are ineffective mechanisms of behavioral modification. They exist, he claims, in part to allow those who use them to avoid the accusation of control.[8] Others have emphasized the failure of manipulative methods to secure genuine compliance. Galbraith, for example, writes of the "illusion of power," the inaccurate assumption that conditioned power actually produces submission. The rise of conditioned power, Galbraith contends, has meant that "there is now much less submission of some to the purposes of others."[9] Dennis Wrong adds that the effects of even manipulative power, with its "awesome" reputation for modifying behavior and belief, "seem to be fairly limited in extensiveness, comprehensiveness and intensity."[10]

To those who would depreciate the importance of democratic social engineering by comparing it with other systems or mechanisms of authority I have no very helpful response, except to suggest the enormous difficulties inherent in such epic comparisons. My goal has been the simpler one of placing democratic social engineering in the lexicon of authority, alongside other significant mechanisms. The suggestion that democratic social engineering is more a "school" than a central component of the culture rests on a reading of this book to which I obviously do not subscribe. Certain aspects of the story — the centrality of Dewey, the concentration of theory in New York City in the 1920s, the apparent primacy of certain social sciences — lend credence to this view. Yet the label "school" suggests a kind of intellectual influence without social substance — thought without praxis — that was not true of democratic social engineering. Furthermore, the method has appeared under such disparate auspices — from a Woodrow Wilson address to a Dale Carnegie anecdote — that to catalogue its practitioners as representatives of a "school" seems needlessly restrictive. Perhaps the best rejoinder to the "school" argument is to emphasize once again how centrally located democratic social engineering has been in a cultural sense.

If democracy has, indeed, been the religion of the twentieth century, it seems logical that a system of social engineering built upon it would also be of general importance.

Galbraith's defense of persuasive mechanisms depends in part on a pluralist reading. He paints the environment of discourse as a cacophony of competing interest groups, each unable to exert undue influence in the sociopolitical sphere. But this *inter*group approach has nothing to say about *intra*group politics (the subject of this book). Moreover, Galbraith grants a neutrality or objectivity to intragroup processes that did not exist, for example, in foremen's clubs or youth groups. Although conditioned power increases participation (more people become involved in more organizations), it also, therefore, opens up new avenues of social control; ironically, participation itself becomes one such avenue. The point is simple but of great importance: to describe a system of authority, one must do more than count organizations, chart their ties to one another, and catalogue their external influence. One must look inside the organizations, at internal processes.

Nor are the group processes labeled democratic social engineering harmless because the tools of social interaction are available to all. Since the turn of the century, interactive skills have become the province of experts. That is one meaning of the phrase "social science"; knowledge of social skills has been appropriated by scientists. Sociologists, social psychologists, educators, and others now understand leadership, small-group interaction, discussion, inquiry, and other aspects of human relations far more precisely and completely than do ordinary people.[11] Moreover, democratic social engineers *knew* they had power not available to others; in fact, the methodology was often employed by an educated middle class of business or the professions toward a subgroup (e.g., the "masses," older persons, children, immigrants) lacking in the social skills learned from participation in group functions.[12] In short, the objects of democratic social engineering were often those least able to resist its appeal.

The contention that democratic social engineering (or some variant of it, such as Galbraith's conditioned power) is ineffective is just that — a mere contention. For Skinner it is a necessary contention, for without it his operant conditioning would be unnecessary. Moreover, while Skinner accurately perceives how democratic social engineering has been presented as a mechanism of individualism, he practically defines away its manipulative quality by overestimating its use of the simplest persuasive techniques. One can grant Galbraith's point — that it is difficult to *measure* the effectiveness of conditioned power — without concluding that it is, in fact, ineffective.[13]

And what of the argument that social engineering systems are rendered ineffective by the opposition of those who are supposed to be governed by them? Certainly if the people did not participate, or perceived group processes as manipulative, the effectiveness of such methods would be reduced. Yet evidence of noncooperation is meager; it can be briefly summarized. In the 1920s, efforts to bring Philadelphia blacks into clubs foundered when participants decided they were being patronized. Sponsors of foremen's clubs found that foremen now and then refused to take part in discussions in the presence of supervisors. During World War II, juvenile group-work agencies were vandalized, and some first-generation Japanese resisted concentration-camp leisure activities because they realized that these activities were designed to separate them from their children. According to an American Youth Commission study carried out in the early 1940s, perhaps a majority of the nation's high school students elected not to participate in the clubs and organizations which would have made them vulnerable to democratic social engineering. Nor were postwar efforts to engineer the behavior of Buffalo youth entirely successful. Some students refused to comply with the student-formulated dress code; others understood how little democratic reality was present in student councils and student courts.[14] And one could argue — with logic, if not evidence — that the beats, juvenile delinquents, and high school dropouts were all in some sense motivated by hostility toward the participatory ethos of the culture and its educational institutions.

Yet these examples are few in number and contain little evidence that such resistance as took place was motivated by an understanding of the manipulative nature of democratic group process. Some people, of course, notably children, did not even have the option of nonparticipation. And not until the Port Huron Statement of 1962 did any group directly affected by democratic social engineering clearly and explicitly denounce the method itself. Additional research — of a kind, unlike my own, designed precisely to probe the extent of resistance — might well uncover more evidence of an articulate opposition. But it would take a great deal of new information to significantly revise the conclusion that resistance to democratic social engineering has been marginal. On this ground, too, the system was not harmless.

A third set of arguments characterizes democratic social engineering as a mild, advanced, and particularly legitimate system of authority, administered by the nation's most socially responsible citizens. Buttressing the latter claim is the undeniable fact that the theorists and practitioners of democratic social engineering were not, on the whole, demagogues, grasping capitalists, notorious social conservatives, or even Republicans. They were, indeed, mostly liberals. Their ranks included Dewey and William H. Kilpatrick, Grace Coyle and Eduard C. Lindeman, Woodrow

Wilson and Lyndon Johnson. Even if democratic social engineering has not been free from manipulation, surely — one could claim — it is a benign manipulation, in the hands of our best and brightest.

According to this argument, the liberal version of authority is progressive and humane, analogous to liberal remedies in the political sphere. Just as the welfare state was designed to protect citizens from the ravages of unemployment and old age, so, too, does democratic social engineering represent a clear advance over other, more primitive, forms of power. The liberals' choice of a method is far superior to violence or threatened violence, to the economic power applied so callously in the nineteenth century, or to the operant conditioning of a B. F. Skinner. While there may well be forms of authority that are *theoretically* more benign than democratic social engineering, the latter is the highest and most progressive form of authority ever put into *practice* on a broad scale. As such, it can be criticized only from a utopian perspective.

According to another portion of this "beneficial" argument, the legitimacy of democratic authority is said to derive from its persuasive essence. Arguments are presented by A, and B evaluates them. B is completely free to accept or reject those arguments and is under no obligation to comply with A's wishes. Should B fail to agree or comply, B will be neither punished nor deprived.[15] To suggest that this process is a form of "engineering," with its connotation of manipulation, is tantamount to denying that free will, intelligence, and reason are distributed among all persons in some reasonable measure.

The "beneficial" argument, too, is seriously flawed. To claim — correctly, on the whole — that most democratic social engineers were neither capitalists nor roaring conservatives tells us little about those who practiced group-process methods. Some, including the Rockefellers' Ivey Lee, served corporate capitalism in the most direct way. Others, such as Dale Carnegie, and even Benjamin Spock, produced a literature that encouraged or facilitated participation in the corporate and bureaucratic institutions of capitalism.[16]

The meaning of liberalism in the context of democratic social engineering can also be grasped by looking at the career movement of its practitioners from one field to another. In the first third of this century, many — Mary Parker Follett, Meyer Bloomfield, Ordway Tead, Lee, and Elton Mayo — made the transition from some form of social work to the business world. It would be a mistake, however, to interpret this movement in ideological terms, as a transition from liberal "reformism" to business "conservatism." As business rather than immigration gradually became the key arena of social problems and adjustment, forward-looking social workers changed fields — but not ideologies or methods. Thus, in the 1920s struggle between business and labor, the liberals — Follett, Tead, Mayo, and Edward Filene among them — sought to improve productivity and to maintain the social order with democratic weapons, while conservatives such as William Taft and the nation's coal operators were content with more traditional devices such as the yellow-dog contract, Pinkertons, and the injunction. It may be that liberals can best be distinguished from conservatives by examining the means they employed rather than the ends they espoused.

The essential social conservatism of the democratic social engineers is also apparent in their shared negative assessment of the reason and judgment of common people. The infant/child described in Benjamin Spock's *Baby and Child Care* was, as we have seen, a volcano of behavioral problems, ready to erupt at the slightest parental provocation; aggression was never far below the surface. Both persons responsible for the intellectual rationale behind the Golden Age Clubs believed that ordinary people were easily susceptible to mass appeals and demagoguery. Oskar Schulze's model for the behavior of the mass was profoundly influenced by his perception that older Germans victimized by the inflation of 1923 were later to be found in Hitler's legions. Grace Coyle's group-work theories were based in part on the belief that rapid social change had destabilized social life and contributed to a "'milling about' process," as she called it. "Many continue to 'mill,'" Coyle wrote in 1926, "guided only by instinctive tendencies and emotions and usually keeping in the routine of the crowd."[17] Similar perceptions of the mass motivated the propaganda efforts of the Creel Committee during World War I and permeated the activities of Bruno Lasker's influential organization of the 1920s, The Inquiry. Follett, whose work would provide a theoretical basis for corporate experiments in democratic methods, also wrote of the "masses" and the "crowd."[18]

Of course, generalizations of this magnitude inevitably oversimplify problems of individual motivation and obscure differences in purpose. Clearly, for example, Schulze cared for the happiness of Cleveland's elderly, while Lee's work was done in service to Rockefeller rather than to help the mine workers. Buffalo school administrators may have wanted to use democratic techniques to thwart delinquency, but they also believed this was in the best interests of all students. Yet even the most socially conscious of the democratic social engineers appears to have been concerned with encouraging stability, order, and adherence to fundamental social values. Whether liberal or not, they were a conservative force.

Nor, I think, should democratic social engineering be interpreted as the product of a historical evolution toward more sensible and beneficial forms of authority. Whatever historical "progress" has been made in mechanisms of social control has been in the direction of subtlety. Democratic social engineering was subtle in its location. Power lodged in the state could be easily grasped; that real power could be located in a YMCA club, a student council, a Sunday school class, and other informal and even voluntary organizations was more difficult to fathom. It was also subtle in method, its lessons wrapped in layer upon layer of disguises. Science (viz., inquiry) was one disguise, process (viz., discussion) another, democracy (viz., participation) a third. It was subtle, too, in that even its practitioners and advocates might be only dimly aware of what it was they were doing. Just as the carriers of George Orwell's Doublethink could be "conscious of complete truthfulness while telling carefully constructed lies,"[19] many democratic social engineers believed that they were involved not in control but in its negation, not in manipulation but in benign persuasion.

Were democratic social engineers engaged, then, in simple persuasion of the kind described in the A/B example above? I think not. Invariably, democratic social engineering was employed in an environment laced with inequalities in status, knowledge, influence, age, and interactive skills. As a result, the objects of this form of authority remained unaware of the intent of the subject to exert influence or, more commonly, of the methods being employed. This lack of awareness was shared by children in relationship to parents, workers in relationship to employers, buyers in relationship to sellers.[20]

Even as presented in the example, however, the technique of "persuasion" is not necessarily wholly legitimate. Although the relationship seems to be one of equals, one party to it (A) is more active than another (B). Moreover, we are not told how A came to this active position. Did B authorize A to present arguments? Although we are informed that B can reject A's arguments with complete impunity, such a situation is difficult, if not impossible, to imagine. In order to imagine it, we would have to conceptualize A as entirely unconcerned with the outcome of the persuasive process. But if A were entirely unconcerned, there would seem to be no reason for A to be involved. A persuasive environment implies needs, goals, desires, and the potential, at least, for punishment or deprivation.

I am often called upon to suggest alternatives to democratic social engineering, as if the act of criticism entails the obligation to shore up the system one has put in disrepair. Faced with such requests, I usually offer two ideal worlds. In one direction is an ideal system of genuinely democratic relations. In such a system, workers would join management to make decisions about such basic matters as production and distribution; students would share in curriculum decisions; and golden-agers would be treated as responsible adults rather than as capricious children. This solution, in short, would involve significantly redistributing power — a goal unlikely to meet with general approbation.

In the other direction lies another solution, at once less comprehensive and more practical. This solution involves moving away from the false democracy of democratic social engineering toward more direct and obvious mechanisms of authority. This might, for example, mean a return to more authoritarian parenting and an end to pseudodemocratic family conferences. Or it could involve the abolition of essentially functionless student councils — and the recognition that all important decisions are made by the school principal, anyway. Since this solution, as opposed to the first, involves only a more realistic appraisal of where authority lies, rather than an actual redistribution, it may seem more reasonable. Nonetheless, it is not much more likely to be embraced by those who have power, most of whom would rather that its operation remain somewhat mysterious. And even the objects of democratic social engineering might, if given a choice, prefer the subtle agency of group process to the more direct, even corporal, methods of the past.

Yet I am not at all convinced that the provision of "solutions" — even solutions developed at great length and in fine detail — is a legitimate or worthwhile exercise. I have no desire to engage in the endless imagining required to sketch out an alternative system of authority nor, given the continued if diminished hold of democratic ideas on American culture, am I sure that alternatives could be imagined. Although this book is a product of my peculiar mix of ethics and politics, I see no compelling need to translate those personal values into a traditional statement of political reformism. My goal has been the more limited one of penetrating and labeling a subtle system of authority, operating through groups and group processes, embedded within the discourse of democracy, and central to twentieth-century American culture.

Notes
Index

Notes

CHAPTER ONE. ORIGINS

1. Thomas L. Haskell, *The Emergence of Professional Social Science: The American Social Science Association and the Nineteenth-Century Crisis of Authority* (Urbana, Ill., 1977), pp. 15–16, 30–31, 39.

2. Haskell, *Emergence of Professional Social Science*, p. 31; Sheldon S. Wolin, *Politics and Vision: Continuity and Innovation in Western Political Thought* (Boston, 1960), p. 357; Jacques Ellul, *Propaganda: The Formation of Men's Attitudes* (New York, 1972), pp. 92–93; Richard Sennett, *Authority* (New York, 1981), p. 44.

3. Mary P. Ryan, *Cradle of the Middle Class: The Family in Oneida County, New York, 1790–1865* (Cambridge, England, 1981), pp. 231–32; David Riesman, with Nathan Glazer and Reuel Denney, *The Lonely Crowd: A Study of the Changing American Character* (1950; abridged ed. New York: Doubleday Anchor, 1953), pp. 57–58.

4. Group life insurance, for example, combined community (people in a similar situation helping each other) with a good dose of social efficiency (spreading risk through a pool of persons lacking other ties).

5. Mark E. Kann, "Consent and Authority in America," in John P. Diggins and Mark E. Kann, eds., *The Problem of Authority in America* (Philadelphia, 1981), pp. 70–72.

6. John P. Diggins, "The Three Faces of Authority in American History," in *Problem of Authority in America*, pp. 19–20.

7. Kann, "Consent and Authority in America," p. 72.

8. Diggins, "Three Faces of Authority in American History," p. 22; Sheldon Wolin, "The Idea of the State in America," in *Problem of Authority in America*, p. 48.

9. Ibid., p. 46.

10. John P. Diggins and Mark E. Kann, "Introduction" to *Problem of Authority in America*, p. 14; Wolin, "Idea of the State in America," p. 45; Kann, "Consent and Authority in America," p. 72.

Another important development in the history of consent in the eighteenth and nineteenth centuries was the dissemination of Adam Smith's free-market ideology. This ideology did not, on the face of it, have anything to do with democracy or democratic authority. In fact, it is not at all difficult to see Americans' embrace of Smith's laissez-faire economics as a manifestation of the nation's historical aversion to genuine authority.

Read another way, the nineteenth-century adherence to the free market was not so much a flight *from* authority as a flight *to* a system of authority predicated on consent — in this case, the consent of the consumer. Just as political democracy located the source of authority in decisions made by voter-citizens, so did economic individualism locate the source of authority in thousands of decisions made by individual consumers. If politicians acted irresponsibly, or the factories made the wrong mix of goods, there was no one to blame but the voters who had elected the politicians or the consumers who had purchased the goods.

From the beginning there were problems with making voters and consumers — ordinary Americans — responsible for the shape of political and economic systems. With the rise of giant corporations in the late nineteenth century, these problems became more acute. The contrast between ideal and real, between the power ordinary people were supposed to have and the power they actually had, became all too obvious. At the same time, it became clear, as John Kenneth Galbraith writes in *The Anatomy of Power* (Boston, 1983), that the "celebration of the market" was "an effective solvent — and concealment — of the power of industrial capitalism. Prices were set by the market. Wages were set by the market. . . . On none of these matters did the industrialist have power; hence there could be no legitimate concern as to its exercise" (p. 119). Market power was "visible" power. The worker, for example, could see that the wage was an inducement for his labor. But raised to the level of ideology, the market system also obscured the fact that Americans did not in any significant way consent to low wages, to an unsafe work place, or even to the prevailing mix of goods and services. Democracy, I shall argue, served much the same function of concealment in the twentieth century.

11. Kann, "Consent and Authority in America," p. 73.

12. Wolin, *Politics and Vision*, pp. 290–91, 301, 308, 343, 348 (quotation); Sennett, *Authority*, pp. 93, 168; Haskell, *Emergence of Professional Social Science*, p. 43; Michel Foucault, *Power/Knowledge: Selected Interviews and Other Writings, 1972–1977*, ed. Colin Gordon, trans. Colin Gordon, Leo Marshall, John Mepham, Kate Soper (New York: Pantheon, 1980), pp. 152–53.

Several scholars have centered investigations of societal authority on Rousseau's theoretics of participation. Robert Nisbet's recent study of authority presents Rousseau as the progenitor of an oblique fascism, the advocate of an authority both pervasive and paralyzing of the individual will. Carole Pateman finds nothing quite so sinister even in Rousseau's famous statement that a man might be "forced to be free." What Rousseau had in mind, Pateman emphasizes, was forcible education, but through participation in democratic decision-making processes — a function, she believes, innocent and appropriate enough. Robert Nisbet, *Twilight of Authority* (New York, 1975), p. 196; Carole Pateman, *Participation and Democratic Theory* (Cambridge, England, 1970), pp. 24–26.

13. Diggins, "Three Faces of Authority in American History," pp. 21, 26.

14. Alexis de Tocqueville, *Democracy in America* (1835 and 1840; New York: Modern Library, 1981), pp. 141, 301.

15. Galbraith, *Anatomy of Power*, pp. 20–21; Sennett, *Authority*, pp. 93–94; Myra C. Glenn, *Campaigns against Corporal Punishment: Prisoners, Sailors, Women, and Children in Antebellum America* (Albany, 1984), pp. 10–12, chap. 7.

According to Antonio Gramsci, the taming of an industrial working class was accomplished in its early stages largely through coercion, then, later, through Puritan ideologies "which give an external form of persuasion and consent to the intrinsic use of force." In the 1920s, Gramsci explained, factory labor was made suitable for the assembly line and scientific management through a variety of hegemonic processes, including Prohibition, psychoanalysis (for the repression of sexuality), and subtle propaganda. Antonio Gramsci, *Selections from the Prison Notebooks of Antonio Gramsci*, ed. and trans. Quintin Hoare and Geoffrey Nowell Smith (New York, 1971), p. 299. See also Haskell, *Emergence of Professional Social Science*, pp. 65, 89.

16. Michael Paul Rogin, *Fathers and Children: Andrew Jackson and the Subjugation of the American Indian* (New York, 1975), p. 215.

17. Myra C. Glenn, "The Naval Reform Campaign against Flogging: A Case Study in Changing Attitudes toward Corporal Punishment, 1830–1850," *American Quarterly* 35 (Fall 1983): 414–15, 421, 418; Glenn, *Campaigns against Corporal Punishment*, chap. 5.

18. Glenn, "Naval Reform Campaign against Flogging," pp. 411–13.

19. Ibid., pp. 421 (quotation), 423.

20. Burton J. Bledstein, *The Culture of Professionalism: The Middle Class and the Development of Higher Education in America* (New York, 1976), pp. 213–15, 248.

21. Bledstein, *Culture of Professionalism*, p. 217; Kenneth E. Reid, *From Character Building to Social Treatment: The History of the Use of Groups in Social Work* (Westport, Conn., 1981), pp. 70, 53; David I. Macleod, *Building Character in the American Boy: The Boy Scouts, YMCA, and Their Forerunners, 1870–1920* (Madison, 1983); Paul Boyer, *Urban Masses and Moral Order in America, 1820–1920* (Cambridge, Mass., 1978), p. 34.

22. See also Richard Sennett's analysis of self-discipline and self-possession as forms of autonomous authority in *Authority*, chap. 3.

23. Robert T. Golembiewski, *The Small Group: An Analysis of Research Concepts and Operations* (Chicago, 1962), p. 1, table of small-group research by decade.

24. Henry F. May, *The End of American Innocence: A Study of the First Years of Our Own Time, 1912–1917* (New York, 1959), pp. 6, 10, 145, 148–49; Robert Allen Skotheim, *Totalitarianism and American Social Thought* (New York, 1971), pp. 23–25.

25. See Edward A. Purcell, Jr., *The Crisis of Democratic Theory: Scientific Naturalism and the Problem of Value* (Lexington, Ky., 1973), p. 11.

There is disagreement regarding the timing of these changes. May believes that the old world, with its certainty of moral values and its belief in inevitable progress, disappeared quickly after 1910. Purcell argues that scientific naturalism weakened democratic theory more gradually, producing a "new democratic theory" only in the decade after 1935. Both authors discuss the work of pragmatists Dewey and James. May argues that Dewey's influence diminished throughout the twentieth century. Purcell makes Dewey central to the forging of a new democratic theory but denies that the philosopher had much success until the Great Depression in America and authoritarianism in Europe made possible a naturalistic theory of democracy. I prefer to interpret the crises of the 1910s and 1930s as chronological pressure points in a larger process by which the culture rejected certain existing methods of perceiving and validating truth (and maintaining social control) and developed new ones. This larger process began at least as early as the mid-nineteenth century and continues to the present day. The group-process movement was not synonymous with this phenomenon; there were many who abandoned the old assumptions who had no interest in any kind of group theory. Nonetheless, democratic social engineering was central to the destruction of the old morality and the building of the new. See May, *End of American Innocence*, p. 150; Purcell, *Crisis of Democratic Theory*, pp. 11–12, 200, 204–8; Boyer, *Urban Masses and Moral Order in America*, pp. 132–33.

26. Boyer, *Urban Masses and Moral Order in America*, pp. 169, 173, 196, 278.

27. Skotheim, *Totalitarianism and American Social Thought*, p. 25; May, *End of American Innocence*, pp. 147–48; 150; William H. Kilpatrick, "The Project Method," *Teachers College Record* 19 (September 1918): 320; R. Jeffrey Lustig, *Corporate Liberalism: The Origins of Modern American Political Theory, 1890–1920* (Berkeley, 1982), p. 124. See also Purcell, *Crisis of Democratic Theory*, p. 25, and Donald B. Meyer, *The Protestant Search for Political Realism, 1919–1941* (Berkeley, 1960), p. 162.

28. May, *End of American Innocence*, p. 28.

29. Quoted in Henry Thomas, *Biographical Encyclopedia of Philosophy* (Garden City, New York, 1965), pp. 132–33. One may argue that Papini's metaphor contains a false conclusion. If one defines the corridor as the process of inquiry, he who controls that process controls the corridor.

30. Kilpatrick, "Project Method," pp. 320, 322, 329.

31. Leon Bramson, *The Political Context of Sociology* (Princeton, 1961), p. 31.

32. Haskell, *Emergence of Professional Social Science*, p. 65; Bramson, *Political Context of Sociology*, chap. 3. See also Gramsci, *Selections from the Prison Notebooks*, p. 276; Foucault, *Power/Knowledge*, p. 151; and Wolin, *Politics and Vision*, p. 420.

33. See Serge Moscovici, *The Age of the Crowd: A Historical Treatise on Mass Psychology* (1981; Cambridge, England, 1985).

34. Boyer, *Urban Masses and Moral Order in America*, pp. 225–27; Randall Collins and Michael Makowsky, *The Discovery of Society* (1972; 2d ed. rev., New York: Random House, 1978), esp. pp. 98–104, on Durkheim; Reid, *From Character Building to Social Treatment*, pp. 84–91.

35. Edward A. Ross, *Social Control: A Survey of the Foundations of Order* (1901; New York: Macmillan, 1928), pp. 394, 430–31. See also J. David Hoeveler, Jr., "Personality and Progressivism: E. A. Ross and American Sociology," paper delivered at the 1983 annual meeting of the Organization of American Historians, and David E. Price, "Community and Control: Critical Democratic Theory in the

Progressive Period," *American Political Science Review* 68 (December 1974): 1663–78.

36. Bramson, *Political Context of Sociology*, pp. 96–97; Edward A. Shils, "The Study of the Primary Group," in Daniel Lerner and Harold D. Lasswell, eds., *The Policy Sciences* (Stanford, Cal., 1951), pp. 44–69.

37. Michael S. Olmsted, *The Small Group* (New York, 1959), pp. 17–18; A. Paul Hare, "The History and Present State of Small Group Research," in Hare, ed., *Handbook of Small Group Research*, 2d ed. (New York, 1976), pp. 385–86; Joseph E. McGrath and Irwin Altman, *Small Group Research: A Synthesis and Critique of the Field* (New York, 1966), pp. 3–4.

38. R. Jackson Wilson, *In Quest of Community: Social Philosophy in the United States, 1860–1920* (New York, 1968), pp. 2, 26–27, 31, 41, 44, 65–66, 90, 105–6, 174.

Jean B. Quandt's *From the Small Town to the Great Community* (1970) is the only historical study which attempts to find common ground among several Progressive Era intellectuals — Jane Addams, Mary Parker Follett, Dewey, Charles Horton Cooley, and Robert Park — associated with the group-process movement. She argues that they shared "a common origin and a common response to social change. Bred in small-town America, moving on to New York, Chicago, Boston and Cleveland carrying the intellectual baggage acquired abroad in American universities, they wanted to perpetuate the qualities of intimate community in the new environment in which they found themselves." Quandt criticizes these intellectuals for rejecting "fundamental social change" for a utopian reliance on education and the religion of communication. Their particular vision of local community, she argues, had little impact on America after 1920.

Quandt's subjects did come from America's small towns, many with an unabashed fondness for life in those communities. Certainly Dewey emerged from his Vermont childhood struck by the power of a local community. Beyond this point, however, the trail of causal relationships leading from small-town America to group process becomes more difficult to follow. What was the reality of small-town life? Was the only lesson to be learned that towns were democratic, and participation in their governance essential? Michael Frisch's study of Springfield, Massachusetts, suggests that in the 1840s and 1850s, small-town Springfield was characterized by a system of governance that was "at once strongly elitist and deeply communitarian," by a "curious blend of aristocracy and egalitarianism, 'democracy without democrats' . . ." As late as the 1870s, these traditions continued to be put at the service of Springfield's goal of "consensus." Frisch's Springfield, unlike Quandt's hypothetical small town, had leaders and followers and was constantly in the process of maintaining harmony and consensus. Far from being a pure and static democracy, Springfield was a working arrangement that was both participatory and elitist. The lesson to be learned from growing up in such a place was not that there were no differences between people, or that people could govern themselves in small units, but that even the most idyllic of democracies had leaders as well as followers, managers as well as ordinary participants.

One can appreciate the "communitarians" as social conservatives without relegating them to the dustbin of nostalgia. Some of them no doubt experienced the dramatic change and flux of the late nineteenth century as anxiety, uncertainty, and doubt, and looked to science, the social sciences, the professions, and expertise for help in understanding change, in tracking down causes, in controlling flux, and ultimately in reducing the level of personal insecurity. But to move from that analysis to the conclusion that the communitarians were limited utopians is tantamount to denying the impact of the sciences and social sciences as mechanisms of social engineering. This is, in fact, what Quandt does; she underestimates the power of education and communication, the chosen methods of her Progressive Era intellectuals. As a result, she locates the mid-1960s version of the communitarian impulse in hippie communes and other examples of retreat, rather than in the mass media or in the ongoing use of social psychology in factories, schools, and families. More important, Quandt assumes that the communitarians sought to bring about basic social change, only to be seduced by the new technology into methods which bypassed the basic issues of group conflict, social structure, and private property. In fact, the communitarians got exactly what they wanted: the consensual society. They wanted to avoid conflict, not bring it about; to maintain private property rather than threaten it; to avert group conflict rather than clarify it. Far from seduced by communication or by "the curative powers of the local community," the communitarians (Quandt's term; i.e., democratic social engineers) chose precisely those tools suited to their goals.

Jean B. Quandt, *From the Small Town to the Great Community: The Social Thought of Progressive Intellectuals* (New Brunswick, N.J., 1970), pp. 4–5, 24–25, 30, 41, 50, 59, 72, 73, 75, 157–59; John Blewett, *"Democracy as Religion: Unity in Human Relations,"* in Blewett, ed., *John Dewey: His Thought and Influence* (1960; rpt., Westport, Conn., 1973), p. 38; Michael H. Frisch, *Town into City: Springfield, Massachusetts, and the Meaning of Community, 1840–1880* (Cambridge, Mass., 1972), pp. 33–34, 48, 220; Bledstein, *Culture of Professionalism,* pp. 196, 213–17; Haskell, *Emergence of Professional Social Science,* pp. 13–15, 254; Wolin, *Politics and Vision,* pp. 398–402, 414–15.

39. George Albert Coe, *Education in Religion and Morals* (New York, 1904), pp. 137, 14, 75, 78, 93; George Walter Fiske, *Boy Life and Self-Government* (New York, 1910), pp. 38, 95–96; Edward Heard Kilpatrick, *Education for a Changing Civilization: Three Lectures Delivered on the Luther Laflin Kellogg Foundation at Rutgers University, 1926* (New York, 1926), pp. 78–85; William Clayton Bower, *Religious Education in the Modern Church: A Textbook in the Standard Leadership Training Curriculum Outlined and Approved by the International Council of Religious Education* (St. Louis, 1929), pp. 54–55.

40. Paul F. Boller, Jr., *Freedom and Fate in American Thought: From Edwards to Dewey* (Dallas, 1978), pp. 232, 159, 163, 176–77.

A 1935 appraisal of the Girl Scout program contains this statement on the conflict between the individual and the collective: "The Program Study staff assumes that 'man is not born human.' Characteristics which are distinctively human and which distinguish man from the animals are acquired through the interaction which occurs between the original nature of the individual and the social or cultural milieu into which he is born. The interests of the individual and of the community are in conflict to begin with and remain so in varying degrees thereafter. However, a working compromise is gradually effected between the individual and the community whereby the interests of both obtain partial realization. This compromise is effected first in the family, then in the play group and in the neighborhood. . . . It is at this point that group work agencies, such as the Girl Scouts, enter the picture." "Program Study Prospectus," 4 September 1935, Grace Coyle Papers, Case Western Reserve University Archives, Case Western Reserve University, Cleveland, Ohio, box 1, folder "Bibliographies — Group Work 1934–1956."

41. Eric Foner, *Free Soil, Free Labor, Free Men: The Ideology of the Republican Party before the Civil War* (New York, 1970), pp. 9, 11, 42.

42. The twentieth-century interest in groups and group life was not caused by a paucity of existing groups. America's reputation as a nation of joiners was well established when Alexis de Tocqueville made note of it in *Democracy in America*, and it had lost none of its luster by the end of the nineteenth century. Americans continued to show a remarkable inclination to group life, coming together in fraternal and religious associations, labor unions, clubs, town meetings, nationwide industrial oligopolies, and dozens of other varieties of organization. Tocqueville, *Democracy in America*, pp. 141–42. See also Ryan, *Cradle of the Middle Class*, pp. 236–37.

Readers will find much of interest in R. Jeffrey Lustig's superb account of the group thinkers as political theorists. While I share Lustig's political posture and cynicism, my own interpretation departs from his in one crucial respect. Although Lustig does not entirely dismiss the pragmatists' devotion to method and process, he interprets this focus as indicative of the desire of the group thinkers to avoid dealing in the hard realities of economic power and social exploitation (168, 170). Consistent with this analysis of method as a system of denial, Lustig argues that the group thinkers failed to enunciate a "democratic theory" (148) or to develop a "democratic reason" (168) and, indeed, wrote off "the interior of group life" (135, 172). In contrast, I argue that the seminal contribution of the group thinkers was to generate a new, democratic theory and system of social engineering and to locate that system within a praxis of group life. Lustig, *Corporate Liberalism*.

43. Herman Harrell Horne, *The Leadership of Bible Study Groups* (New York, 1912), pp. 36, 39. Herman Horne entry, *The National Cyclopaedia of American Biography* (New York, 1962).

44. Charles C. Cooper, "An Adventure in Religion," in Cooper, ed., *Religion and the Modern Mind* (New York, 1929), pp. 4, 9, 10. The Hungry Club's emphasis on precedent may be seen as analogous to the common law in the nineteenth-century American legal system.

45. Ibid., p. 158; Tay Hohoff, *A Ministry to Man: The Life of John Lovejoy Elliott* (New York, 1959), pp. 17–18, 30, 35–36, 41, 53.

46. Hohoff, *Ministry to Man*, pp. 75–78.

47. John Lovejoy Elliott, "Religion from the Standpoint of the Ethical Culture Movement," in *Religion and the Modern Mind*, pp. 159–60, 162–63.

48. *The Random House Dictionary of the English Language: College Edition* (New York, 1968).

49. Henry M. Busch, *Conference Methods in Industry: A Practical Hand-*

book of Basic Theory of Group Thinking and Tested Applications to Industrial Situations (n.p., 1949), pp. 10–11.

50. Quoted in Blewett, "Democracy as Religion," p. 45.

51. See David A. Hollinger's discussion of pragmatism's interest in the methodology of inquiry in "The Problem of Pragmatism in American History," *Journal of American History* 67 (June 1980): 92–100. R. Jackson Wilson describes Charles Sanders Peirce's devotion to a "community of inquiry" in *In Quest of Community*, pp. 41–44.

52. Boller, *Freedom and Fate in American Thought*, p. 239. One facet of this ideology of inquiry, and one historical example of it, was the belief in the function of "debate" in the Progressive Era. For a vivid example of the popularity of an institution we no longer cherish so fully, see Scott Nearing, *The Making of a Radical: A Political Autobiography* (New York, 1972), pp. 60–70 passim.

Historian David Hollinger describes pragmatism's bias as "anti-elitist." According to the pragmatic tradition, writes Hollinger, "inquiry was accessible on meaningful levels by the rank-and-file membership of an educated, democratic society." "Problem of Pragmatism in American History," pp. 99–100. Although I am much less convinced than Hollinger of the ability of ordinary Americans to use and control group discussions, conferences, forums, debates, and other mechanisms of group process, there is no question of the theoretical accessibility and the ubiquity of pragmatic inquiry. It was and is a critical ingredient of twentieth-century American culture. Inquiry may have a legal counterpart in twentieth-century legal realism. Committed to democracy and suspicious of elitism, the realists moved away from judicial review, with its connotations of expertism, guidance, and leadership, and toward a reliance on the legislative institutions that they thought better represented the people. Rather than search for some principle or some system of shared values to give meaning to the law, the realists focused on the ostensibly neutral realm of procedure (i.e., process). I am grateful to Alfred Konefsky for bringing this relationship to my attention. See his "Men of Great and Little Faith: Generations of Constitutional Scholars," *Buffalo Law Review* 30 (Spring 1981): 365–84.

53. Henry Sloane Coffin, *A Half Century of Union Theological Seminary, 1896–1945: An Informal History* (New York, 1954), pp. 155–56, 158.

54. Bruno Lasker Memoir, Columbia University Oral History Collection, Butler Library, Columbia University, New York, 2: 201–2 and 1: 167–68. Hohoff, *Ministry to Man*, p. 77; George Dykhuizen, *The Life and Mind of John Dewey* (Carbondale, Ill., 1973), pp. 104–5, 146–47; Quandt, *From the Small Town to the Great Community*, pp. 48–49; William Adams Brown, *Imperialistic Religion and the Religion of Democracy: A Study in Social Psychology* (New York, 1923), p. 194. The entry in the *Dictionary of American Religious Biography* describes Brown as a "liberal" who "struggled to formulate religious principles compatible with both denominational traditions . . . and secular standards of a scientific age." See *Dictionary of American Religious Biography* (Westport, Conn., 1977), pp. 71–72. Dewey was deeply and concretely interested in the Henry Street and Hull House settlements.

55. Catherine S. Vance, *The Girl Reserve Movement of the Young Women's Christian Association: An Analysis of the Educational Principles and Procedures*

Used throughout Its History, Teachers College, Columbia University, Contributions to Education No. 730 (New York, 1937), p. 88; discussion following Walter J. Rhodes, "Company Foremen's Clubs," in Albert Sobey and Walter J. Rhodes, eds., *Foremen's Clubs*, American Management Association, Production Executives Series No. 45 (New York, 1926), p. 22.

56. "Informal Conference Regarding the Work of the Commission on Christianity and Race Relations of the National Conference on the Christian Way of Life," 3 November 1923, in Bruno Lasker Papers, Columbia University Archives, Division of Special Collections, Butler Library, Columbia University, New York, Notebook, Vol. 1; "Interview with Professor Robert E. Park," 26 October 1923, Notebook, "1923." See also Lasker's critique of a discussion method he considered excessively open and uncontrolled, in "BL to ECC," Notebook, Vol. 1, no date. In addition, see Diggins' discussion of Talcott Parsons' concept of authority in "The Socialization of Authority and the Dilemmas of American Liberalism," *Social Research* 46 (Autumn 1979): 472.

57. Bower, *Religious Education in the Modern Church*, pp. 144–45, 148.

58. Macleod, *Building Character in the American Boy*, pp. 271–73.

59. Bower, *Religious Education in the Modern Church*, pp. 157–58, 146–47.

60. George Albert Coe, *Education in Religion and Morals*, pp. 313, 314, 323; Coffin, *Half Century of Union Theological Seminary*, p. 71.

61. Clarence A. Barbour, ed., *Making Religion Efficient* (New York, 1912), pp. 47–48; Men and Religion Forward Movement, Committee of Ninety-Seven, *Report of Committee of Ninety-Seven to the Christian Conservation Congress of the Men and Religion Forward Movement*, Carnegie Hall, 19 April 1912 (n.p., n.d.), pp. 24–25, 27. See also Charles F. McKinley, *Educational Evangelism: The Religious Discipline of Youth* (New York, 1905), p. 236; Fiske, *Boy Life and Self-Government*, pp. 95–97, 208, chap. 12; Horne, *Leadership of Bible Study Groups*, pp. 34–46; Lena Madesin Phillips, *Onward Leader* (New York, 1937), pp. 5, 6.

62. Ann Douglas, *The Feminization of American Culture* (New York, 1977), pp. 23, 25. Diggins, "Socialization of Authority," pp. 460, 482–83; Kenneth Cauthen, *The Impact of American Religious Liberalism* (New York, 1962), pp. 14–18.

63. Douglas, *Feminization of American Culture*, pp. 26, 36, 42–43.

64. Arthur Mann, *Yankee Reformers in the Urban Age: Social Reform in Boston, 1880–1900* (New York: Harper Torchbooks, 1966), pp. 73–79; May, *End of American Innocence*, p. 12.

65. Wilson, *In Quest of Community*, p. 105. See also the discussion of continuity in Cauthen, *Impact of American Religious Liberalism*, pp. 46–48, 54.

66. Quoted in Haskell, *Emergence of Professional Social Science*, p. 83; Henry Ward Beecher entry in *Dictionary of American Religious Biography*, pp. 35–37.

67. Bower, *Religious Education in the Modern Church*, pp. 51–52.

68. Barbour, *Making Religion Efficient*, pp. 37–38. Clarence Augustus Barbour entry, *Dictionary of American Biography*, Vol. 22, supplement 2 (New York, 1958), pp. 20–21.

69. Sherwood Eddy, *New Challenges to Faith: What Shall I Believe in the Light of Psychology and the New Science* (New York, 1926), pp. 231–32, see also

p. 90; Sherwood Eddy, *A Century with Youth: A History of the Y.M.C.A. from 1844 to 1944* (New York, 1944), p. 121; Vance, *Girl Reserve Movement of the Young Women's Christian Association*, p. 75. See also Meyer, *Protestant Search for Political Realism*, p. 21; Coe, *Education in Religion and Morals*, p. 272.

70. Eddy, *Century with Youth*, pp. 50–51.

71. Bower, *Religious Education in the Modern Church*, p. 159. See also Vance, *Girl Reserve Movement of the Young Women's Christian Association*, pp. 28–29.

72. George Albert Coe entry, *Dictionary of American Biography*, Supplement 5 (New York, 1977), pp. 115–16.

73. Coe, *Education in Religion and Morals*, pp. 5, 394, 17, 74–75, 78, 93, 137; Dykhuizen, *Life and Mind of John Dewey*, pp. 143–44. See also Wilson, *In Quest of Community*, pp. 133–37, on G. Stanley Hall.

74. Coe, *Education in Religion and Morals*, pp. 273–75.

75. Ibid., pp. 271–72. See also Meyer, *Protestant Search for Political Realism*, pp. 110, 138–42.

76. Fiske, *Boy Life and Self-Government*, pp. 96–97; George Walter Fiske entry, *National Cyclopaedia of American Biography*, Vol. 35 (New York, 1949), p. 241; Charles E. Germane and Edith Gayton Germane, *Character Education: A Program for the School and the Home*, 2 pts. (New York, 1929), 2: 179. Fiske's vocabulary and Coe's theoretical framework are apparent in Benjamin Spock, *The Common Sense Book of Baby and Child Care* (New York, 1946).

77. I have not attempted to generate numerical estimates for Bible clubs, Bible study classes, or Sunday schools. The Men and Religion Forward Movement, an interdenominational evangelistic movement launched in Buffalo in 1910, made Bible study one of its five programs. Among the leaders of that program was William Adams Brown, a religious educator knowledgeable in social psychology. In the decade after 1910, a number of local YWCAs established self-governing Bible clubs. See Men and Religion Forward Movement, *Report of Committee of Ninety-Seven*, p. 11; Allyn K. Foster, "The Dream Come True," in *Making Religion Efficient*, pp. 19–20; Vance, *Girl Reserve Movement of the Young Women's Christian Association*, p. 16.

78. McKinley, *Educational Evangelism*, pp. 241–42, 244; Barbour, *Making Religion Efficient*, p. 54. Charles Ethelbert McKinley entry, *Who Was Who in America*, Vol. 5 (Chicago, 1973).

79. Edwin F. See, *The Teaching of Bible Classes: Principles and Methods, With Special Reference to Classes of Young Men and Boys* (New York, 1905), pp. 2, 3, 104, 39, 108; Barbour, *Making Religion Efficient*, pp. 58, 55; Horne, *Leadership of Bible Study Groups*, pp. iii, 5, 34–36; McKinley, *Educational Evangelism*, p. 246.

80. Barbour, *Making Religion Efficient*, p. 38.

81. E. F. See, "The Social Element," in Young Men's Christian Association, *Mountain Lake Papers: General Secretaries' Conference, 1902* (New York, 1902), pp. 3, 12, 14–15; Louis D. Hartson, "The Psychology of the Club: A Study in Social Psychology," *Pedagogical Seminary* 18 (September 1911): 357–71, 411.

82. Fiske, *Boy Life and Self-Government*, pp. 106, 110–11, 213; McKinley, *Educational Evangelism*, p. 244; Barbour, *Making Religion Efficient*, pp. 41–42.

See also Coe, *Education in Religion and Morals*, p. 323, and Robert E. L. Faris, *Chicago Sociology, 1920–1932* (San Francisco, 1967), p. 42.

The fondness for study of spontaneous organizations reflects the belief that because these groups were spontaneously created they were models of pure group life and thus especially fine vehicles for social engineering. See Hartson, "Psychology of the Club," pp. 381–84. The focus on gangs was also a product of an increased interest in adolescence following the publication of G. Stanley Hall's *Adolescence* in 1904. Hall argued that adolescence was a time of transition from individual to collective concerns. See Wilson, *In Quest of Community*, pp. 133–34, 137.

83. Foster, "Dream Come True," pp. 8–9, 12, 17, 19; Men and Religion Forward Movement, *Report of Committee of Ninety-Seven*, pp. 3–7, 10–11, 20, 24–25, 27.

84. George Albert Coe, *The Psychology of Religion* (Chicago, 1916), pp. 1, 171, 152, 394; Kilpatrick, "Project Method," p. 320; *The Encyclopedia of Education*, Vol. 2 (New York, 1971), p. 588. In addition, Kilpatrick's project method was a problem-solving approach, in which students presumably absorbed a method applicable to other areas and problems.

85. Samuel Tenenbaum, *William Heard Kilpatrick: Trail Blazer in Education* (New York, 1951), pp. 23, 26, 31, 35, 37, 135; Riesman, *The Lonely Crowd*, pp. 76–85.

CHAPTER TWO. A NEW RELIGION

1. Tay Hohoff, *A Ministry to Man: The Life of John Lovejoy Elliott* (New York, 1959), pp. 75, 77; George Walter Fiske, *Boy Life and Self-Government* (New York, 1910), p. 23; Clarence A. Barbour, ed., *Making Religion Efficient* (New York, 1912), p. 47.

2. Follett was a transitional figure in the group-process movement. Although the substance of *The New State* was worked out in a traditional setting—the Roxbury Neighborhood House in Boston—her ideas were widely influential. See "Notes on the Life of Mary Parker Follett," in Eduard C. Lindeman Papers, Columbia University Archives, Division of Special Collections, Butler Library, Columbia University, New York, box 2, file "Sheffield."

3. A. Paul Hare, "The History and Present State of Small Group Research," in Hare, ed., *Handbook of Small Group Research*, 2d ed. (New York, 1976), appendix 2, p. 384.

4. Goodwin Watson, *Youth after Conflict* (New York, 1947), p. 88.

5. George Albert Coe, *The Motives of Men* (New York, 1928), p. 237; Sherwood Eddy, *Eighty Adventurous Years: An Autobiography* (New York, 1955), p. 217; Mary Parker Follett, *The New State: Group Organization the Solution of Popular Government* (New York, 1918), p. 99.

6. Emory S. Bogardus, *Democracy by Discussion* (Washington, D.C., 1942), pp. iv–v, 37; Harrison S. Elliott, *A New World Democracy: An Outline Study of the New World Order in the Light of Jesus' Ideals* (New York, 1918), pp. 41–44.

7. David M. Kennedy, *Over Here: The First World War and American Society* (New York, 1980), p. 48.

8. Elliott, *New World Democracy*, p. 7.

9. The speech is printed in Henry Steele Commager, ed., *Documents of American History*, 2 vols., 7th ed. (New York, 1963), 2: 128–32.

10. Eric Foner, *Free Soil, Free Labor, Free Men: The Ideology of the Republican Party before the Civil War* (New York, 1970).

11. John Blewett, "Democracy as Religion: Unity in Human Relations," in Blewett, ed., *John Dewey: His Thought and Influence* (1960; rpt. Westport, Conn., 1973), pp. 45–46; Samuel Tenenbaum, *William Heard Kilpatrick: Trail Blazer in Education* (New York, 1951), pp. 3–4, 10, 13; Goodwin Watson Memoir, Columbia University Oral History Collection, Butler Library, Columbia University, New York, 1: 9, 31, 36–37, 2: 197–201.

12. Coyle obituary, *New York Times*, 10 March 1962, p. 22; "Assembly Talk by Grace L. Coyle," 18 May 1933, Grace Coyle Papers, Case Western Reserve University Archives, Case Western Reserve University, Cleveland, Ohio, box 6, file "Speeches, 1930s."

13. In his study of the University of Chicago sociologists, Robert Faris notes the theological background of several members of the faculty and adds: "The wild enthusiasm which not long before had generated a serious intention to Christianize the entire world in a single generation became transferred in these men to the more secular but similarly inspiring aims of higher education and the creation of a new science of social behavior." Robert E. L. Faris, *Chicago Sociology, 1920–1932* (San Francisco, 1967), p. 26. See also John P. Diggins, "The Socialization of Authority and the Dilemmas of American Liberalism," *Social Research* 46 (Autumn 1979): 482–86.

14. Croly's statement originally appeared in the *New Republic*. It is quoted in Coyle, "Some Personal and Social Values in Adult Education," Coyle Papers, box 6, file "Speeches, 1930s."

15. Donald Harring to Bowman, 4 February 1954, LeRoy Bowman Papers, Columbia University Archives, Division of Special Collections, Butler Library, Columbia University, New York, box 1, file "Miscellaneous Correspondence"; *Cleveland Plain Dealer*, 12 December 1965, sec. F, p. 3.

16. Bruno Lasker, "Contact and Conduct," *International Journal of Ethics* 38 (January 1928): 153–66. The quotation is from "Luncheon at Hudson Guild, Chicago," 26 November 1924, Bruno Lasker Papers, Columbia University Archives, Division of Special Collections, Butler Library, Columbia University, New York, Notebook, "1923."

17. R. M. MacIver, *As a Tale That Is Told: The Autobiography of R. M. MacIver* (Chicago, 1968), pp. 2, 33, 130–31, 129.

18. L. Cody Marsh, "Group Treatment of the Psychoses by the Psychological Equivalent of the Revival," *Mental Hygiene* 15 (April 1931): 330, 333, 341; American Group Psychotherapy Association, Committee on History, "A Brief History of the American Group Psychotherapy Association, 1943–1968," *International Journal of Group Psychotherapy* 21 (October 1971): 406–7.

19. Stephen Vaughn, *Holding Fast the Inner Lines: Democracy, Nationalism,*

and the Committee on Public Information (Chapel Hill, 1980), pp. 52, 2, 43, 45, 104, 238. Vaughn asserts that the CPI was established to preserve "American democracy," implying that this "democracy" had identifiable content. Although his book contains suggestions that such a content existed, the thesis is by no means proved. See pp. xii, 237–38 for Vaughn's positive evaluation of the work of the CPI.

20. Kennedy, *Over Here*, p. 20; Vaughn, *Holding Fast The Inner Lines*, pp. 238, 47 (italics added).

21. Quoted in Vaughn, *Holding Fast the Inner Lines*, p. 13. Bullard's background prepared him well for understanding the new religion of democracy. His father was a Presbyterian minister, and Bullard had worked in a settlement on New York's Lower East Side. See pp. 7–8.

22. Kennedy, *Over Here*, pp. 43, 47, 60; Vaughn, *Holding Fast the Inner Lines*, p. 10.

23. Kennedy, *Over Here*, pp. 43 (Allen quotation), 75, 47, 60; Vaughn, *Holding Fast the Inner Lines*, pp. 213, 230, 7, 18, 10.

24. Vaughn, *Holding Fast the Inner Lines*, pp. 20 (Creel), 10 (Bullard). See also the remarks by Newton D. Baker in Kennedy, *Over Here*, p. 60.

25. Vaughn, *Holding Fast the Inner Lines*, pp. 22, 194, 213.

26. Kennedy, *Over Here*, p. 61; David Kennedy, "Curing the Body Politic's Ills: Is America Governable?" *Stanford Observer*, January 1981, p. 3.

27. Kennedy, "Curing the Body Politic's Ills," p. 3.

28. John Dewey, *Democracy and Education: An Introduction to the Philosophy of Education* (New York, 1916), pp. 25, 99, 101.

29. Religious educator George Albert Coe captured the mood of 1917 when he wrote that "a democracy cannot afford to use in its public schools the methods that an autocratic state finds adapted to its purposes. . . . A divine-human democracy cannot grow up through educative processes that have in their nostrils the breath of autocracy." *A Social Theory of Religious Education.*

30. William H. Kilpatrick, "The Project Method," *Teachers College Record* 19 (September 1918): 320–23, 329, 334.

31. Kennedy, *Over Here*, p. 92.

32. David W. Eakins, "The Origins of Corporate Liberal Policy Research, 1916–1922: The Political-Economic Expert and the Decline of Public Debate," in Jerry Israel, ed., *Building the Organizational Society: Essays on Associational Activities in Modern America* (New York, 1972), pp. 163–79; Kennedy, *Over Here*, p. 92; Robert Allen Skotheim, *Totalitarianism and American Social Thought* (New York, 1971), p. 21; Roderick Nash, *The Nervous Generation: American Thought, 1917–1930* (Chicago, 1970), pp. 52–62.

33. William E. Leuchtenburg, *The Perils of Prosperity, 1914–32* (Chicago, 1958), p. 153.

34. Eddy, *Eighty Adventurous Years*, pp. 101, 117. See also Follett, *New State*, p. 3; Elliott, *New World Democracy*, pp. 41–43.

35. Kilpatrick diary entry for 27 October 1930, printed in Tenenbaum, *William Heard Kilpatrick*, p. 274; Coe, *Motives of Men*, p. 15. Coe notes that this conception of man predated the war (p. 19).

36. Watson, *Youth after Conflict*, pp. 105–9, 29; Charles C. Cooper, ed.,

Religion and the Modern Mind (New York, 1929), pp. 9–10; Sherwood Eddy, *A Century with Youth: A History of the Y.M.C.A. from 1844 to 1944* (New York, 1944), p. 86.

37. Watson, *Youth after Conflict*, pp. 83 (quotation), 122, 19–26.

38. Follett, *New State*, p. 231; Harold L. Sheppard, "The Social and Historical Philosophy of Elton Mayo," *Antioch Review* 10 (September 1950): 396; Watson, *Youth after Conflict*, pp. 95–96.

There is little doubt that political activity, especially at the national level of government, decreased substantially in the 1920s. But what one makes of this fact depends on the context in which it appears. Given a "progressive" paradigm, in which one assumes that political activity represents reform, the decade takes on a conservative cast. Given a "social-engineering" paradigm, in which one assumes that political activity represents only one possible mechanism of reform and/or control, the decade takes on an entirely different tone. The viewpoint presented here is that during the 1920s, political forms of control were replaced and augmented by other forms of control, some of them "democratic." This shift from politics to democratic social engineering was one important characteristic of the decade. It is captured in a letter written by LeRoy Bowman, well known for his expertise in democratic group leadership. "I don't like politics," Bowman said, "it requires compromises I dislike and resist." Bowman to Rex D. Hopper, 24 April 1962, Bowman Papers, box 1, file "Miscellaneous Correspondence."

39. Notebook, "1936," in Eduard C. Lindeman Papers, Social Welfare History Archives, Minneapolis, Minnesota, box 2, folder 7, pp. 16–17; Watson, *Youth after Conflict*, pp. 96–98; William Heard Kilpatrick, *Education for a Changing Civilization: Three Lectures Delivered on the Luther Laflin Kellogg Foundation at Rutgers University, 1926* (New York, 1926), pp. 71–72.

40. Watson, *Youth after Conflict*, p. viii (by Kilpatrick); Tenenbaum, *William Heard Kilpatrick*, p. 283; Character Education Association, *Character Education Methods: The Iowa Plan $22,000 Award, 1922* (Washington, D.C., n.d.), p. 9; William Adams Brown, *Imperialistic Religion and the Religion of Democracy: A Study in Social Psychology* (New York, 1923), pp. 64, 85.

41. Mary Parker Follett entry, *Dictionary of American Biography*, Vol. 21, Supplement 1 (New York, 1944), pp. 308–9.

42. Follett, *New State*, pp. 3, 89; Kilpatrick, *Education for a Changing Civilization*, p. 67. See also Tenenbaum, *William Heard Kilpatrick*, p. 194.

43. Alfred Dwight Sheffield, recorder, *Training for Group Experience: A Syllabus of Materials from a Laboratory Course for Group Leaders Given at Columbia University in 1927* (New York, 1929), pp. 30–31.

44. "Some Obstacles to Race Cooperation," speech by Bruno Lasker to the Urban League, Columbus, Ohio, 14 December 1924, Lasker Papers, Notebook, Vol. 1; "Conference with Girl Reserve Field Workers," 23 April 1924, in Lasker Papers, Notebook, "1923." See also MacIver, *As a Tale That Is Told*, p. 94.

45. Active efforts to decentralize the structure of government are best exemplified in the community center movement, essentially an attempt to revitalize neighborhoods by employing the public schools as neighborhood community centers. See Robert Fisher, "From Grass-Roots Organizing to Community Service: Com-

munity Organization Practice in the Community Center Movement, 1907–1930," Unpublished paper, 1980; Follett, *New State*, pp. 192, 205, 230, 321.

46. On Elliott, see Henry Sloane Coffin, *A Half Century of Union Theological Seminary, 1896–1945: An Informal History* (New York, 1954), p. 155. On Watson, see Watson Memoir, 1: 103, 2: 125–26, 195–96, and Watson, *Youth after Conflict*, pp. 150–51.

47. Catherine S. Vance, *The Girl Reserve Movement of the Young Women's Christian Association: An Analysis of the Educational Principles and Procedures Used throughout Its History*, Teachers College, Columbia University, Contributions to Education No. 730 (New York, 1937), pp. 14, 19–20; Gisela Konopka, *Eduard C. Lindeman and Social Work Philosophy* (Minneapolis, 1958), pp. 12, 33–34. On Dewey's *How We Think*, see Harrison S. Elliott, *The Leadership of Red Triangle Groups: A Consideration of the Organization and Conduct of Bible Study or Life Problem Groups in Army Camps* (New York, 1918), p. 18; Watson, *Youth after Conflict*, pp. 150–51; Kenneth Lewis Heaton, *Character Building through Recreation: A Training Course in Recreational Leadership* (Chicago, 1929), p. 10.

48. Tenenbaum, *William Heard Kilpatrick*, pp. 185–87; William Heard Kilpatrick entry, *Dictionary of American Biography*, Supplement 7, 1961–65 (New York, 1981), pp. 434–36.

49. Tenenbaum, *William Heard Kilpatrick*, p. 190; Watson Memoir, 1: 36, 2: 197–98; Coffin, *Half Century of Union Theological Seminary*, p. 155; Lasker Memoir, 2: 273–74; Sheffield, *Training for Group Experience*, p. 25; Vance, *Girl Reserve Movement of the Young Women's Christian Association*, pp. 83–85.

50. Coffin, *Half Century of Union Theological Seminary*, pp. 73, 71, 87–89, 106, 155.

51. Ibid., p. 27; Barbour, *Making Religion Efficient*, chap. 3; Donald B. Meyer, *The Protestant Search for Political Realism, 1919–1941* (Berkeley, 1960), pp. 48–49.

52. Coffin, *Half Century of Union Theological Seminary*, pp. 155–57; Harrison Sackett Elliott and Ethel Cutler, *Student Standards of Action* (New York, 1914).

53. Elliott, *Leadership of Red Triangle Groups*, pp. 1–2, 9–10, 18, 23, 38, 52, 55, 58.

54. Watson Memoir, 2: 120, 121, 89; Watson, *Youth after Conflict*, p. 114; Entry 25 July 1924, Lasker Papers, Notebook, "1923"; Sheffield, *Training for Group Experience*, p. iv; Lasker Memoir, 3: 568, n. 32; National Conference on the Christian Way of Life (NCCWL), "Summary of Minutes of the Executive Committee," 13 November 1924, in Lasker Papers, Notebook, "1923"; Sheffield to Lindeman, 28 April 1925, in Lindeman Papers, box 2, file "Sheffield"; Coe, *Motives of Men*, pp. 234–35; miscellaneous bibliographies in Coyle Papers, box 1, file "Bibliographies — Group Work." On Elliott's use of nondirective discussion methods in his classes at Union, see Coffin, *Half Century of Union Theological Seminary*, pp. 156–58.

55. Lasker Memoir, 2: 233–37, 244, 3: 568, n. 32; Sheffield to Lindeman, 28 April 1925, Lindeman Papers, box 2, file "Sheffield"; "Conference on Printed Discussion," 3 March 1925, Lasker Papers, Notebook, "1923"; Entry 15 April 1924, Lasker Papers, Notebook, "1923"; Entry 25 July 1924, Lasker Papers, Notebook, "1923." See also Robert MacIver's account of The Inquiry in Robert MacIver

Memoir, Columbia University Oral History Collection, Butler Library, Columbia University, New York, pp. 27–28.

56. Lasker Memoir, 1: 13, 1, 2, 19, 48, 9, 52, 76–77.

57. Ibid., pp. 10, 96–119; B. Seebohm Rowntree, *The Human Factor in Business* (London, 1921).

58. Lasker Memoir, 1: 180–81, 167–68.

59. Ibid., pp. 141, 148.

60. Ibid., 2: 191, 207, 210, 213–14.

61. Lindeman to Follett, 10 December 1922, Lindeman Papers, box 2, file "Mary Follett."

62. Text of article written for the *Survey*, 15 April 1924, Lasker Papers, Notebook, Vol. 1; "Commission on Race Relations," 26 October 1923, Lasker Papers, Notebook, Vol. 1; "Minutes of Hull House/Riverside Conference," 6–11 November 1924, Lasker Papers, Notebook, "1923"; "Notes on Luncheon at Hudson Guild," 26 November 1924, Lasker Papers, Notebook, "1923"; "Notes on Conference with Girl Reserve Field Workers," 23 April 1924, Lasker Papers, Notebook, "1923"; "Some Obstacles to Race Cooperation," speech by Lasker to Urban League, Columbus, Ohio, 14 December 1924, Lasker Papers, Notebook, Vol. 1.

63. "Minutes of Discussion of Prejudice as a Social Phenomenon," 2 January 1925, Lasker Papers, Notebook, "1923–24" (Race Commission, Vol. 2); "Second Discussion on Prejudice as a Social Phenomenon," 30 January 1925, ibid. By 1927, Lasker had accepted an underlying economic basis to interracial conflict. Nonetheless, he retained an optimistic bias toward psychological solutions. Though racial hostility was set in a genuine economic conflict of interest, it could be "attacked successfully only by a psychological revolution." See "Economic Aspects of Interracial Questions," address before the National Industrial Committee of the YWCA, 24 March 1927, Lasker Papers, Notebook, Vol. 4, "1927."

64. Lasker Memoir, 2: 269–70.

65. The Inquiry, "The Worker and His Job: Outlines for the Use of Workers' Groups" (New York, n.d.); Lasker Memoir, 2: 271.

66. Sheffield to Eduard C. Lindeman [1924], Lindeman Papers, box 2, file "Sheffield."

67. "Informal Conference Regarding the Work of the Commission on Christianity and Race Relations of the National Conference on the Christian Way of Life," 3 November 1923, Lasker Papers, Notebook, Vol. 1.

68. BL [Bruno Lasker] to ECC, no date, Lasker Papers, Notebook, Vol. 1; "Interview with Professor Robert E. Park," 26 October 1923, Lasker Papers, Notebook, "1923"; Sheffield to Lindeman, 8 October 1923, Lindeman Papers, box 2, file "Sheffield."

69. "Minutes of Third Meeting, Committee on Race Attitudes in Children," 12 November 1925, Lasker Papers, Notebook, "1923–24" (Race Commission, Vol. 2).

70. Sheffield, *Training for Group Experience*, pp. iv, v.

71. "Notes on Meeting in Cleveland," 12 and 13 November 1924; entry for 25 November 1924; "Case Studies"; "Conference on Printed Discussion," 3 March 1925, all in Lasker Papers, Notebook, "1923."

72. Entry 27 March 1924, re Charles Teller, Stuyvesant Neighborhood House, New York City, and entry for 15 April 1924, re Forest B. Washington of Armstrong Association of Philadelphia, both in Lasker Papers, Notebook, "1923."

73. "Notes on Atlanta — October 18 to 20, 1923," Lasker Papers, Notebook, "1923." The Inquiry was funded by the direct, nonfoundation contributions of Mr. and Mrs. John D. Rockefeller, Jr. (the budget in 1925 was about $61,000). See Lasker Papers, Notebook, "1923–24" (Race Commission, Vol. 2), following "Second Discussion on Prejudice as a Social Phenomenon," and Lasker Memoir, 2: 235. Contributors to the organization included Cleveland H. Dodge, Dwight W. Morrow, Mary Simkhovitch, William P. Hapgood, Samuel G. Inman, Graham Taylor, and Mrs. Willard Straight. See NCCWL, "Summary of the Minutes of the Executive Committee," 13 November 1924, Lasker Papers, Notebook, "1923."

74. Vance, *Girl Reserve Movement of the Young Women's Christian Association*, pp. 5, 52; Abel J. Gregg, *Group Leaders and Boy Character: A Manual for Leaders of Groups of Boys* (1924; rev. ed. New York, 1927); Lasker Memoir, 2: 233; entry for 25 March 1924, Lasker Papers, Notebook, "1923."

The intellectual sources which fueled this surge of interest in group process in the 1920s are, on the whole, familiar ones. Mary Parker Follett's *Creative Experience* (1924) is cited in the YMCA and YWCA literature, as is the work of Harrison Elliott. Both the Girl Reserves and Gregg, in his leadership manual, demonstrate an obligation to William Kilpatrick and his project method. See Vance, *Girl Reserve Movement of the Young Women's Christian Association*, pp. 76, 58–59, 96, 99; Sherwood Eddy, *New Challenges to Faith: What Shall I Believe in the Light of Psychology and the New Science* (New York, 1926), pp. 90–92; Gregg, *Group Leaders and Boy Character*, pp. 174–89, 52. A unitary theory of personality, rooted in Dewey and Gardner Murphy, is also apparent in the sources. See Vance, *Girl Reserve Movement of the Young Women's Christian Association*, p. 75, and Eddy, *New Challenges to Faith*, p. vii.

75. Vance, *Girl Reserve Movement of the Young Women's Christian Association*, pp. 14, 19, 28–29, 22.

76. Ibid., pp. 36, 39, 88, 94; Gregg, *Group Leaders and Boy Character*, p. 66.

77. Robert Fisher, "From Grass-Roots Organizing to Community Service: Community Organization Practice in the Community Center Movement, 1907–1930," unpublished paper, 1980, pp. 15–16.

78. Heaton, *Character Building through Recreation*; Tenenbaum, *William Heard Kilpatrick*, pp. 287–88; William H. Kilpatrick Memoir, Columbia University Oral History Collection, Butler Library, Columbia University, New York, p. 134; Lawrence A. Cremin, *The Transformation of the School: Progressivism in American Education, 1876–1957* (New York, 1961), pp. 224–31.

CHAPTER THREE. THE BUSINESS OF AMERICA . . .

1. Milton Derber, *The American Idea of Industrial Democracy, 1865–1965* (Urbana, Ill., 1970), pp. 104, 140.

2. Claude S. George, Jr., *The History of Management Thought* (Englewood Cliffs, N.J., 1972), pp. 136–43, 182–83.

3. On the change from a producer to a consumer economy, see Stuart Ewen, *Captains of Consciousness: Advertising and the Social Roots of the Consumer Culture* (New York, 1976).

4. Frank Presbrey, *The History and Development of Advertising* (1928; rpt. Greenwood Press: Englewood Cliffs, N.J., 1968), illustration section following p. 618.

5. Quoted in Ewen, *Captains of Consciousness*, p. 92.

6. Edward L. Bernays, *Biography of an Idea: Memoirs of Public Relations Counsel Edward L. Bernays* (New York, 1965), p. 384; Ewen, *Captains of Consciousness*, p. 93.

7. "Ivey Ledbetter Lee," *Dictionary of American Biography*, Vol. 21, Supplement 1 (New York, 1944), p. 489.

8. Peter Collier and David Horowitz, *The Rockefellers: An American Dynasty* (New York: Signet Books, 1977), p. 43.

9. Ibid., pp. 65–66, 116.

10. Ibid., pp. 116, 120.

11. Ibid., pp. 127–28; Dale Carnegie, *How to Win Friends and Influence People* (1936; New York: Pocket Books, 1964), preface, pp. 135, 136.

12. Carnegie, *How to Win Friends and Influence People*, p. 136 (italics added); Collier and Horowitz, *Rockefellers*, p. 115.

13. Bernays, *Biography of an Idea*, pp. 155, 187–92, 194.

14. Edward L. Bernays, *Crystallizing Public Opinion* (New York, 1923); Walter Lippmann, *Public Opinion* (New York, 1922).

15. Lippmann, *Public Opinion*, pp. 12–14, 30.

16. Ibid., pp. 31, 383, 386–87.

17. Ibid., pp. 248–49, 402–3.

18. Bernays, *Crystallizing Public Opinion*, pp. 34–35, 62, 126.

19. Ibid., pp. 109, 104–5, 63–64, 140–43, 159.

20. Ibid., pp. 159–60.

21. Ibid., pp. 128–29.

22. Ibid., p. 212.

23. Craig Lloyd, *Aggressive Introvert: A Study of Herbert Hoover and Public Relations Management, 1912–1932* (Columbus, Ohio, 1972), pp. 107–109, 170, 158, 156, 194, 45–52; John Kenneth Galbraith, *The Great Crash: 1929* (Boston: Sentry Edition, 1961), pp. 142–46.

24. Lloyd, *Aggressive Introvert*, pp. 185–86, 160, 102, 107.

25. Clarence Darrow, "Salesmanship," *American Mercury*, August 1925, excerpted in George E. Mowry, ed., *The Twenties: Fords, Flappers and Fanatics* (Englewood Cliffs, N.J., 1963), pp. 20, 19.

26. Gail Thain Parker, "*How to Win Friends and Influence People*: Dale Carnegie and the Problem of Sincerity," *American Quarterly* 29 (Winter 1977): 506–18.

27. Carnegie, *How to Win Friends and Influence People*, pp. 28, 92–93, 144. Among the sources Carnegie gave for his ideas were pragmatists John Dewey and William James (pp. 14, 31).

28. Ibid., pp. 113, 112, 118.

29. Ibid., pp. 157 (Roosevelt example), 155–56 (sales example). See also p. 160.

30. Ibid., p. 54.

31. Quoted in Derber, *American Idea of Industrial Democracy,* pp. 174–75.

32. Quoted in ibid., p. 168.

33. Ibid., pp. 214, 206–29. See also Frank Tannenbaum's vision of a fully cooperative system of industrial governance, in *The Labor Movement: Its Conservative Functions and Social Consequences* (New York, 1921). The book was dedicated to Dewey.

34. Clarence J. Hicks, *My Life in Industrial Relations: Fifty Years in the Growth of a Profession* (New York, 1941), pp. 47, 50.

35. George, *History of Management Thought,* pp. 146–54; David F. Noble, *America by Design: Science, Technology, and the Rise of Corporate Capitalism* (New York: Oxford University Press, 1979), pp. 257–98.

36. Frederick Winslow Taylor, *The Principles of Scientific Management* (New York, 1911), pp. 40–47.

37. Derber, *American Idea of Industrial Democracy,* pp. 208–9.

38. Ordway Tead, *Instincts in Industry: A Study of Working-Class Psychology* (New York, 1918), pp. 131–32, 216.

39. Ibid., pp. 130, 145–46, 179–83, 185, 207, 219.

40. William H. Kilpatrick, "The Project Method," *Teachers College Record* 19 (September 1918): 319–35.

41. M. P. Follett, *The New State: Group Organization the Solution of Popular Government* (New York, 1918), pp. 5, 89, 180, 208, 212, 229, 230, 368, 6, 31, 159 (quotation).

42. Jean B. Quandt, *From the Small Town to the Great Community: The Social Thought of Progressive Intellectuals* (New Brunswick, N.J., 1970), pp. 37–42; Follett, *New State,* pp. 196, 202, 205, 230.

43. See the biography in the introduction to *Dynamic Administration: The Collected Papers of Mary Parker Follett,* ed. Henry C. Metcalf and L. Urwick (London, 1941), pp. 10–29.

44. Ibid., pp. 17–19, 27–28.

45. Ibid., pp. 30–33, 71–73, 32 (quotation).

46. Ibid., pp. 58–59.

47. Ibid., pp. 59, 102, 258, 263, 288.

48. "Elton Mayo," in *International Encyclopedia of the Social Sciences,* 18 vols. (New York, 1968), 10: 82–83.

49. Loren Baritz, *The Servants of Power: A History of the Use of Social Science in American Industry* (Middletown, Conn., 1960), pp. 88–89; Paul Blumberg, *Industrial Democracy: The Sociology of Participation* (New York: Schocken Books, 1973), pp. 15, 21.

50. Elton Mayo, *The Psychology of Pierre Janet* (1952; rpt. Westport, Conn., 1972), pp. 10–13, 15, 53, 77, 89, 91, 104–5, 107, 124–25; Mayo, *The Social Problems of an Industrial Civilization* (Boston, 1945), pp. ix, 14–15.

51. Harold L. Sheppard, "The Social and Historical Philosophy of Elton Mayo," *Antioch Review* 10 (September 1950): 400.

52. Baritz, *Servants of Power,* pp. 123–24.

53. Ibid., pp. 112, 134; Elton Mayo, "What Every Village Knows," *Survey Graphic* 26 (December 1937): 697–98; Sheppard, "Social and Historical Philosophy of Elton Mayo," p. 398; Elton Mayo, *The Political Problems of Industrial Civilization* (Boston, 1947), p. 23.

According to Paul Blumberg's recent reevaluation of the Hawthorne experiments, the relationship between democracy and productivity was downplayed in subsequent studies carried out at the Western Electric facilities and has been virtually ignored by later writers summarizing the experiments for texts in sociology and industrial sociology. Blumberg believes that this neglect occurred because neither Mayo nor his successors cared to face the radical implication that "self-determination" would increase productivity; to have done so would have entailed consideration, at least, of major modifications in industrial governance.

While plausible enough, Blumberg's analysis contains the vulnerable assumption that the issue at Hawthorne was between a genuinely democratic methodology and existing managerial prerogatives. In fact, when Mayo's results were published, business had been working with participatory techniques for more than a decade, through the most conservative period in the recent history of industrial relations. The influential journalist John Fitch had in 1924 suggested participatory solutions to the problem of factory work that was "monotonous" and "distasteful." Blumberg knows nothing of this history, and little of the efforts by establishment businessmen to use democracy to serve their own ends. Because Blumberg defines these efforts as unworthy of Mayo's original "radical" suggestion, he dismisses a 1930s literature on supervision, and experiments with T-groups in the 1960s, as somehow adulterative of the original democratic concept. Blumberg, *Industrial Democracy,* pp. 30–31, 40–41, 28–29, 129; John A. Fitch, *The Causes of Industrial Unrest* (New York, 1924), pp. 378, 383–85.

54. Baritz, *Servants of Power,* pp. 186, 185.

55. Henry M. Busch, *Conference Methods in Industry: A Practical Handbook of Basic Theory of Group Thinking and Tested Applications to Industrial Situations* (n.p., 1949), pp. ix, x, 5.

56. Alfred J. Marrow, *The Practical Theorist: The Life and Work of Kurt Lewin* (New York, 1969), pp. 15, 141–42; anonymous manuscript on Lewin, dated 6/28/67 and 7/5/67, in Kurt Lewin Papers, Archives of the History of American Psychology, University of Akron, Akron, Ohio, box 948, file 67.

57. Quoted in Marrow, *Practical Theorist,* p. 144.

58. Charles Hendry to Alfred Marrow, 5 September 1947, Lewin Papers, box M946.

59. "Prospectus concerning the Future of the National Training Laboratory on Group Development," Grace Coyle Papers, Case Western Reserve University Archives, Case Western Reserve University, Cleveland, Ohio, box 3, file "National Training Laboratory on Group Development, Bethel, Maine — 1948–1950"; National Training Laboratory on Group Development, "Explorations in Human Relations Training: An Assessment of Experience, 1947–1953" (n.p., n.d.), LeRoy Bowman Papers, Columbia University Archives, Division of Special Collections, Butler Library, Columbia University, New York, box 12, file "Group Work," p. 3.

60. "Preliminary Report of the First National Training Laboratory on Group Development," Bethel, Maine, 16 June to 4 July 1947, National Training Laboratory Papers, Archives of the History of American Psychology, University of Akron, Akron, Ohio, box 220, folder "Preliminary Report of the First National Training Laboratory on Group Development"; "Prospectus concerning the Future of the National Training Laboratory," Coyle Papers; Coyle to Frank Hertel, 13 December 1948, Coyle Papers, box 4, "Correspondence, 1948–49"; "Explorations in Human Relations Training," Bowman Papers.

61. Grace Coyle, "The Relation of 'Group Dynamics' to Group Work," Coyle Papers, box 4, "Correspondence, 1948–49."

62. Gordon W. Allport, "The Genius of Kurt Lewin," typescript, 5 May 1967, Lewin Papers, box M944, folder 1.

63. Coyle, "Relation of 'Group Dynamics' to Group Work."

64. Ronald Lippitt, evaluation of Lewin, 10 May 1967, Lewin Papers, box M944.

65. Coyle, "Relation of 'Group Dynamics' to Group Work."

66. Boy Scouts of America, *Handbook for Scoutmasters: A Manual of Leadership*, 2d ed. (New York, 1920), pp. 269, 270, 272.

67. "Preliminary Report of the First National Training Laboratory"; "Chapter III NTL Document . . . Establishing an Appropriate Environment for Training Operations," NTL Papers, box 220, file "Misc. AHAP#1." See also "Explorations in Human Relations Training," Bowman Papers.

68. "Chapter III NTL Document," NTL Papers.

69. Thomas B. Fordham, "The Invisible Sign," typescript, Dayton Public Library, Dayton, Ohio, p. 17; Sherwood Eddy, *A Century with Youth: A History of the Y.M.C.A. from 1844 to 1944* (New York, 1944), pp. 59–61.

70. J. W. Reinhardt, "The Foreman's Club Comes Back," *Personnel* 13 (May 1937): 156; Fordham, "Invisible Sign," p. 17; National Association of Foremen, *The Foremen's Club Manual* (Chicago, 1938), p. 17; Edward Tingley comments in Albert Sobey and Walter J. Rhodes, eds., *Foremen's Clubs*, American Management Association, Production Executives' Series No. 45 (New York, 1926), pp. 12–13; George Frederick Buxton, "Report of Foremanship Training Program in Indiana Industries, 1919–1936," Purdue University, Engineering Extension Department, Extension Series No. 36 (Lafayette, Ind., 1936), p. 3.

71. Tingley comments, in Sobey and Rhodes, "Foremen's Clubs," p. 11. Standard Oil of New Jersey created a club in Bayonne, New Jersey, the site in 1915 of a serious labor disturbance. See Russell N. Keppel, "Development of Foremen," in Frank P. Cox, Russell N. Keppel, and George Mettam, "Development of Foremen," American Management Association, Production Executives' Series No. 44 (New York, 1926), p. 17, and Hicks, *My Life in Industrial Relations*, p. 54.

72. NAF, *Foremen's Club Manual*, p. 17; Albert Sobey, "Community Foremen's Clubs," in Sobey and Rhodes, "Foremen's Clubs," p. 3; Harry G. Lefever, "The Involvement of the Men and Religion Forward Movement in the Cause of Labor Justice, Atlanta, Georgia, 1912–1916," *Labor History* 14 (Fall 1973): 521–35; Reinhardt, "Foreman's Club Comes Back," p. 156. Efforts to unionize foremen in the decade after 1936 can be traced through the files of *Personnel* and *Personnel*

Journal. See, for example, Frank Rising, "Union for Foremen?" *Personnel* 16 (1939–40): 93–96, and Ira B. Cross, Jr., "When Foremen Joined the C.I.O.," *Personnel Journal* 18 (February 1940): 274–83.

73. John Carl Cabe, *Foremen's Unions: A New Development in Industrial Relations,* University of Illinois, Bureau of Economic and Business Research, Bulletin No. 65 (Urbana, Ill., 1947), p. 7; Katherine Stone, "The Origins of Job Structures in the Steel Industry," *Review of Radical Political Economics* 6 (Summer 1974): 146–47.

74. Cabe, *Foremen's Unions,* pp. 8–9, 19, 29, 31.

75. Walter J. Rhodes, "Company Foremen's Clubs," in Sobey and Rhodes, "Foremen's Clubs," pp. 20 (quotation), 17–18; Sobey, "Community Foremen's Clubs," in Sobey and Rhodes, "Foremen's Clubs," p. 5; Tingley comments, in Sobey and Rhodes, "Foremen's Clubs," p. 12.

76. Protheroe comments, in Sobey and Rhodes, "Foremen's Clubs," p. 22.

77. Fordham, "Invisible Sign," pp. 38, 18, 40, 17. Although written in the 1940s, Fordham's account was based on lectures delivered to foremen's clubs in the early 1920s. In 1924, Fordham was superintendent of the Delco Light Company.

78. Thomas Cochran, "The Sloan Report: American Culture and Business Management," *American Quarterly* 29 (Winter 1977): 476–86.

79. Reinhardt, "Foreman's Club Comes Back," p. 155; Rhodes, "Company Foremen's Clubs," p. 17; Protheroe comments, in Sobey and Rhodes, "Foremen's Clubs," p. 22.

80. National Foremen's Institute, Inc., *Conducting Foremen's Meetings,* 2 vols., Vol. 1: *Leadership Methods* (Chicago, 1929), pp. 37, 24, 9, 21.

81. Keppel, "Development of Foremen," p. 15; Donald Meyer, *The Positive Thinkers: Religion as Pop Psychology from Mary Baker Eddy to Oral Roberts* (New York: Pantheon Books, 1980), pp. 191–92.

82. National Association of Foremen, *Manual for Conference Leaders on the N.A.F. Code of Ethics for Foremen* (Dayton, Ohio, 1944), foreword and preceding page.

83. Reinhardt, "Foreman's Club Comes Back," pp. 153–54, 157.

84. NAF, *Manual for Conference Leaders on the N.A.F. Code of Ethics for Foremen,* p. 9.

85. NAF, *Foremen's Club Manual,* p. 33.

86. Young Men's Christian Associations, *Foremanship: The Standard Course of the United YMCA Schools,* 4 vols., Vol. 1: *The Foreman and His Job,* by Wallace Clark and Harry Tipper (New York, 1921), pp. 40, 200–201, 193, 90, 190, 189, 94. Fitch makes an argument similar to that of the YMCA in *Causes of Industrial Unrest,* pp. 378–85.

87. Fordham, "Invisible Sign," p. 45; Young Men's Christian Associations, *Foremanship: The Standard Course of the United YMCA Schools,* 4 vols., Vol. 4: *Organization and Management,* by Walter N. Polakov and Harry Tipper (New York, 1921), p. 165; Sobey, "Community Foremen's Clubs," p. 4. The word "driving" is distinguished from "suggestion" in the 1920 handbook for scoutmasters. See Boy Scouts of America, *Handbook for Scoutmasters,* p. 269.

The fullest exposition of the theoretical basis for this approach was Mary Parker Follett, "The Giving of Orders," paper delivered January 1925, printed in *Dynamic Administration*, pp. 50–70. Follett dealt explicitly with the relationship between the foreman and the rank and file (p. 59).

88. NAF, *Manual for Conference Leaders on the N.A.F. Code of Ethics for Foremen*, p. 43. See also A. L. Kress, "The Foreman as a Leader," in Carl Heyel, ed., *The Foreman's Handbook* (New York, 1943), p. 22.

89. Reinhardt, "Foreman's Club Comes Back," p. 155; Clark and Tipper, *Foreman and His Job*, p. 94.

90. Buxton, "Report of Foremanship Training Programs in Indiana Industries," pp. 5, 16; Keppel, "Development of Foremen," pp. 12–14; "Minutes of Foremanship Training Leaders Conference," Richmond, Virginia, 10–17 January 1940, Record Group 69, "Records of the Works Progress Administration," National Archives, Washington, D.C., 211.41 (1939–40), file "Foremanship Training"; NAF, *Manual for Conference Leaders on the N.A.F. Code of Ethics for Foremen*, p. 46; NAF, *Foremen's Club Manual*, p. 8.

91. Polakov and Tipper, *Organization and Management*, pp. 165, 194–95, 198; National Foremen's Institute, *Leadership Methods*, pp. 17, 12.

92. Kress, "Foreman as a Leader," pp. 20, 28 (italics added).

93. National Foremen's Institute, *Conducting Foremen's Meetings*, 2 vols., Vol. 2: *Discussion Plans* (Chicago, 1929), pp. 39, 9; and Vol. 1: *Leadership Methods*, pp. 35, 37.

94. NAF, *Manual for Conference Leaders on the N.A.F. Code of Ethics for Foremen*, p. 12.

95. Ibid., pp. 16 (quotation), 15, 11, 33, 22.

96. Ibid., p. 46 (italics added).

97. Ibid., pp. 20, 22.

98. Stephen Vaughn, *Holding Fast the Inner Lines: Democracy, Nationalism, and the Committee on Public Information* (Chapel Hill, 1980), pp. 141–42, 336 nn. 9 and 11; "Ivey Ledbetter Lee," *Dictionary of American Biography*; "Dale Carnegie," in *Dictionary of American Biography*, Supplement 5, 1951–55 (New York, 1977), pp. 101–2.

99. Follett, *Dynamic Administration*, pp. 11, 13, 16–18; "Notes on the Life of Mary Parker Follett," Eduard C. Lindeman Papers, Social Welfare History Archives, Minneapolis, Minnesota, box 2, file "Sheffield."

100. "Meyer Bloomfield," in *Dictionary of American Biography*, Supplement 2 (New York, 1958), pp. 45–46.

101. *Who's Who in America*, Vol. 24 (1946–47), p. 2338.

102. The Inquiry, "The Worker and His Job: Outlines for the Use of Workers' Groups" (New York, n.d.).

103. In about 1915, Lasker toured the United States, apparently researching a series of reports for the Rowntree Trust. As part of this tour, he interviewed Bloomfield and was intrigued by what he understood of Bloomfield's participatory notions of factory management. "There were people like Bloomfield," he recalled, "who were well worth interviewing because they had developed new and

original ideas about how to avert strikes and how to give the workers a more genuine stake in their work." Bruno Lasker Memoir, Columbia University Oral History Collection, Butler Library, Columbia University, New York, 1: 152, 159.

104. Although Grace Coyle did not make the transition from social-welfare activity to industrial relations as completely as many others, she was not uninterested in the labor problem. See Grace Longwell Coyle, *Social Process in Organized Groups* (New York, 1930), pp. 181, 222.

105. Lasker Memoir, 1: 10.

106. Ibid., pp. 10, 178; Christopher Lasch, *The New Radicalism in America, 1889–1963: The Intellectual as a Social Type* (New York: Vintage Books, 1965), pp. 36–37.

107. On the transformation of work, see Daniel T. Rodgers, *The Work Ethic in Industrial America, 1850–1920* (Chicago, 1978), and James B. Gilbert, *Work without Salvation: America's Intellectuals and Industrial Alienation, 1880–1910* (Baltimore, 1977).

108. Jane Addams, *Twenty Years at Hull House* (New York, 1910), pp. 439–40, 235–37.

CHAPTER FOUR. DEPRESSION, WAR, AND THE STATE

1. See, for example, Harry N. Scheiber, *Ohio Canal Era: A Case Study of Government and the Economy, 1820–1861* (Athens, Ohio, 1969), and Carter Goodrich, *Government Promotion of American Canals and Railroads, 1800–1890* (New York, 1960).

2. James Weinstein, *The Corporate Ideal in the Liberal State, 1900–1918* (Boston, 1968); Gabriel Kolko, *The Triumph of Conservatism: A Reinterpretation of American History, 1900–1916* (New York, 1963).

3. Christopher G. Wye, "The New Deal and the Negro Community: Toward a Broader Conceptualization," *Journal of American History* 59 (December 1972): 621–39; Gabriel Kolko, *Wealth and Power in America: An Analysis of Social Class and Income Distribution* (New York, 1962), pp. 30–35; Edward D. Berkowitz and Kim McQuaid, "Businessman and Bureaucrat: The Evolution of the American Social Welfare System, 1900–1940," *Journal of Economic History* 38 (March 1978): 130–40; William Graebner, *A History of Retirement: The Meaning and Function of an American Institution, 1885–1978* (New Haven, Conn., 1980), chap. 7.

4. Charles Forcey, *The Crossroads of Liberalism: Croly, Weyl, Lippmann, and the Progressive Era, 1900–1925* (New York, 1961), pp. 301–3.

5. Clarke A. Chambers, *Seedtime of Reform: American Social Service and Social Action, 1918–1933* (Minneapolis, 1963), pp. 102–4; William E. Leuchtenburg, *Franklin D. Roosevelt and the New Deal, 1932–1940* (New York: Harper Torchbooks, 1963), pp. 125–30; Robert H. Bremner, *American Philanthropy* (Chicago, 1960), p. 160; Roy Lubove, *The Professional Altruist: The Emergence of Social Work as a Career, 1880–1930* (Cambridge, Mass., 1965), pp. 108–9.

6. R. Jackson Wilson, *In Quest of Community: Social Philosophy in the United States, 1860–1920* (New York, 1968), pp. 5, 10–13. Lindeman's fascination with Emerson is apparent in his notebooks, in the Eduard C. Lindeman Papers, Social Welfare History Archives, Minneapolis, Minnesota.

7. Lindeman Papers, Notebook, "1932–33," box 1, folder 1, p. 233; Eduard C. Lindeman, *The Meaning of Adult Education* (New York, 1926), p. 56.

8. Lindeman, *Meaning of Adult Education*, pp. 56–57.

9. Lindeman Papers, Notebook, "1932–33," box 1, folder 1, p. 207, "My Social Philosophy"; ibid., p. 234; Lindeman, *Meaning of Adult Education*, p. 57; Notebook, "1934–35," box 1, folder 5, pp. 8, 10, 21, and speech at College Club, Philadelphia, p. 231.

10. Lindeman Papers, Notebook, "1936," box 2, folder 7, pp. 16–17; "1937," box 2, folder 10 (pages not numbered), folder 11, p. 179; "1936," box 2, folder 7, p. 145.

11. Lindeman to J. Brewster Jones, 24 August 1936, Record Group 68, Records of the Works Progress Administration, National Archives, Washington, D.C., 216, 1935–38, file I-J-K.

12. Lindeman Papers, Notebook, "1936," box 2, folder 7, p. 146; "1937," box 2, folder 10.

13. Lindeman's credentials as a social engineer include familiarity with three leaders in industrial relations: T. North Whitehead, Ordway Tead, and Mary Parker Follett. On Whitehead, see Lindeman Papers, Notebook, "1936," box 2, folder 7, pp. 130, 132; on Follett, see Notebook, "1936," box 2, folder 7 (1937 material). Lindeman's relationship with Tead, who in the mid-1930s edited a Harper & Row series on economics, is documented in Lindeman to Tead, 27 January 1938, Record Group 68, WPA, 216, 1935–38 (E-K), file E-F.

14. Memorandum, Lindeman to Dorothy Cline, 1 November 1936, Record Group 68, WPA, 216, 1935–38 (L-M), file "Eduard C. Lindeman."

15. Memorandum Lindeman to Leonard C. Rennie, Chief Exhibit Section, 7 May 1937, Record Group 68, WPA, 216, 1935–38 (L-M), file "Eduard C. Lindeman," 1 January 1937; "Report of the Inter-State Recreational Conference: Works Progress Administration," Hotel Fort Des Moines, Des Moines, Iowa, 3, 4, 5, 6 August 1936, typescript, WPA, 216, 1935–38 (C-D), file "Des Moines Conference, August 1936"; Lindeman to Max Otto, no date, Lindeman Papers, box 2, file "Max Otto"; Speech by Irma Ringe, asst. director of recreation, WPA, 16 April 1938, in WPA, 216.911, file "July 1937–June 1938"; Report of Dr. Harold Meyer on a Dramatic Workshop Experiment in Georgia, 1 March 1937, WPA, 216, 1935–38 (E-K), file E-F. On leadership, see Memorandum Lindeman to Dorothy Cline, 1 November 1936, WPA, 216, 1935–38 (L-M), file "Eduard C. Lindeman."

16. See Charles E. Reed, "Notes from the District Conferences," Record Group 68, WPA, 211.6, 1941–43 (N-R), file "National Recreational Association," September 1941–March 1942, and "Services in Children," WPA, 211.59–211.6, 1939–40, file "Recreation," H-J 1940. Lindeman's letter of resignation is Lindeman to Aubrey Williams, 30 November 1937, Lindeman Papers, box 2, file "Dewey Letters."

17. Federal Works Agency, Works Progress Administration, Division of Professional and Service Projects, "Workers' Service Program," WPA Technical

Series, Workers' Service *Circular* No. 1, 4 March 1940 (Washington, D.C., n.d.), copy in Record Group 68, WPA, 211.43, 1939–40 (G-Z), file "Workers Education," C-F; Hilda Smith to Grace Coyle, 30 November 1940, and Ida Solar to Hilda Smith, 18 December 1939, both in WPA, 211.43, 1939–40 (G-Z), file "Workers Education," A-B; [ ] P. Hubbard to Hilda Smith, 15 May 1940, WPA, 211.43, 1939–40 (G-Z), file "Workers Education," C-F.

18. "Workers' Service Program," cited note 17; " 'Now We've Got It': The Workers Service Program Hits Its Stride," drafted by Hilda W. Smith, in Record Group 68, WPA, 211.43, 1939–40 (G-Z), file "Hilda W. Smith," pp. 16–17; "The Voice of a W.P.A. Adult Education Teacher," typescript, WPA, 211.44, 1941–43 (E-L), file "Department of Justice, January–September 1941"; Hilda W. Smith to Jacqueline Farrell, 16 May 1940, WPA, 211.43, 1939–40 (G-Z), file "Workers Education," C-F. On the devotion of the WSP to group-work ideas, see WPA, Illinois, "Report of the National Training Conference for State Supervisors of the Workers' Service Program," Hull House, Chicago, 30 September–13 October 1940, mimeograph, in WPA, 211.43, 1939–40 (G-Z), file "Workers Education, Hull House, November 1940," pp. 28, 30, 36.

19. "Voice of a W.P.A. Adult Education Teacher," cited in note 18; Smith to Farrell, cited note 18; Memorandum, Ernestine L. Friedmann to C. E. Triggs, 18 December 1939, Record Group 68, WPA, 211.43, 1939–40 (A-F), file "Ernestine Friedmann, 1939–40"; "Report of the National Training Conference," cited note 18, p. 36; "Now We've Got It," cited note 18, pp. 16–17; Mark Starr to Hilda Smith, 9 April 1941, WPA, 211.43, ⁻941–42 (A-Z), file "Mark Starr, 1941"; William H. Kilpatrick, "The Project Method," *Teachers College Record* 19 (September 1918): 319–35.

20. "Third Corps Area Advisers in Throes of Lengthy Parley," *Happy Days*, 27 July 1935, p. 1; "Of, by, for the Advisers," *Happy Days*, 17 August 1935, p. 6; George Frederick Buxton, "Report of Foremanship Training Program in Indiana Industries, 1919–1936," Purdue University, Engineering Extension Department, Extension Series No. 36, May 1936 (Lafayette, Ind., n.d.), pp. 4, 19.

21. Editorial, Edward Averill, "Leadership," *Happy Days*, 7 September 1935, p. 12.

22. "Self-Government in Camp Works for Abundant Life," *Happy Days*, 12 October 1935, p. 1; "Self Government," *Happy Days*, 2 November 1935, p. 6; "Sixth Corps Area's Big Camp Skokie Valley Has Biggest Canteen in CCC," *Happy Days*, 6 July 1935, p. 16. The fifth article of the Solomonsville Constitution read: "All the wishes, and all the regulations of the commanding officer of this camp . . . are hereby declared the supreme law of this organization." Quoted in "Self Government."

23. "Third Corps Area Men Work at Powder Plant; Chaplain's Club Booms," *Happy Days*, 6 July 1935, p. 6.

24. "Study of Civilian Conservation Corps by the American Youth Commission," mimeograph, Record Group 95, Records of the Civilian Conservation Corps, National Archives, Washington, D.C., box "CCC Selection Division, Education, Am. Youth Comm. Project, Ind. and W. Va. Corres. File," pp. 21, 23; "The Experi-

mental Program of the American Youth Commission in the Ten CCC Camps of the Fifth Corps Area," same box as above, pp. 21–22.

25. CCC Educational Report, 29 July 1938, for Checotah, Oklahoma Camp, in Record Group 95, CCC, box "Oklahoma, scs-25-sp-14, 172," file "Oklahoma/scs-26/Checotah Co." I examined fifteen such reports and found only one other that contained such a reference. But the question soliciting the information was so vaguely worded that it was often answered in entirely different terms.

26. "Educational Directive," 20 March 1942, from Second Corps Area Education Committee, in Record Group 95, CCC, "C.C.C. Educational Program 1933–42, corres. Courses – General," box 871, file "Educational Program General." See also "Summary of Training Policy and Procedure for CCC Personnel Training (Enrollees)," 2 May 1940, CCC, "Forest Service CCC Camp Files, 1933–1942," box 52, file "CCC – Personnel/Training/(Circulars)." On Tead, see Chapter 3, above.

27. Hilda Smith to Florence Kerr, 16 August 1940, Record Group 68, WPA, 211.43, 1939–40 (G-Z), file "Workers Education," R-S; Walter J. Stein, *California and the Dust Bowl Migration* (Westport, Conn., 1973), pp. 166, 170, 174, and notes; G. Ott Romney to Morris Miller, 11 January 1940, WPA, 211.6, 1941–43 (F-H), file "Housing Authority January–May"; National Association of Housing Officials, Committee on Community Relations in Housing Developments, "Community Relations in Urban Low-Rent Housing," May 1940, WPA, 211.6, 1941–43 (F-H), file "Housing Authority, June–August 1940."

28. George A. Warner, *Greenbelt: The Cooperative Community, An Experience in Democratic Living* (New York, 1954), pp. 41, 64–65, 84–85, 74 (quotation).

29. Edward A. Purcell, Jr., *The Crisis of Democratic Theory: Scientific Naturalism and the Problem of Value* (Lexington, Ky., 1973), pp. 11 (quotation), 9, 10, 22, 25 (quotation), 34.

30. Ibid., pp. 128 (quotation), 148 (quotation), 153, 180–81, 191–93.

31. Ibid., pp. 200–201. In a series of conferences organized in the early 1940s, Dewey, Sidney Hook, Bruce Bliven, Horace M. Kallen, Eduard C. Lindeman, Thomas Smith, and other "naturalist" (i.e., relativist) intellectuals elaborated on these identities. See ibid., pp. 204–5, 208.

32. Mark Starr to Hilda W. Smith, 17 June 1940, Record Group 68, WPA, 211.43, 1939–40 (G-Z), file "Workers Education, R-S"; Lindeman address, on Nazi schools, delivered to Conference on the Conservation and Development of Human Resources, Washington, D.C., 3, 4, 5 March 1938, WPA, 216.911, file "July 1937–June 1938"; Boy Scouts of America, *Staff Management Manual for the Use of Local Council Leaders* (New York, 1941), pp. 55, 60.

33. William H. Kilpatrick, ed., *The Teacher and Society*, First Yearbook of the John Dewey Society (New York, 1937), pp. 56, 61–64; LeRoy E. Bowman, "Dictatorship, Democracy, and Group Work in America," *National Council of Social Work, Proceedings*, 62d Annual Session, Montreal, 9–15 June 1935 (Chicago, 1935), pp. 387–92 (quotation p. 392); Lindeman Papers, Notebook, "1934–35," box 1, folder 5, p. 8.

After 1935, business used democratic methods more frequently and more self-consciously. Small, problem-solving groups were used for policymaking, communication, foreman training, and grievances. The influence of Nazi Germany was apparent in much of this activity. As late as 1949, a manual on conference methods rejected the "efficiency of the chain gang, the Nazi drill squad, or the group of individuals driven by inescapable grim necessity" in favor of procedures taken straight from Dewey. Its author compared the conference method to the scientific method: "In both the basic attitude is honest inquiry, not partisan defense. Both require analysis of a problem, a search for a solution which squares with all the facts at hand, and practical testing of the solution."

At least one American businessman — Tom Watson of International Business Machines — reacted quite differently to the European dictators. Watson had become chief executive officer of the company in 1922, and during the early years at least paid lip service to democratic managerial ideas. "The farther we keep away from the 'boss' proposition," Watson said in a 1925 address, "the more successful we are going to be." Leadership — meaning guidance rather than command — had a place in the Watson lexicon. "The leader," writes Watson's biographer, "was instructed not to tell people what to do but to help them to do it."

Nonetheless, Watson was early drawn to managerial methods that democratic theorists would hardly have recognized as their own, and to a goal — loyalty — that democratic managers would have felt free to articulate only in wartime. While democratic theorists universally condemned emotion and irrationality as harbingers of "mob rule," Watson's IBM was the burned-over district of American business. At conventions and sales meetings, the Methodist-raised Watson led his employees in song and anthem and delivered charged addresses that can only be described as sermons. On many occasions, Watson spoke passionately of the virtues of loyalty. The "great lubricant of life," loyalty evoked a corporate tone at odds with individualism and with democratic, participatory decision making. "Loyalty," said Watson, "saves the wear and tear of making daily decisions as to what is best to do. . . . The man who is loyal to his work is not wrung nor perplexed by doubts, he sticks to the ship, and if the ship founders, he goes down like a hero with colors flying at the masthead and the band playing."

It was a small step from this notion of loyalty to admiration for the European dictators. Early in the 1930s, Watson journeyed to Italy for an IBM sales convention in Florence, there to pay tribute to Benito Mussolini. In a speech liberally laced with the words "leader" and "leadership," Watson described Mussolini as a "great leader," a "pioneer" in securing loyalty and cooperation. Perhaps a related sense of admiration led Watson to accept the Order of Merit of the German Eagle with Star (given to "foreign nationals who have made themselves deserving of the German Reich") in Berlin in 1937. See Loren Baritz, *The Servants of Power: A History of The Use of Social Science in American Industry* (Middletown, Conn., 1960), pp. 178, 185; William Rodgers, *Think: A Biography of the Watsons and IBM*, rev. ed. (New York: Mentor, 1974), pp. 89, 122–23, 127–28, 106, 115, 129–30.

34. Barry D. Karl, *The Uneasy State: The United States from 1915 to 1945* (Chicago, 1983), p. 107.

35. Emory S. Bogardus, *Democracy by Discussion* (Washington, D.C., 1942), pp. 19–22. See also Frank Ernest Hill and W. E. Williams, *Radio's Listening Groups: The United States and Great Britain* (New York, 1941). The American Youth Com-

mission recommended that groups for radio listening and discussion be made a part of the CCC program. See "The Experimental Program of the American Youth Commission in the Ten CCC Camps of the Fifth Corps Area," Record Group 95, CCC, box "CCC Selection Division, Education, Am. Youth Comm. Project, Ind. and W. Va. Corres. File," pp. 21–23.

36. Mary L. Ely, *Why Forums?* (New York, 1937), pp. vii, 2, 7; U.S. Department of the Interior, Office of Education, "A Step Forward for Adult Civic Education," Bulletin No. 16, 1936 (Washington, D.C., 1936), pp. 2, 3, 5; U.S. Department of the Interior, Office of Education, *Forum Planning Handbook,* by J. W. Studebaker and Chester S. Williams, Bulletin No. 17, 1939 (Washington, D.C., 1939), pp. 6, 7.

37. Office of Education, "Step Forward for Adult Civic Education," p. 27.

38. Bogardus, *Democracy by Discussion,* p. iv.

39. John W. Studebaker, *The American Way: Democracy at Work in the Des Moines Forums* (New York, 1935), pp. 30, 117–121.

40. Verbatim Notes of Meeting of the American Association for the Study of Group Work, 23 July 1940, in National Association of Social Workers (NASW) Papers, Social Welfare History Archives, Minneapolis, Minnesota, box 75, folder 822; Verbatim Notes of Meeting of the Committee on an Emergency Program, American Association for the Study of Group Work, 25 July 1940, NASW Papers, box 75, folder 822.

41. This statement was qualified with the addition of "but constantly to keep on the alert to bring democratic controls back into practice in every conceivable way now and in the future."

42. American Association for the Study of Group Work, Committee on an Emergency Program, "Group Workers in the Present Emergency," tentative draft, August 1940, NASW Papers, box 75, folder 822.

Although the Selective Training and Service Act of 1940 created no participatory mechanisms save the local draft boards, the Welfare Federation of Cleveland was ready in 1941 to handle the problem of draftee morale by interpreting the act "through discussion groups with informed leaders." Welfare Federation of Cleveland, Group Work Council, "Recreation in Relation to National Defense: An Inventory of Community Needs," 5 May 1941, copy in Record Group 68, WPA, 211.6, 1941–43 (C-F), file "Cleveland Welfare Federation."

43. U.S., Department of Agriculture, Bureau of Agricultural Economics, "Group Discussion and Its Techniques: A Bibliographical Review," Farmer Discussion Group Pamphlet (n.p., n.d.), copy in LeRoy Bowman Papers, Columbia University Archives, Division of Special Collections, Butler Library, Columbia University, New York, box 8, file "Discussion," pp. 1, 7, 11–12.

44. "The Relative Effectiveness of a Lecture Method and a Method of Group Decision for Changing Food Habits," Preliminary Report on a Study Directed by Kurt Lewin, Child Welfare Research Station, University of Iowa, in Kurt Lewin Papers, Archives of the History of American Psychology, University of Akron, Akron, Ohio, box M948, folder 56.

45. Evaluations of Lewin by Gardner Murphy (8 May 1967) and Margaret Mead (8 May 1967), Kurt Lewin Papers, box M944, folder 1. For another example

of the use of small-group discussions in agriculture during the war, see Virginia Agricultural Experiment Station, "Virginia Rural Youth Talking and Doing," Rural Sociology Report No. 18, January 1942, by William E. Garnett, Margaret MacDonald Ward, and Charles G. Burr (Blacksburg, Va., 1942).

46. "Administrative Instruction No. 73," in Record Group 210, "Records of the War Relocation Authority," National Archives, Washington, D.C., Headquarters-Subject-Classified General Files (HSCGF), 67.010, file #1, "General Recreational Problems (GRP), June 1942–February 1943"; Memorandum Edward B. Marks, Jr., to John H. Provinse, 20 August 1943, in WRA, HSCGF, 67.010, file #4, "GRP, July 1943–February 1944"; "Progress Report on Community Education Program at the War Relocation Authority Center, Topaz, Utah," 21 October 1943, typescript, WRA, HSCGF, 67.010, file #4, "GRP, July 1943–February 1944."

47. Edwin B. Marks, Jr., "Visit to Hart Mountain July 28 to August 2, 1943," Record Group 210, WRA, HSCGF, 67.010, file #4, "GRP, July 1943–February 1944"; "Special Supplementary Report Community Activities," 9 July 1943, Benson Arkansas, WRA, HSCGF, 67.010, file #3, "GRP, June 1943–July 1943."

48. Memorandum Marks to Provinse, 20 August 1943, cited note 46; "Progress Report on Community Education Program at the War Relocation Authority Center, Topaz, Utah," cited note 46; "Report of Community Activities Section, Granada Project," 23 July 1943, by W. Ray Johnson, Record Group 210, WRA, HSCGF, 67.010, file #4, "GRP, July 1942–February 1944"; "Administrative Instruction No. 73," cited note 46.

49. Memorandum Marks to Provinse, 20 August 1943, cited note 46; "Report on Leadership Training Institutes Sponsored by the Advisory Committee of National Agencies to the War Relocation Authority," by Juanita Luck, Record Group 210, WRA, HSCGF, 67.010, file #6, "GRP, 1 January–April 1945."

I have no necessary objection to the claim that Japanese community and family structures might have helped the Japanese resist full and immediate assimilation; a similar case has been made for other families in Richard Sennett, "Middle-Class Families and Urban Violence: The Experience of a Chicago Community in the Nineteenth Century," and Virginia Yans McLaughlin, "Patterns of Work and Family Organization: Buffalo's Italians," both reprinted in Michael Gordon, ed., *The American Family in Social-Historical Perspective* (New York, 1973). However, to forcibly isolate a group from the cultural mainstream, and then claim that its failure to fit in is a function of its own institutions, strikes me as perverse.

Group work was also used in the WRA's Emergency Refugee Shelters, which took in European immigrants during and after the war. For an excellent statement of the philosophy of group work, see "Final Report of the Community Activities Section," Emergency Refugee Shelter, Fort Ontario, New York, 9 February 1946, Record Group 210, WRA, Emergency Refugee Shelter, Parts I, II, III, Reports, box 1, file "Final Report, Copy 1." My thanks to Sharon Lowenstein for this citation.

50. "USO Local Operations and Personnel as of December 29, 1941," in Record Group 225, "Records of the Joint Army and Navy Committee on Welfare and Recreation (JANCWR)," National Archives, Washington, D.C., General Subject Files (GSF), 1941–42, box 15, file "USO 1941." Some of the funds for these programs

came from the Carnegie Corporation of New York. See "Procedure to be Followed in the Development of Experimental Programs," 10 December 1941, in Grace Coyle Papers, Case Western Reserve University Archives, Case Western Reserve University, Cleveland, Ohio, box 4, file "Correspondence, 1928, 1929, 1940–47."

Many USOs, especially those operated by the YWCA, had youth programs. Grace Coyle to Kathryn Close, 3 February 1944, Coyle Papers, box 4, file "Correspondence, 1928, 1929, 1940–47."

51. While recruiting an adviser on adult-education activities, the USO interviewed two candidates. One was LeRoy Bowman, considered, as the USO director of program services commented, "something of an authority on forums and discussion methods." David Danzig to Francis Keppel, no date, Record Group 225, JANCWR, GSF, 1942–46, box 45, file "United Service Organizations, Inc., David Danzig."

52. Robert M. Heininger, "Developing Effective Programs," Release #2, Conference of Regional Staff, USO, Inc., 5 November 1942, Record Group 225, JANCWR, GSF, 1942–46, box 45, file "United Service Organizations, Inc., Ray Johns."

53. Heininger, "Developing Effective Programs," cited note 52; see also Ray Johns statement, in USO, Inc., Field Staff Conference, 4–6 November 1942, Release #3, Record Group 225, JANCWR, GSF, 1942–46, box 45, file "United Service Organizations, Inc., Ray Johns," and USO National Program Committee, "Music: USO," *Bulletin* (n.p., n.d.), copy in JANCWR, GSF, 1942–46, box 46, file "United Service Organizations, Inc., Raymond Kendall," p. 14.

54. Ray Johns statement, cited note 53; Coyle to Mollie Condon, 25 January 1943, Coyle Papers, box 4, file "Correspondence, 1928, 1929, 1940–47."

The military experimented with group psychotherapy on a large scale during World War II; and the USO, working with the National Committee on Mental Hygiene, developed a program of psychiatric counseling. There is no evidence, however, that these programs were commingled or that the USO counseling program involved group methods. See Memorandum, Helen Phillips to Member Schools of the Conference of Professional Schools of Recreation and Group Work, in Coyle Papers, box 3, file "Conference of National Agencies and Schools of Group Work and Recreation . . . ," and "Conference Re: Counseling for USO Staff," 8 April 1942, Record Group 225, JANCWR, GSF, 1941–42, box 15, file "USO-General."

55. "Minutes of Mobile Service Conference Held in Norfolk, Va., February 11, 1943," Record Group 225, JANCWR, GSF, 1942–46, box 45, file "United Service Organizations, Inc., Carleton E. Cameron."

56. L. Cody Marsh, "Group Treatment of the Psychoses by the Psychological Equivalent of the Revival," *Mental Hygiene* 15 (April 1931): 338–39.

57. "Music: USO," pp. 4, 5, 9.

58. For a succinct and powerful description of the role of social scientists in W.W. II, see "Summary of Work Done during and after World War II by Social Scientists Some of Whom Would Be Available for the Research Institute's Programs," Lewin Papers, box M946, file 20.

59. Geoffrey Perrett, *Days of Sadness, Years of Triumph: The American People, 1939–1945* (1973; Baltimore: Penguin Books, 1974), calls the self-government features of the Japanese camps a "sham" (p. 225).

CHAPTER FIVE. SOCIAL ENGINEERING THROUGH RECREATION

1. Handwritten notes of Oskar Schulze (hereafter referred to as Schulze notes); Benjamin Rose Institute of Cleveland, "Annual Report of Executive Director for 1955," mimeographed, p. 8; clippings, "Oldsters' Club Fills Need in Community," *Cleveland Press,* 8 November 1944; Bud Weidenthal, "Golden Age Clubs Mark 10 Years," *Cleveland Press,* 4 January 1952; clippings, *Cincinnati Times Star,* 6 April 1946, and *Cleveland Plain Dealer,* 8 July 1946; BRI, "Annual Report Executive Director, 1955," p. 8, all in Benjamin Rose Institute Papers, Cleveland (hereafter referred to as BRI Papers). The clubs were originally called Old Age Clubs. The Golden Age name was affixed early, by a member. See Margaret W. Wagner, foreword to James H. Woods, *Helping Older People Enjoy Life* (New York, 1953), p. xi.

The Golden Age Clubs had predecessors. These included the Three-Quarter Century Clubs, established in the 1920s, and the Threescore, or Best to Be, Clubs of Miami and New York City. *Three-Quarter Century Club* 1 (January 1928): 1, and Leta Browning, " 'The Best Is Yet to Be,' " *Magazine of Michigan* 2 (March 1930): 13, 28–29, in Three-Quarter Century Club Papers, Michigan Historical Collections, Bentley Historical Library, University of Michigan, Ann Arbor; *New York Times,* 19 November 1932, p. 17.

2. Geoffrey Blodgett, "Frederick Law Olmsted: Landscape Architecture as Conservative Reform," *Journal of American History* 62 (March 1976): 869–89; Bernard Mergen, "The Discovery of Children's Play," *American Quarterly* 27 (October 1975): 399–420; Kenneth E. Reid, *From Character Building to Social Treatment: The History of the Use of Groups in Social Work* (Westport, Conn., 1981), pp. 94–101; Robert Fisher, "From Grass-Roots Organizing to Community Service: Community Organization Practice in the Community Center Movement, 1907–1930," unpublished paper, 1980; Robert Goldman and John Wilson, "The Rationalization of Leisure," *Politics and Society* 7 (1977): 157–87; Eduard C. Lindeman, *The Meaning of Adult Education* (New York, 1926).

On the "new leisure" of the 1920s and 1930s, a compound of unemployment, productivity, and ideology, see George Barton Cutten, *The Threat of Leisure* (Washington, D.C., 1926); Paul T. Frankl, *Machine-Made Leisure* (New York, 1932); L. C. Walker, *Distributed Leisure: An Approach to the Problem of Overproduction and Underemployment* (New York, 1931); Roger Payne, *Why Work? Or the Coming "Age of Leisure and Plenty"* (Boston, 1939); George W. Alger, "Leisure — for What?" *Atlantic Monthly* 135 (April 1925): 483–84.

3. Sara Elizabeth Maloney, "The Development of Group Work Education in Schools of Social Work in the United States," Ph.D. diss., Western Reserve University, 1963), pp. 37–38, 76, 216, 314–15; W. I. Newstetter, "What Is Social Group

Work?" *National Conference of Social Work, Proceedings,* 62d Annual Session, Montreal, 9–15 June 1935 (Chicago, 1935), p. 298; Lucia Johnson Bing, *Social Work in Greater Cleveland: How Public and Private Agencies Are Serving Human Needs* (Cleveland, 1938), pp. 117–18; Reid, *From Character Building to Social Treatment,* pp. 117–21, 140–42.

4. Reid, *From Character Building to Social Treatment,* pp. 58–71. See also "Summary of material on Clubs from Elliott course at Columbia – 1927," Grace Coyle Papers, Case Western Reserve University Archives, Case Western Reserve University, Cleveland, Ohio, box 1, file "Group Work Class Materials."

5. Other youth-focused club efforts can be traced in Paul Boyer, *Urban Masses and Moral Order in America, 1820–1920* (Cambridge, Mass., 1978), pp. 180, 246; " 'Harmony in Camp' is Aim of Missouri Leaders' Club," *Happy Days,* 13 July 1940, p. 4. For a description of typical nondirective club activity in one city, see Charles E. Reed, "Notes from the District Conferences," Record Group 68, "Records of the Works Progress Administration," National Archives, Washington, D.C., 211.6, 1941–43 (N-R), file "National Recreation Association, September 1941–March 1942."

6. *Life* 10 (13 January 1941): 65, 68.

7. "Assembly Notes," in Kensington High School, *Compass* (Buffalo, 1941), p. 19.

8. Compiled from clipping, *Cleveland Plain Dealer,* 20 March 1977, pt. 4, p. 16, BRI Papers; Margaret Wagner interview by William Graebner, 13 April 1977.

9. Benjamin Rose Institute, "Brief History of the Benjamin Rose Institute, 1908–1976," BRI Papers, p. 1; BRI, "Annual Report Executive Director, 1955," BRI Papers, p. 2.

10. M. L. Brown to Franklin D. Roosevelt, 12 October 1933; Brown to Roosevelt, 10 November 1933, Franklin Delano Roosevelt Papers, Franklin Delano Roosevelt Library, Hyde Park, New York, President's Personal File 683, "Old Age Pensions."

11. Margaret W. Wagner, "Older Persons Come of Age," Address presented at the Meeting of the Committee on Older Persons, Welfare Federation of Cleveland, 1 February 1965, p. 2, copy in author's possession. John Culver, Professor Emeritus, Department of History, Case Western Reserve University, made this document available to me.

12. Ibid., pp. 2–3; BRI, "Annual Report Executive Director, 1955," BRI Papers, p. 9.

13. Wagner, "Older Persons Come of Age," p. 3; Wagner interview by Graebner; Arthur J. Altmeyer, *The Formative Years of Social Security* (Madison, Wis., 1966), pp. 75–76; *Cleveland Plain Dealer,* 11 January 1939, p. 8.

Wagner would not cast a vote for Franklin D. Roosevelt until 1944, and she supported the Social Security Act of 1935 less as a welfare measure than as a repudiation of the poorhouse; it "enabled many individuals to live independently," she later wrote. Wagner foreword in Woods, *Helping Older People Enjoy Life,* p. ix; Wagner interview by Graebner.

14. *Cleveland Plain Dealer,* 20 July 1936, p. 6 (editorial); 18 July 1936, p. 2; 28 March 1936, p. 8 (editorial); 17 January 1936, p. 8; Wagner interview by Graebner.

As a generic term, the Townsend movement included Francis Townsend's Old Age Revolving Pension Plan and a variety of lesser organizations. The most significant legislative expression of the movement was a measure introduced in the House by California representative John McGroarty, calling for pensions of $200 per month to retired persons over sixty years of age.

15. Goodrich House, "Minutes of Meeting of Board of Trustees," 1 December 1937, Goodrich Social Settlement Papers, Western Reserve Historical Society Library, Cleveland, box 1, file 5; Judith Ann Trolander, *Settlement Houses and the Great Depression* (Detroit, 1975), pp. 84–85.

16. Script, "Taking Off on Townsend Plan," presented at the Hiram House Workers Christmas Party, 21 December 1935, in Hiram House Papers, Western Reserve Historical Society Library, Cleveland, box 43, file 7.

17. BRI, "Annual Report Executive Director, 1955," BRI Papers, pp. 3, 4, 8; Tamara K. Hareven, *Eleanor Roosevelt: An American Conscience* (Chicago, 1968); Margaret Stage, "Resumé of Report of Conference on Youth Problems," 18 August 1935, Hiram House Papers, box 38, file 5.

18. This material is adapted from William Graebner, "Grace Coyle," *Dictionary of American Biography*, Supplement 7, 1961–65 (New York, 1981), pp. 151–52. See especially obituary, *New York Times*, 10 March 1962, p. 22 and Ben Zion Shapiro, "Grace Longwell Coyle: Contributions to the Philosophy and Practice of Social Work," Seminar Paper, 1965, in the Library of the School of Applied Social Sciences, Case Western Reserve University, Cleveland.

19. Thomas F. Campbell, *SASS: Fifty Years of Social Work Education: A History of the School of Applied Social Sciences* (Cleveland, 1967), p. 37; Rev. Joel B. Hayden, "The Need for People Who Know and Can and Do," Cleveland, n.d., in "Course Work, 1926–31," in Case Western Reserve University Archives, Cleveland.

20. "Minutes of the Committee of Eighteen," 13 July 1932, in School of Applied Social Sciences Papers, Case Western Reserve University Archives, Cleveland, General Office Files, box 1, file "Minutes of the Committee of Eighteen, 1932–33"; "Summary of Thinking of Joint Committee of the Case Work and Group Work Councils," 3 April 1935, Coyle Papers, box 3, file "Committees on Professional Education. . . ." The idea of group work as an adjustment mechanism did not disappear. A 1945 description of group work defined it as "concerned with the adjustment of the individual to other persons and to society and with improvements in society." Mildred C. Barry, "The Group Work Council of the Welfare Federation of Cleveland, 1935–1945," 8 January 1945, Hiram House Papers, box 8, file 8, p. 1. The applicability of recreational theory to children's play is ably discussed in Charles E. Hendry and Irma Ringe, "Memorandum on Play, Recreation and Leisure," 10 October 1939, National Association of Social Workers Papers, Social Welfare History Archives, Minneapolis, Minnesota, file 806.

21. Grace Longwell Coyle, *Social Process in Organized Groups* (New York, 1930); Coyle, "Group Work and Social Change," *National Conference of Social Work, Proceedings*, 62d Annual Session, Montreal, 9–15 June 1935 (Chicago, 1935), pp. 393–405; and the very revealing document, "Some Personal and Social Values in Adult Education," Coyle Papers, box 6, file "Speeches, 1930's." On the Chicago

sociologists, see Robert E. L. Faris, *Chicago Sociology, 1920–1932* (San Francisco, 1967). Early academic work on small groups is described in A. Paul Hare, "The History and Present State of Small Group Research," in Hare, ed., *Handbook of Small Group Research*, 2d ed. (New York, 1976), appendix 2, pp. 384–95.

22. "Annual Report on Alta Social Settlement by W. T. McCullough, Headworker, January, 1937," Alta Social Settlement Papers, Western Reserve Historical Society Library, Cleveland, box 1, file 1, p. 2; "Proposal to the Board of Trustees Relating to the Case Work–Group Work Project," Alta Papers, box 1, file 1, p. 2.

23. Bing, *Social Work in Greater Cleveland*, p. 117. For references on social-group work and youth, see the bibliographies compiled by Coyle in Coyle Papers, box 1, file "Bibliographies — Group Work."

24. Compiled from Schulze vita; clipping, *Cleveland Plain Dealer*, 8 July 1946; Oskar Schulze to Miss Wagner, 14 May 1940; Dr. Goerdeler to [unknown], 21 September 1933; Dr. Goerdeler to [unknown], 4 June 1935, all in BRI Papers, file "Schulze, Oskar."

25. Oskar Schulze, "A Neglected Age of Social Group Work," mimeographed address delivered ca. 1940, BRI Papers, file "Articles by Oskar," p. 2; statements by Schulze in *Rose Leaves* 2, no. 8 (October 1941); 3, no. 1 (January 1942); 2, no. 9 (November 1941), BRI Papers, file "Oskar Schulze Papers."

26. Emil Lederer, *State of the Masses: The Threat of the Classless Society* (1940; rpt. New York, 1967), pp. 206, 26–29.

27. Ibid., pp. 107, 44–45; LeRoy E. Bowman, "Dictatorship, Democracy, and Group Work in America," *National Conference of Social Work, Proceedings*, 62d Annual Session, Montreal, 9–15 June 1935 (Chicago, 1935), pp. 391–92.

28. Charles E. Hendry, "Social Group Work," *Social Work Year Book: 1941*, Vol. 6 (New York, 1941), p. 526; Coyle, "Group Work and Social Change," p. 394. See also Mary K. Simkhovitch, *Group Life* (New York, 1940), pp. 74–75.

29. See Susan H. Kubie and Gertrude Landau, *Group Work with the Aged* (New York, 1953).

30. Talcott Parsons, "Age and Sex in the Social Structure of the United States," *American Sociological Review* 7 (October 1942): 616, 616n; undated statement on ideals of group work and its function in eliminating "road-blocks of personality," in East End Neighborhood House Papers, Western Reserve Historical Society Library, Cleveland, box 1, file 2.

31. Schulze vita; clipping, *Chicago Daily News*, 15 May 1972, pt. 3, p. 23, BRI Papers; Wagner interview by Graebner; Oskar Schulze, "Live Long and Like It: A Brief Description of Recreational Services for Older People," address given at the National Convention of the Associated Lutheran Charities of Minneapolis, Minnesota, 20 May 1947, mimeograph, BRI Papers, file "Articles by Oskar," p. 2.

32. Oskar Schulze, "Neglected Age of Social Group Work," BRI Papers, file "Articles by Oskar," pp. 3–8; Mrs. Edwin Eells to Grace Coyle, 22 May 1940, BRI Papers, file "Schulze, Oskar."

33. Schulze, "Neglected Age of Social Group Work," p. 7.

34. Schulze notes, BRI Papers; Wagner interview by Graebner.

35. *Cleveland Plain Dealer*, 23 April 1937, p. 20.

36. Schulze notes, BRI Papers; Oskar Schulze, "Recreation for the Aged,"

Journal of Gerontology 4 (October 1949): 310; Cleveland Foundation, "Recreation for the Aged," Cleveland, 1945, copy in BRI Papers; Benjamin Rose Institute, "Minutes of the Board of Trustees," 13 October 1941, BRI Papers (copies in author's possession).

37. BRI, "Minutes of the Board of Trustees," 10 June 1940, BRI Papers.

38. Wagner interview by Graebner; BRI, "Minutes of the Board of Trustees," 9 June 1941, BRI Papers; *Cleveland Plain Dealer*, 12 December 1965, sec. F, p. 3, BRI Papers; Goodrich Social Settlement, "Minutes of the Annual Meeting," 6 November 1940, Goodrich Papers, box 1, file 5, p. 2; Goodrich Social Settlement, *Annual Report: 1940–1941* (n.p., n.d.), BRI Papers, file "Oskar Schulze Papers"; BRI, "Annual Report Executive Director, 1955," BRI Papers, p. 8.

39. Compiled from clipping, John Collier, "Low-Cost Recreation Shown," *New Orleans Item*, 24 October 1947; Schulze, "Live Long and Like It," p. 3; Schulze notes; clippings, Martha Lee, "You Can Help to Entertain Settlement House Old Folks," *Cleveland News*, 18 February 1944; Mrs. Maxwell, "Oldsters' Club Fills Need in Community," *Cleveland Press*, 8 November 1944; Eleanor Prech, "Golden Age Club Brings Sunshine into Lives of Oldsters at Goodrich House," *Cleveland Press*, 29 May 1941, Schulze, "Recreation for the Aged," pp. 311–12, all in BRI Papers; Wagner interview by Graebner; Jewish Community Centers of Cleveland, "Report on Golden Age Program," 18 October 1950, Papers of the Cleveland Section of the National Council of Jewish Women (NCJW), Western Reserve Historical Society Library, Cleveland, box 12, file 4.

40. Lindeman, *Meaning of Adult Education*, pp. 56–57. On Lindeman's background, see Gisela Konopka, *Eduard C. Lindeman and Social Work Philosophy* (Minneapolis, 1958).

41. Boyd H. Bode, "The Confusion in Present-Day Education," in William H. Kilpatrick, ed., *The Educational Frontier* (New York, 1933), p. 19.

42. M. P. Follett, *The New State: Group Organization the Solution of Popular Government* (New York, 1918), pp. 106, 368, 370; Bruno Lasker, *Democracy through Discussion* (New York, 1949), pp. vi–vii; Coyle, "Group Work and Social Change," pp. 399, 403–04; Simkhovitch, *Group Life*, pp. 18–27, 97–98; Joseph Ernest McAfee, "Middle-Aged White-Collar Workers on the Economic Rack," *Annals of the American Academy of Political and Social Science* 154 (March 1931): 34–36; Elton Mayo, *The Social Problems of an Industrial Civilization* (Boston, 1945), pp. 22, 30–32.

43. Konopka, *Eduard C. Lindeman and Social Work Philosophy*, p. 53.

44. Wagner interview by Graebner; clipping, unidentified Philadelphia paper, BRI Papers.

45. Schulze, "Live Long and Like It"; Schulze, "Recreation for the Aged," p. 312; Jewish Community Centers of Cleveland, "Golden Age Program," Papers of Cleveland Section, NCJW, box 12, file 4; BRI, "Annual Report Executive Director, 1955," BRI Papers, p. 9.

46. Woods, *Helping Older People Enjoy Life*, pp. 4, 5; clipping, Weidenthal, "Golden Age Clubs," BRI Papers; BRI, "Annual Report Executive Director, 1955," BRI Papers, pp. 8–9; *Cleveland Section Bulletin* 14 (May 1942), BRI Papers.

47. Woods, *Helping Older People Enjoy Life*, pp. 63–64; Jessie Ruth Robinson,

"Dictators," *Golden Age Center News* 2 (July 1957): 9; *Golden Age Center News* 1 (October 1955), in Ernest Bohn Collection, Freiberger Library, Case Western Reserve University, Cleveland; James H. Woods, "Fun in the Golden Years," typescript, July 1948–February 1950, Cleveland Foundation Papers, box 7, file "Welfare Federation — Recreation for Aged," p. 46; Leavenworth to Trustees of Cleveland Foundation, 14 July 1954, Cleveland Foundation Papers, Western Reserve Historical Society Library, Cleveland, box 4, file "The Golden Age Center of Cleveland."

The persistence of the rhetoric and ideology of democratic social engineering is also apparent in a 1952 history of the Neighborhood House Golden Age Clubs of Minneapolis. According to the history, early meetings of the Neighborhood House club, established in 1949, were characterized by authoritarian patterns: "The President was an aggressive person who assumed a 'boss' role and made decisions for the group. She did not know how to delegate or share responsibility." A new adviser (social worker) "made an effort to get group members to assume responsibilities for group life. . . . The group learned . . . that it could make its own decisions." In less than a year, the club had demonstrated additional responsibility by drawing up a constitution. "History of Neighborhood House Golden Age Clubs," 1952, National Federation of Settlements Papers, Social Welfare History Archives, Minneapolis, Minnesota, box 188.

48. Philip Eisenberg and Paul F. Lazarsfeld, "The Psychological Effects of Unemployment," *Psychological Bulletin* 35 (June 1938): 359–60, 364, 370, 375; Dan H. Mater, "Effects of Seniority upon the Welfare of the Employee, the Employer and Society," *Journal of Business* 14 (October 1941): 417–18.

49. Frank G. Dickinson, "Economic Aspects of the Aging of Our Population," in T. Lynn Smith, ed., *Problems of America's Aging Population*, Southern Conference on Gerontology, Institute of Gerontology Series, Vol. 1 (Gainesville, Fla., 1951), p. 80, also pp. 78–79. See also Paul Niven, "Youth versus Age: A New Class Struggle," *Social Frontier* 4 (January 1938): 117–20.

50. Clyde V. Kiser, "The Demographic Background of Our Aging Population," in *The Social and Biological Challenge of Our Aging Population: Proceedings of the Eastern States Health Education Conference*, 31 March–1 April 1949 (New York, 1950), pp. 65–66; California, Legislature, Senate, Interim Committee on Social Welfare, *Report of the Interim Committee on Social Welfare*, Regular Session, 1949, pt. 1 (n.p., n.d.), pp. 57, 97; Albert Q. Maisel, "The Pension Preacher: He Wants to be President," *Look* 14 (31 January 1950): 21–24; California, Governor, *Proceedings of the Governor's Conference on the Problem of the Aging*, Sacramento, Cal., 15 and 16 October 1951 (n.p., n.d.), p. 240.

51. From *Essays in Sociological Theory: Pure and Applied* (Glencoe, Ill., 1949), quoted in G. C. Hoy, "The Life of the Retired in a Trailer Park," *American Journal of Sociology* 59 (January 1954): 361; Abraham Holtzman, "Analysis of Old Age Politics in the United States," *Journal of Gerontology* 9 (January 1954): 56–58; Frank A. Pinner, Paul Jacobs, and Philip Selznick, *Old Age and Political Behavior: A Case Study* (Berkeley, 1959), pp. 27, 55, 61, 82.

52. *Senior Citizen* 1 (October 1955): 3–4; *Harvest Years* 1 (May 1961): 44; Fred Cottrell, "Your Rights and Duties as a Citizen," ibid., 1 (July 1961): 17–19;

Dorothy Andrews, "Make Your Vote Count More," ibid., 2 (October 1962): 17–19; W. Naleszkiewicz, "Cast a *Quality* Vote," ibid., 4 (November 1964): 46–48; Florence E. Vickery, "Having Fun at a Senior Center," ibid., 1 (March 1961): 3–5.

53. Eduard C. Lindeman, "The Sociological Challenge of the Aging Population," in *Social and Biological Challenge of Our Aging Population*, pp. 177–79; Eugene Staley, ed., *Creating an Industrial Civilization: A Report on the Corning Conference*, Held under the Auspices of the American Council of Learned Societies and Corning Glass Works, 17–19 May 1951, Corning, New York (New York, 1952), p. 128; Harold L. Wilensky, "Life Cycle, Work Situation, and Participation in Formal Associations," in Robert W. Kleemeier, ed., *Aging and Leisure: A Research Perspective into the Meaningful Use of Time* (New York, 1961), p. 238; Edward L. Bortz, "The 'Threat of Leisure' at Age 65," *Personnel Journal* 38 (June 1959): 64–65; Pinner, Jacobs, and Selznick, *Old Age and Political Behavior*, pp. 66–68; Fred Cottrell, "Aging and the Political System," in John C. McKinney and Frank T. de Vyver, eds., *Aging and Social Policy* (New York, 1966), pp. 92–93; typescript, address by Charles E. Reed, Manager Field Department, National Recreation Association, to Southwest Recreation Executives Conference, Fort Worth, 26–29 March 1941, in Record Group 68, WPA, 211.6, 1941–43 (H-N), file "National Recreation Association, January–August 1941."

54. Lindeman, "Sociological Challenge," in *Social and Biological Challenge of Our Aging Population*, p. 174.

55. *Retirement Planning News* 6 (October 1961): 1, 7; (8 May 1963): 3; Holtzman, "Analysis of Old Age Politics in the United States," pp. 63–64.

CHAPTER SIX. INVADING THE FAMILY

1. Benjamin Spock, *The Common Sense Book of Baby and Child Care* (New York, 1946). See also Benjamin Spock interview by Milton J. E. Senn, 20 November 1974, interview 67A, transcript, Senn Oral History Collection, National Library of Medicine, Bethesda, Md., pp. 35, 14.

2. It is possible to come away from a close reading of *Baby and Child Care* with other interpretations of Benjamin Spock's advice. Michael Zuckerman interprets Spock as a spokesman for a bureaucratic society that has lost its hard, competitive edge. According to Zuckerman, the Spock baby is born amiable, suited to a post–World War II environment in which fellowship is the primary virtue. Michael Zuckerman, "Dr. Spock: The Confidence Man," in Charles Rosenberg, ed., *The Family in History* (Philadelphia, 1975), pp. 179–207. Because the baby book speaks with more than one voice and because Spock has never successfully integrated his own thinking, a historical approach, designed to clarify the text of *Baby and Child Care* and identify the sources of Spock's thought, seemed essential.

3. Spock, *Baby and Child Care*, pp. 20, 147, 24, 50, 81, 220.

4. Ibid., pp. 195–96.

5. Ibid., pp. 252–53, 250, 263, 325, 268; Benjamin Spock, *Decent and Indecent: Our Personal and Political Behavior* (New York, 1970), pp. 71, 86. Charles Anderson Aldrich and Mary M. Aldrich described the newborn as a "self-centered barbarian" in their child-rearing manual (*Babies Are Human Beings: An Interpretation of Growth* [New York, 1938], p. 20). Cf. Zuckerman, "Dr. Spock"; Lynn Z. Bloom, *Doctor Spock: Biography of a Conservative Radical* (Indianapolis, 1972), p. 128, and Martha Wolfenstein, "Fun Morality: An Analysis of Recent American Child-Training Literature," in Margaret Mead and Martha Wolfenstein, eds., *Childhood in Contemporary Cultures* (Chicago, 1955), pp. 169–73.

6. S. R. Slavson, "Some Psycho-social Foundations of Group Work," in Slavson et al., *They Say: About Group Work* (Hartford, 1940), p. 28; John Dollard et al., *Frustration and Aggression* (New Haven, 1939).

7. Lois B. Murphy interview by Milton J. E. Senn, 14 May 1969, interview 50, transcript, Senn Oral History Collection, pp. 33–34. Others whose work may be linked to Spock's used some form of aggression analysis. David Levy, for example, was an instructor at the New York Psychoanalytic Institute, where Spock was a student in the mid-1930s. See David M. Levy, *Maternal Overprotection* (New York, 1943), pp. 161–62, 37, and Milton J. E. Senn, "Insights on the Child Development Movement in the United States," *Monographs of the Society for Research in Child Development* 40 (August 1975): 39, 41, 42n. New York City pediatricians Ruth Morris Bakwin and Harry Bakwin argued that parental overprotection could produce a child given to aggression or submission. ("Psychologic Care of the Preschool Child, III," *Journal of Pediatrics* 16 [March 1940]: 359).

8. Kurt Lewin, *Resolving Social Conflicts: Selected Papers on Group Dynamics*, ed. Gertrud Weiss Lewin (New York, 1948), p. 83; Senn, "Insights on the Child Development Movement in the United States," pp. 48, 50; Alfred J. Marrow, *The Practical Theorist: The Life and Work of Kurt Lewin* (New York, 1969), pp. 146, 110, 120–22, 124. German-born Kurt Lewin emigrated to the United States in the early 1930s.

9. Milton J. E. Senn, "A Tribute to Lawrence K. Frank," speech, October 1967, Senn Oral History Collection, file 22, "Lawrence K. Frank"; Lois Murphy interview, pp. 13, 34; Margaret Mead interview by Senn, 3 September 1970, interview 46, transcript, Senn Oral History Collection, pp. 1–4, 7; Spock interview by Senn, p. 32; Senn, "Insights on the Child Development Movement in the United States," pp. 11–24; Bloom, *Doctor Spock*, p. 85; Benjamin Spock interview by William Graebner, 13 December 1977, notes in author's possession. For a time in the 1940s Lawrence K. Frank was director of the Institute of Human Development (IHD), the research and workshop facility established by Caroline Zachry in New York City in 1939. At the same time, Spock served on the IHD board of directors. See Catherine MacKenzie, "Dr. Caroline Zachry's Name Added to Unit as Memorial to City Worker for Child Aid," *New York Times*, 1 October 1945, p. 16.

10. Robert A. Jones, "Freud and American Sociology, 1909–1949," *Journal of the History of the Behavioral Sciences* 10 (January 1974): 26; Lawrence K. Frank, "Social Order and Psychiatry," *American Journal of Orthopsychiatry* 11 (October 1941): 621; Frank, "Freedom for the Personality," *Psychiatry* 3 (August 1940): 344–47. See also A. Michael Sulman, "The Humanization of the American Child:

Benjamin Spock as a Popularizer of Psychoanalytic Thought," *Journal of the History of the Behavioral Sciences* 9 (July 1973): 258–65, and Hamilton Cravens, "The Laura Spelman Rockefeller Memorial, the Child Welfare Institutes, and the Creation of the Science of the Child, 1917–1940," paper presented at the annual meeting of the American Historical Association, New York City, December 1979.

11. Spock, *Baby and Child Care,* pp. 259, 26, 39.

12. Ibid., pp. 145, 3, 20. See also Aldrich and Aldrich, *Babies Are Human Beings,* p. 22.

13. Mead interview, p. 4; Margaret Mead, "Group Psychotherapy in the Light of Social Anthropology," *International Journal of Group Psychotherapy* 1 (September 1951): 195.

14. Mead interview, p. 19; Bloom, *Doctor Spock,* p. 85; Margaret Mead, *Blackberry Winter: My Earlier Years* (New York, 1972), p. 248. Spock was familiar with at least three of Margaret Mead's books, including *Coming of Age in Samoa* (1928), and with *Patterns of Culture* (1934), a major essay by Mead's colleague and close friend, Ruth Benedict. Spock interview by Graebner.

15. Erik H. Erikson, *Childhood and Society* (New York, 1963), pp. 412–13, 282; Spock interview by Senn, p. 35. For Erik H. Erikson's critique of geographic and social mobility, see Erikson, *Childhood and Society,* pp. 280, 35, 42–43. On the one known occasion when Spock commented on an Erikson paper, the baby doctor was in virtually complete agreement. See the transactions arising from the Fourth Conference on Problems of Infancy and Childhood (1950) sponsored by the Josiah Macy, Jr., Foundation, *Symposium on the Healthy Personality: Transactions of Special Meetings of Conference on Infancy and Childhood, June 8–9 and July 3–4, 1950, New York, N.Y.,* ed. Milton J. E. Senn (New York, 1950), pp. 18, 21, 31–32, 74–78, 85, 88. At one point in the discussion that followed Erikson's paper, Spock argued that among better-educated people, the "inhibition against . . . brisk, direct, impulsive methods has played a part in pushing parents into more civilized and more damaging techniques."

16. Erikson, *Childhood and Society,* pp. 115–16, 132–33, 141, 154–55.

17. Others whose work merges the themes of rapid social change and/or disruption with an element of attachment to a simpler past include Frank Walser, *The Art of Conference* (New York, 1933), pp. 3–5, and Elton Mayo, "What Every Village Knows," *Survey Graphic* 26 (December 1937): 695–98. This matrix of ideas is also present in Aldrich and Aldrich, *Babies Are Human Beings,* pp. xi, 22. According to the Aldriches, the adult "ability to feel secure in a world of change" is to be achieved through child-rearing techniques that conform to the child's natural patterns of growth and development.

18. David Elkind, "Giant in the Nursery — Jean Piaget," *Annual Editions: Readings in Human Development, '73–'74* (Guilford, Conn., 1973): 2–13. See also Erikson, *Childhood and Society,* pp. 65, 67.

19. Arnold Gesell and Frances L. Ilg, *Infant and Child in the Culture of Today: The Guidance of Development in Home and Nursery School* (New York, 1943).

20. Susan Isaacs, *Social Development in Young Children: A Study of Beginnings* (London, 1933), pp. 393–94; Spock, *Decent and Indecent,* p. 16; *Symposium on the Healthy Personality,* p. 85; Spock, *Baby and Child Care,* p. 315.

21. Spock, *Baby and Child Care*, pp. 212, 267, 254, 258, 268–69. See also pp. 213, 261, 284, 269–70. To bring this off, of course, the adult must have clear expectations of the child's behavior — a real problem, as Spock realized. *Symposium on the Healthy Personality*, p. 78. For an analogous justification of standards in higher education, see Robert Maynard Hutchins, *The Higher Learning in America* (New Haven, 1936).

22. Bloom, *Doctor Spock*, pp. 17–18, 21.

23. Isaacs, *Social Development in Young Children*, pp. 420, 270–71, 417, 395; Levy, *Maternal Overprotection*, p. 211; Gesell and Ilg, *Infant and Child in the Culture of Today*, p. 49; Bakwin and Bakwin, "Psychologic Care of the Preschool Child, III," p. 359; Ruth Morris Bakwin and Harry Bakwin, "Psychologic Care of the Preschool Child, II," *Journal of Pediatrics* 16 (February 1940): 224. For the argument that a leader must have "a strongly developed sense of a dominant purpose and direction," see Ordway Tead, *The Art of Leadership* (New York, 1935), p. 94.

24. Erikson, *Childhood and Society*, p. 117; Erik Erikson, "Observations on Sioux Education," *Journal of Psychology* 7 (1937): 101–56.

25. Lawrence K. Frank, "Children in a World of Violence," *Progressive Education* 17 (October 1940): 393; Frank, "The Fundamental Needs of the Child," *Mental Hygiene* 22 (July 1938): 370. There is a related ambivalence in the 1939 World's Fair slogan, "Unity without Uniformity."

26. Spock, *Baby and Child Care*, pp. 272, 211–13, 273, 268.

27. Ibid., pp. 263, 242–43.

28. Ibid., pp. 329–30. Aldrich and Aldrich state: "True Progressive education begins with the nursing bottle and the potty, not with formal schooling." *Babies are Human Beings*, p. 62.

29. Bloom, *Doctor Spock*, pp. 85–86; Lois Meek Stolz interview by Milton J. E. Senn, 2 October 1968, interview 71, transcript, Senn Oral History Collection, pp. 5, 11, 27; Caroline B. Zachry and Margaret Lighty, *Emotion and Conduct in Adolescence* (New York, 1940); *New York Times*, 8 July 1938, p. 10; 6 April 1939, p. 27; 24 February 1945, p. 11; Eunice Bernard, "Mothers' Autocratic Care of Children Found Hurtful," ibid., 26 February 1939, sec. 2, p. 5; Zachry, "Orthopsychiatry and the Profession of Education: Section Meeting, 1942," *Journal of Orthopsychiatry* 13 (April 1943): 279. In 1969, at the height of student agitation against the Vietnam War, Spock explained his thirty-year adherence to an educational theory that many considered excessively radical and destructive of discipline and social order. Not so, wrote Spock, "Children don't have to be forced or even strictly guided. . . . They will advance their emotional and social as well as their intellectual maturity by creative activities including those carried out in cooperation with each other." The teacher could encourage "democratic discussion," even allow a group to "make mistakes that are not dangerous." *Decent and Indecent*, p. 190. See also Bakwin and Bakwin, "Psychologic Care of the Preschool Child, II," p. 223.

30. Milton J. Senn comments, n.d., interview 65, transcript, Senn Oral History Collection, p. 29; Spock interview by Graebner.

31. Marrow, *Practical Theorist*, pp. 123–27.

32. Spock interview by Graebner. It is not surprising that Lewin had this impact on Spock. Gordon W. Allport recalled in 1967: "More clearly than anyone else, [Lewin] has shown us in concrete, operational terms what it means to be a democratic leader, and to create a democratic group structure." "The Genius of Kurt Lewin," typescript, 5 May 1967, in Kurt Lewin Papers, Archives of the History of American Psychology, University of Akron, Akron, Ohio, box M944, folder 1.

33. Marrow, *Practical Theorist*, pp. 144, 108–10; Lewin, *Resolving Social Conflicts*, pp. 73–76. The possible trade-off between democracy and efficiency was also at issue in the executive-reorganization movement in the late 1930s. See Barry D. Karl, *Executive Reorganization and Reform in the New Deal: The Genesis of Administrative Management, 1900–1939* (Cambridge, Mass., 1963), pp. 24–25, xiii.

34. See the foreword by Gordon Allport in Lewin, *Resolving Social Conflicts*, p. xi. According to Allport, "Dewey . . . is the outstanding philosophical exponent of democracy, Lewin its outstanding psychological exponent."

35. George Albert Coe, *Education in Religion and Morals* (New York, 1904), pp. 271–75.

36. Harold Anderson interview by Milton J. E. Senn, 8 December 1970, interview 2, transcript, Senn Oral History Collection, pp. 23–24, 35, 9–13. See also M. P. Follett, *Creative Experience* (New York, 1924), pp. 150–51; Eduard C. Lindeman Papers, Notebook "1932–33," Social Welfare History Archives, Minneapolis, Minnesota, box 1, folder 1, p. 201.

37. Walser, *Art of Conference*, pp. 2, 3, 4, 200.

38. Christopher Lasch, *Haven in a Heartless World: The Family Besieged* (New York, 1977), pp. 111–18. That Spock worked intuitively from industrial relations or at least from a factory/capitalist model is suggested by the close parallels found in Spock's work to that of Ordway Tead, next to Follett the nation's leading advocate of democratic methods of industrial discipline. Tead wrote in *The Art of Leadership* (1935) that "it is better to lead than to boss." The words "lead" and "boss" were used in *Baby and Child Care* to establish Spock's conception of proper parental conduct. (Tead, *Art of Leadership*, pp. vii, 20, 14, 7–9; Spock, *Baby and Child Care*, pp. 156, 263, 272.)

Slavson, an acquaintance of Spock, began using group psychotherapy at the Jewish Board of Guardians in New York City in 1934. He conceptualized the therapy group in family terms, so that the aim of group therapy was "to create an atmosphere and stimulate relationships among its members that will approximate . . . those of an ideal family." Spock would have had to reverse the configuration, conceptualizing the family as a therapeutic group, the parent as therapist. S. R. Slavson, *An Introduction to Group Therapy* (New York, 1943), pp. 18, 39; Slavson, *Creative Group Education* (New York, 1937), pp. 5–6; Walter Schindler, "Family Pattern in Group Formation and Therapy," *International Journal of Group Psychotherapy* 1 (June 1951): 100.

39. *New York Times*, 28 May 1968, p. 46. See also Spock interview by Senn, p. 10; Christopher Jencks, "Is It All Dr. Spock's Fault?" *New York Times Magazine*, 3 March 1968.

40. Spock was quoted in a letter from Corinna Marsh that appeared in *New York Times Magazine*, 21 April 1968, p. 16.

41. See the analysis in Zuckerman, "Dr. Spock," pp. 179–207.

CHAPTER SEVEN. DECLENSION

1. The Buffalo Public Library's card catalogue provides another measure of the strength of postwar democratic social engineering. The catalogue's listing of books designed to assist leaders of democratic institutions includes Harry A. Overstreet and Bonaro W. Overstreet, *Town Meeting Comes to Town* (1938); a volume by former Inquiry head Bruno Lasker, *Democracy through Discussion* (1949); Ruth Haller, *Planning Your Meeting* (1944); Bertram W. Strauss, *New Ways to Better Meetings* (1951); Marquis Fay Stigers, *Making Conference Programs Work* (1949); Sidney Samson Sutherland, *When You Preside* (1952); Russell Halderman Wagner, *Handbook of Group Discussion* (1950); Matthew B. Miles, *Learning to Work in Groups: A Program for Educational Leaders* (1959); and John S. Morgan, *Practical Guide to Conference Leadership* (1966). Few such books appeared after 1970. The 1945–1960 period was also notable for the sheer quantity of published small-group research. See Joseph E. McGrath and Irwin Altman, *Small Group Research: A Synthesis and Critique of the Field* (New York, 1966).

2. Stanley Hochman, *Yesterday and Today: A Dictionary of Recent American History* (New York, 1979), p. 324.

3. Clifford J. Sager and Helen Singer Kaplan, eds., *Progress in Group and Family Therapy* (New York, 1972); S. R. Slavson, ed., *The Fields of Group Psychotherapy* (New York, 1956); Abraham S. Luchins, *Group Therapy: A Guide* (New York, 1964).

4. Kenneth E. Reid, *From Character Building to Social Treatment: The History of the Use of Groups in Social Work* (Westport, Conn., 1981), pp. 163, 161; Grace Coyle to Donald Van Valen, 10 September 1948, Grace Coyle Papers, Case Western Reserve University Archives, Case Western Reserve University, Cleveland, Ohio, box 4, file "Correspondence, 1948–49."

5. Reid, *From Character Building to Social Treatment*, pp. 154–59, 183.

6. James Gilbert, *A Cycle of Outrage: America's Reaction to the Juvenile Delinquent in the 1950s* (New York, 1986), pp. 17–18; Edgar Z. Friedenberg, *The Vanishing Adolescent* (1959; New York: Dell, 1962), p. 72.

7. Angela E. Fraley, *Schooling and Innovation: The Rhetoric and the Reality* (New York, 1981), pp. 78, 82, 131–32.

8. William Graebner, "Coming of Age in Buffalo: The Ideology of Maturity in Postwar America," *Radical History Review* 34 (January 1986): 66, 68. See also "Democracy in U.S. Schools," *Life* 10 (13 January 1941): 65; "Assembly Notes," Kensington High School, *Compass* (Buffalo, 1941), p. 19; Friedenberg, *Vanishing Adolescent*, pp. 136–38, 140–43; and David Riesman et al., *The Lonely Crowd:*

A Study of the Changing American Character (1950; abridged ed. New York: Doubleday Anchor, 1953), pp. 79–85.

9. *Buffalo Courier-Express*, 28 January 1951, sec. 5, p. 14.

10. Ibid.; Victor B. Wylegala, "Home Life Shapes Child's Character," *Buffalo Courier-Express*, 26 February 1952, p. 13.

11. Victor B. Wylegala, "Outside Leadership Important to Child," *Buffalo Courier-Express*, 27 February 1952, p. 13.

12. New York State, Youth Commission, "Making Teen Centers Succeed," by Sidney G. Lutzin (Albany, 1953), pp. 7–8; *Y's Doings* 14 (November 1958): 3; "Leaders Told to Let Youths Run Activities," *Buffalo Courier-Express*, 29 September 1953, p. 6; photo and caption, *Buffalo Courier-Express*, 15 April 1953, p. 11; "Youths Take Over Reins of City Government Today," *Buffalo Courier-Express*, 3 May 1953, p. 20B; "CYC Group 'Takes Over' Reins of City," *Buffalo Courier-Express*, 10 May 1953, p. 40B.

13. "Proposal for the Study of the D. P. Problem by the Jewish Research Institute for the Study of Human Relations," and Kurt Lewin, "Philosophy and Broader Goals of the Commission on Community Interrelations," both in Kurt Lewin Papers, Archives of the History of American Psychology, University of Akron, Akron, Ohio, box M946, file 22; B. F. Skinner, *Beyond Freedom and Dignity* (New York, 1971).

14. "The Research Program of the Commission on Community Interrelations of the American Jewish Congress," Lewin Papers, box M946, file 22.

15. Rachel David DuBois, "Small Talk with Big Results," reprinted from *Freedom and Union*, copy in LeRoy Bowman Papers, Columbia University Archives, Division of Special Collections, Butler Library, Columbia University, New York, box 9, file "Discussion." See also Friedenberg, *Vanishing Adolescent*, pp. 97–98.

16. The American Friends Service Committee, "Speak Truth to Power: Discussion Guide" (n.p., n.d.), in Bowman Papers, box 9, file "Discussion." This question resembles one I learned to ask while selling waterless cookware in the summer of 1967. The name of the game was "closing the sale," and to that end we were provided with a typed list of closing lines. My favorite was "If you were to purchase this set of cookware, which free gift would you like?" Apparently the Friends, too, knew how to close a sale.

17. Norman L. Rosenberg, Emily S. Rosenberg, and James R. Moore, *In Our Times: America since World War II* (Englewood Cliffs, N.J., 1976), p. 3.

18. Lewis Perry, *Intellectual Life in America: A History* (New York, 1984), pp. 414–15; Henry S. Kariel, *In Search of Authority: Twentieth-Century Political Thought* (Glencoe, 1964), p. 210.

19. Kariel, *In Search of Authority*, pp. 206–10.

20. Paul F. Kress, *Social Science and the Idea of Process: The Ambiguous Legacy of Arthur F. Bentley* (Urbana, Ill., 1970), pp. 44–45, 71.

21. Ibid., pp. 82–83, 86.

22. David B. Truman, *The Governmental Process: Political Interests and Public Opinion* (New York, 1951), pp. 11, 21, 129 (quotation), 197–98, 205–6.

23. Ibid., pp. 191, 513, 197–98 (quotation).

24. Ibid., pp. 507–11.

25. Robert A. Dahl, *A Preface to Democratic Theory* (Chicago, 1956), pp. 2–3, 131.

26. Ibid., pp. 150–51.

27. This interpretation is derived from Howell John Harris, *The Right to Manage: Industrial Relations Policies of American Business in the 1940s* (Madison, 1982), pp. 88–89, 93–96, 99, 102, 137–38, 171–75. Harris' account is ambiguous on this point.

28. Edward Alsworth Ross, *Social Control: A History of the Foundations of Order* (1901; New York, 1928), pp. 362–63.

29. Students for a Democratic Society, "The Port Huron Statement," reprinted in Robert D. Marcus and David Burner, eds., *America since 1945*, 2d ed. (New York, 1977), p. 206; Kirkpatrick Sale, *SDS* (1973; New York: Vintage Books, 1974), pp. 51–52.

30. Allen J. Matusow, *The Unraveling of America: A History of Liberalism in the 1960s* (New York, 1984), p. 330; Michael Ferber, "Chiller," *Radical History Review* 28–30 (September 1984): 505.

31. Thomas Hayden, "A Letter to the New (Young) Left," in Mitchell Cohen and Dennis Hale, eds., *The New Student Left: An Anthology*, rev. ed. (Boston: Beacon Press, 1967), pp. 3, 5, 6; Timothy V. Kaufman-Osborn, "John Dewey," in Sohnya Sayres, Anders Stephanson, Stanley Aronowitz, and Fredric Jameson, eds., *The 60s without Apology* (Minneapolis, 1984), pp. 289–90.

32. Sara Evans, *Personal Politics: The Roots of Women's Liberation in the Civil Rights Movement and the New Left* (New York, 1979), p. 116.

33. Tom Wolfe, *The Electric Kool-Aid Acid Test* (1968; New York, Bantam Books, 1969), p. 112.

34. Jerry Farber, *The Student as Nigger* (North Hollywood, Cal., 1969), pp. 17, 27–28, 33, 37, 35; Neil Postman and Charles Weingartner, *Teaching as a Subversive Activity* (New York, 1969); Charles E. Silberman, *Crisis in the Classroom: The Remaking of American Education* (New York: Vintage Books, 1971).

35. Farber, *Student as Nigger*, pp. 114–17.

36. Farber, "The Student and Society: An Annotated Manifesto," in *Student as Nigger*, pp. 17, 27–28, 33, 37, 35. Postman and Weingartner in *Teaching as a Subversive Activity* (1969) and Charles E. Silberman in *Crisis in the Classroom* (1971) also drew on Dewey for inspiration yet backed off from Farber's anticorporate, populist vision. Postman and Weingartner could locate no source of educational authoritarianism more serious than "well-intentioned" educators. Silberman was drawn to informal, process-based education not because it was free or even genuinely informal, but because it was so completely controlling. "In a sense there is no spontaneity at all," he quoted an English headmistress, "since we select the materials that are available. We are structuring all the time; that is what teaching is." Silberman had no interest in Farber's radical restructuring of the social order. He, too, acknowledged a crisis, but it was a crisis of authority, its perpetrators "young rebels" who sought to " 'slough off' the accumulation of past achievements, creations and discoveries that constitutes contemporary culture and, for the older generation, gives it its authority," and who "do not recognize the authority of

knowledge, of skill, of simple truth." Postman and Weingartner, *Teaching as a Subversive Activity*, pp. 27–28; Silberman, *Crisis in the Classroom*, pp. 238, 26, 28, 235–36.

37. Jack Kerouac, *On the Road* (New York, 1957). In his study of black nationalism, Frank Kofsky places cool jazz on the same plane with the beats: "Both Beat literature and cool music have to be seen as the only form of rebellion — that of disaffiliation, as opposed to direct battle with the status quo — available to young, alienated whites during the first years of the Cold War." Kofsky, *Black Nationalism and the Revolution in Music* (New York, 1970), p. 32. See also R. Jeffrey Lustig, *Corporate Liberalism: The Origins of Modern American Political Theory, 1890–1920* (Berkeley, 1982), p. 240.

38. *The Gallup Opinion Index*, Report No. 183, December 1980, p. 67; Students for a Democratic Society, "Port Huron Statement," p. 206. Aging experts were concerned about the withdrawal of older persons from participation in political and social life. See William Graebner, *A History of Retirement: The Meaning and Function of an American Institution, 1885–1978* (New Haven, Conn., 1980), pp. 234–35. High-school dropouts might also be relevant here.

39. "Port Huron Statement," pp. 204, 207. On Lyndon Johnson's manipulative, pseudodemocratic politics, see Doris Kearns, *Lyndon Johnson and the American Dream* (New York: Signet, 1977), pp. 149, 142, 117, 128, 142.

40. Hal Draper, *Berkeley: The New Student Revolt* (New York, 1965), pp. 27, 30, 22–26.

41. Louis Menashe, ed., comp., annot., "Berkeley Teach-In: Vietnam," Folkway Records, Album No. FD5765 (n.d.).

42. Wolfe, *Electric Kool-Aid Acid Test*, pp. 177, 169.

43. Ibid., p. 146.

44. Among other books that were part of a new interest in authority, see Toby Moffett, *The Participation Put-on: Reflections of a Disenchanted Washington Youth Expert* (New York, 1971), and Joe McGinniss, *The Selling of the President, 1968* (1968; New York: Pocket Books, 1970).

45. Skinner, *Beyond Freedom and Dignity*, p. 87.

46. *Newsweek*, 20 September 1971, p. 95; Skinner, *Beyond Freedom and Dignity*, pp. 99, 92–93, 97. See also Skinner's critique of a thirty-five-year-old group-therapy program, Alcoholics Anonymous, on pp. 73–74.

47. Skinner's book, while avidly read, was greeted with unveiled hostility, much of it focused on his denial of free will. *Time*, 20 September 1971, p. 52; *America*, 23 October 1971, pp. 323–24; Charles McCarry, "He Envisions a Happier Age," *McCall's* 99 (November 1971): 35; *New Republic* 166 (1 and 8 January 1972): 14.

48. See, for example, Todd Gitlin, *The Whole World Is Watching: Mass Media in the Making and Unmaking of the New Left* (Berkeley: University of California Press, 1980).

49. Antonio Gramsci, *Selections from the Prison Notebooks of Antonio Gramsci*, ed. and trans. Quintin Hoare and Geoffrey Nowell Smith (New York, 1971), pp. 144, 249, 259, 192–93.

50. Thomas R. Bates, "Gramsci and the Theory of Hegemony," *Journal of the History of Ideas* 36 (April–June 1975): 353.

51. Eugene D. Genovese, *Roll, Jordan, Roll: The World the Slaves Made* (New York: Pantheon, 1974), pp. 147–48; T. J. Jackson Lears, "The Concept of Cultural Hegemony: Problems and Possibilities," *American Historical Review* 90 (June 1985): 569; Gramsci, *Selections from the Prison Notebooks*, pp. 326–27, 333.

52. Gramsci, *Selections from the Prison Notebooks*, pp. 333, 326–27.

53. Lears, "Concept of Cultural Hegemony," p. 570; Gramsci, *Selections from the Prison Notebooks*, pp. 323, 192–93.

54. Gramsci, *Selections from the Prison Notebooks*, pp. 327, 327n; Lears, "Concept of Cultural Hegemony," p. 569.

55. Gramsci, *Selections from the Prison Notebooks*, pp. 242, 268, 259; Bates, "Gramsci and the Theory of Hegemony," p. 363.

56. Bates, "Gramsci and the Theory of Hegemony," p. 363; Gramsci, *Selections from the Prison Notebooks*, pp. 243–44, 193.

57. Sheldon S. Wolin, *Politics and Vision: Continuity and Innovation in Western Political Thought* (Boston, 1960), pp. 301, 314.

58. Christopher Lasch, *The World of Nations: Reflections on American History, Politics, and Culture* (New York, 1973), pp. 279–81. On the importance of clarity in the teaching process, see Friedenberg, *Vanishing Adolescent*, pp. 75–87.

59. Wolin, *Politics and Vision*, pp. 353, 347–48, 358, 360, 368.

60. Michel Foucault, *Power/Knowledge: Selected Interviews and Other Writings, 1972–1977*, ed. Colin Gordon, trans. Colin Gordon, Leo Marshall, John Mepham, Kate Soper (New York: Pantheon, 1980), pp. 60, 125, 119, 7, 61, 39, 74, 1, 7, 8, 27. Friedenberg's account of student courts in *Vanishing Adolescent* is roughly equivalent (pp. 140–43).

61. Richard Sennett, *Authority* (1980; New York: Vintage Books, 1981), p. 94. See also p. 47. One might argue that Sennett's "shame" is the equivalent of Wolin's "society" and of Foucault's visibility.

62. Sennett, *Authority*, pp. 77, 84, 89, 104 (quotation).

63. Ibid., pp. 104, 111–15, 115–16 (quotation).

64. John Kenneth Galbraith, *The Anatomy of Power* (Boston, 1983), pp. 5–6.

65. Ibid., p. 147.

66. David F. Noble, *America by Design: Science, Technology, and the Rise of Corporate Capitalism* (New York: Oxford University Press, 1979), pp. xxii, xxiii, xxv. Noble's definition of technology is from Herbert Marcuse.

67. Ibid., pp. 274 (quotation), 271–73.

68. Peter Lyman, "The Politics of Anger: On Silence, Ressentiment, and Political Speech," *Socialist Review* 57 (May–June 1981): 66–67. On the process by which vernacular language is transformed into a system of control, see Ivan Illich, "The War against Subsistence," *Democracy* 1 (July 1981): 70–85.

69. Steven Lukes, *Power: A Radical View* (New York, 1974), pp. 12–13, 16–19.

70. Ibid., pp. 23–24, 33. As Lukes realized, the difficulty in his position lay in determining the ingredients of this "manipulated consensus." The best he could do was to suggest that even the most widely acceptable form of power and influ-

ence, "rational persuasion" itself, might violate autonomy and thus produce a consensus in name only.

71. Bertram Gross, *Friendly Fascism: The New Face of Power in America* (New York, 1980), p. 5.

72. Ibid., pp. 1, 2, 5, 277, 373.

73. Ibid., pp. 258, 277, 351, 266.

74. Jacques Ellul, *Propaganda: The Formation of Men's Attitudes* (New York: Knopf, 1971), pp. 75, xviii, xvi, 236, 38, 39.

75. Ibid., p. 5 (italics added).

76. Ibid., pp. 62–64, 85, 81–82, 64. Although Wolin employed neither "propaganda" nor "hegemony," his *Politics and Vision* was informed by a similar notion of politics and, specifically, by an understanding of the historical importance of participation. Wolin harbored no illusions about the political function of participation; it was, he wrote, "the basic method for establishing areas of agreement or political consensus." He traced participatory methods through Calvin, Machiavelli, Rousseau, and Durkheim to twentieth-century industrial-relations experts Elton Mayo and Philip Selznick, both of whom he found guilty of elite manipulation. *Politics and Vision*, pp. 62 (quotation), 191, 223, 368, 372, 409–12, 420–21, 428, 433–34.

77. Christopher Lasch, *The Culture of Narcissism: American Life in an Age of Diminishing Expectations* (New York, 1978), pp. 183, 185, 7.

78. Ibid., pp. 181–85, 154–55, 11.

79. Ibid., pp. 230, 229 (quotation). In *The New Radicalism*, Lasch developed the authoritarian and manipulative side of Dewey, Jane Addams, George Creel, and other exponents of the "new radicalism," yet curiously claimed that its methods were "the exclusive possession of a small minority." *The New Radicalism, 1889–1963: The Intellectual as a Social Type* (New York: Vintage Books, 1965), p. 147 (quotation) and chap. 5 ("Politics as Social Control").

80. Riesman, *Lonely Crowd*, p. 54.

81. Ibid., pp. 70, 78, 90–103, quotation on p. 103.

82. Carole Pateman, *Participation and Democratic Theory* (Cambridge, England, 1970), pp. 24–26, 29–34, 36–38, 8–9, 103.

83. Ibid., pp. 2, 105, 53, 44.

84. Robert Nisbet, *Twilight of Authority* (New York: Oxford University Press, 1975), pp. 11, 195, 223–25, 196, 253, 3, 241, 97, 196–97, 249, 270.

85. David Moberg, "Work and American Culture: The Ideal of Self-Determination and the Prospects for Socialism," *Socialist Review* 10 (March–June 1980): 38, 50, 51.

86. Gross, *Friendly Fascism*, pp. 364, 366, 372–73.

87. David Hunt, "Popular Uprisings and the Origins of Socialism in France," *Socialist Review* 8 (July–October 1978): 233, 236.

88. Harry Boyte, "Building the Democratic Movement: Prospects for a Socialist Renaissance," *Socialist Review* 8 (July–October 1978): 18, 22 (Thompson quotation), 23. See also Lustig, *Corporate Liberalism*, p. 262.

89. Sennett, *Authority*, pp. 170, 179, 181, 185.

90. Ian Hacking, "The Archaeology of Foucault," *New York Review of Books* 28 (14 May 1981): 36.

CHAPTER EIGHT. CONCLUSION

1. Dennis H. Wrong, *Power: Its Forms, Bases and Uses* (New York, 1979), pp. 1, 4. See also Christopher Lasch, *The Culture of Narcissism: American Life in an Age of Diminishing Expectations* (New York, 1978), p. 169n.

2. Wrong, *Power*, pp. 248 (Collingwood quotation), 247. Recent scholars of the history of authority apparently agree. Christopher Lasch objects not to all authority, but to authority in therapeutic forms. Patriarchal authority, represented by fathers, teachers, and preachers, is entirely legitimate, even though it functions to strengthen the "social superego." According to John Kenneth Galbraith, power can be "socially malign" or "socially essential," but it cannot be indicted out of hand. "Power, per se," he writes, "is not a proper subject for indignation. The exercise of power, the submission of some to the will of others, is inevitable in modern society; nothing whatever is accomplished without it." Sennett examines authority from the perspective of the individual, rather than social need. "The need for authority is basic," he writes. "Children need authorities to guide and reassure them. Adults fulfill an essential part of themselves in being authorities; it is one way of expressing care for others." Lasch, *Culture of Narcissism*, p. 11; John Kenneth Galbraith, *The Anatomy of Power* (Boston, 1983), p. 13; Richard Sennett, *Authority* (1980; New York: Vintage Books, 1981), p. 15.

3. Seen another way, the distinction between power and socialization is entirely arbitrary — itself, perhaps, a mechanism of social control.

4. Michel Foucault, *Power/Knowledge: Selected Interviews and Other Writings, 1972–1977,* ed. Colin Gordon, trans. Colin Gordon, Leo Marshall, John Mepham, and Kate Soper (New York: Pantheon, 1980), p. 39.

5. On the other hand, it is not clear whether a high level of consciousness makes the system more or less heinous. Should we define democratic social engineering as benign simply because millions of American mothers followed Dr. Spock's instructions without quite knowing why? Does the system become innocuous if one concedes that thousands of scout troop leaders thought they were just giving their charges valuable camping experience? In fact, democratic social engineering probably had more impact when it was administered without self-consciousness.

6. Galbraith, *Anatomy of Power*, pp. 139–40.

7. Ibid., p. 183. See also David A. Hollinger, "The Problem of Pragmatism in American History," *Journal of American History* 67 (June 1980): 92–100.

8. B. F. Skinner, *Beyond Freedom and Dignity* (New York, 1971), pp. 97, 87.

9. Galbraith, *Anatomy of Power*, pp. 158, 180, 164.

10. Wrong, *Power*, p. 31. Aside from theory, a generation of labor historians,

including David Montgomery, Herbert Gutman, and Eugene Genovese, has argued that slaves and industrial workers have maintained an important measure of control over the work process even under the most difficult conditions. See, for example, David Montgomery, *Workers' Control in America: Studies in the History of Work, Technology, and Labor Struggles* (Cambridge, England, 1979).

11. Something analogous happened in the factories, where "scientific" managers developed a science of production, planning, and administration in which workers had no function.

12. Those scholars who have touched on the phenomenon – Lasch, Noble, Gramsci, Bledstein, and Macleod – describe the same persons. Bledstein writes of an upwardly mobile middle class, seeking "respectability, orderliness, control, and discipline" through a university-based culture of professionalism. According to Bledstein, it was the function of this culture of professionalism and of the schools that fostered it to "legitimize the authority of the middle class by appealing to the universality and objectivity of 'science.' The fact that most Americans learned to associate the scientific way with democratic openness and fairness made the relationship convincing." Macleod's study of the YMCA and other character-building and group-work agencies of the late nineteenth and early twentieth centuries identifies the same group: an aggressive middle class, anxious not only to control the working class but, especially, to ensure that its own offspring had the proper combination of self-direction and group participation for rapid upward mobility. Noble identifies a body of "professional engineers" as the agents of technology and corporate capital, but it is quite clear that by the 1920s this group included those with training in psychology and sociology. Gramsci identifies teachers, ministers, club leaders, editors, and political party officials and intellectuals as among those who "engineer" behavior in modern society. While Lasch focuses more on the "helping" professionals, including psychiatrists, social workers, and juvenile court officials, he, like other scholars, describes the agents of social control as the educated middle class. Burton J. Bledstein, *The Culture of Professionalism: The Middle Class and the Development of Higher Education in America* (New York, 1976), pp. 54 (first quotation), 90, 124 (second quotation); David I. Macleod, *Building Character in the American Boy: The Boy Scouts, YMCA, and Their Forerunners, 1870–1920* (Madison, 1983), pp. xv, xvii, xviii, 16, 17, 31, 170; David F. Noble, *America by Design: Science, Technology, and the Rise of Corporate Capitalism* (New York: Oxford University Press, 1979), pp. xxiii, 257–59, 273–74; Thomas R. Bates, "Gramsci and the Theory of Hegemony," *Journal of the History of Ideas* 36 (April–June 1975): 353; Lasch, *Culture of Narcissism*, pp. 154–55. See also Kenneth E. Reid, *From Character Building to Social Treatment: The History of the Use of Groups in Social Work* (Westport, Conn., 1981).

13. Galbraith, *Anatomy of Power*, p. 159.

14. Grace Coyle to Kathryn Close, 3 February 1944, in Grace Coyle Papers, Case Western Reserve University Archives, Case Western Reserve University, Cleveland, Ohio, box 4, file "Correspondence, 1928, 1929, 1940–47"; Charles E. Reed, "Notes from the District Conferences," in Record Group 68, Records of the Works Progress Administration, National Archives, Washington, D.C., 211.6, 1941–43 (N-R), file "National Recreation Association, September 1941–March 1942";

Student Council cartoon, Lafayette High School, *The Oracle*, 1953, p. 34; "Report on 'The Buffalo Plan,'" Joseph Manch Papers, Buffalo, New York, in possession of Joseph Manch.

15. Wrong, *Power*, pp. 32–34.

16. Dale Carnegie, *How to Win Friends and Influence People* (1936; New York: Pocket Books, 1964); Gustav Theodor Schwenning, "A History of the Industrial Work of the Young Men's Christian Association," Ph.D. diss., Clark University, 1925, pp. 130–31; Michael Zuckerman, "Dr. Spock: The Confidence Man," in Charles Rosenberg, ed., *The Family in History* (Philadelphia, 1975).

17. Grace Coyle, "Some Personal and Social Values in Adult Education," c. 1926, Grace Coyle Papers, box 6, file "Speeches, 1930s," p. 4. See also Gregory W. Bush, "The Face in the Crowd: Gerald Stanley Lee and the Engineering of American Attention," paper presented to the Popular Culture Association, Louisville, Ky., April 1982.

18. See also Robert A. Dahl, *A Preface to Democratic Theory* (Chicago, 1956), pp. 150–51.

19. From George Orwell, *1984*, quoted in Wrong, *Power*, p. 109.

20. For Galbraith this is a central feature of his "conditioned" power: "the fact of submission is not recognized." *Anatomy of Power*, p. 6.

Index

absolute values, 3

academia, and ideas of leadership, 26

Addams, Jane, 13, 22, 115; and John Lovejoy Elliott, 20; and social disorganization, 125; and work place, 89; mentioned, 51

Adler, Felix, 20

advertising, 59

aggression, in children, 129

Allen, Frederick Lewis, 43

Allport, Gordon, on Lewin, 77

Alta Social Settlement, 117

American Association for the Study of Group Work, 103, 111

American Friends Service Committee, 145

American Jewish Congress, Commission on Community Interrelations, 144

American Youth Commission, 97, 187

anarchism, 89; mentioned, 15

Anderson, Harold, 137, 138

anger, 160

anti-Semitism, 143; after World War I, 53

assembly line, 89

association, related to conduct, 70

associations, voluntary, 164, 165

authority: crisis of, in late nineteenth century, 7; defined, ix; democratic, opposed, 151; history of, as field of study, x; indirect, 175; internal, 12, 16, 17; internalized, 77; invisible, 155; nature of modern, 164; of parents, 133; patriarchal, 243n2; political, 157–58; religious, under Puritanism, 9; social, 10–11, 13

autocracy, 47; German, 44–45

autonomy, 158

Bachrach, Peter, 160

Bakwin, Harry, 134

Bakwin, Ruth Morris, 134

Baldwin, James Mark, 16

Baptist church: and social personality, 28–29; mentioned, 26, 39

Baratz, Morton, 160

barber shops, 166

Barbour, Clarence, 28–29, 32, 33, 37

Baritz, Loren, 75

Beatles, 153

beats (beatniks), 151–52, 181, 240n37; mentioned, 187

beauty parlors, 166

Beecher, Henry Ward, 28

behavior, engineering of, and manipulation, 5

Benjamin Franklin High School, 112, 174

Benjamin Rose Institute, 112, 113, 114, 120, 121, 122–23

Benne, Kenneth, 76

Bentham, Jeremy, and social authority, 10–11

Bentley, Arthur, 146

Berkman, Alexander, 89

Bernays, Edward L., 59–60, 62, 65, 87; under Herbert Hoover, 66; mentioned, 67, 71

Bible clubs, 31

COMPOSED BY B. VADER DESIGN/PRODUCTION, FORT COLLINS, COLORADO
MANUFACTURED BY BRAUN-BRUMFIELD, INC., ANN ARBOR, MICHIGAN
TEXT AND DISPLAY LINES ARE SET IN PALADIUM

Library of Congress Cataloging-in-Publication Data
Graebner, William.
The engineering of consent.
(History of American thought and culture)
Includes bibliographical references and index.
1. Social engineering — United States — History —
20th century. 2. Authority — History — 20th century.
3. United States — Social conditions. I. Title.
II. Series.
HM291.G659   1987   303.3'6   87-8266
ISBN 0-299-11170-9